# TALKING
# WALKING
ESSAYS IN
CULTURAL
CRITICISM

For my father, Ronnie Bowlby

# TALKING WALKING

## ESSAYS IN CULTURAL CRITICISM

## RACHEL BOWLBY

**sussex**
ACADEMIC
PRESS
*Brighton • Portland • Toronto*

The right of Rachel Bowlby to be identified as Author of this work has been asserted in accordance with the Copyright, Designs and Patents Act 1988.

2 4 6 8 10 9 7 5 3 1

*First published 2018, in Great Britain by*
SUSSEX ACADEMIC PRESS
PO Box 139
Eastbourne BN24 9BP

*Distributed in North America by*
SUSSEX ACADEMIC PRESS
ISBS Publisher Services
920 NE 58th Ave #300, Portland, OR 97213, USA

An Acknowledgements (page 239) provides information on the publication history of some of the articles published in this volume.

*British Library Cataloguing in Publication Data*
A CIP catalogue record for this book is available from the British Library.

*Library of Congress Cataloging-in-Publication Data*
Names: Bowlby, Rachel, 1957– author.
Title: Talking walking : essays in cultural criticism / Rachel Bowlby.
Description: Brighton ; Portland : Sussex Academic Press, [2018] |
   Includes  bibliographical references.
Identifiers: LCCN 2017046724 | ISBN 9781845199111
   (pbk : alk. paper)
Subjects: LCSH: Literature—History and criticism. | Literature,
   Modern—History and criticism.
Classification: LCC PN86 .B69 2018 | DDC 824/.92—dc23
LC record available at https://lccn.loc.gov/2017046724

Typeset and designed by Sussex Academic Press, Brighton & Eastbourne.

# Contents

*Preface*                                                                vii

**Modern Spaces**
1   Talking Walking                                                        3
2   Half Art: Baudelaire's *The Painter of Modern Life*                  18
3   Readable City                                                        28
4   Motoring through History: Woolf's 'Evening over Sussex'              33
5   Shopping for Christmas                                               42
6   Please Enter Your Pin                                                48

**Family Mutations**
7   After Œdipus: Changing Family Stories                                59
8   The Third Parent                                                     76
9   Woolf and Childhood Abuse                                            79
10  Kinship Under All: Judith Butler on *Antigone*                       82
11  James's *Maisie* in Manhattan                                        86

**Critical Languages**
12  Domestication                                                        93
13  The Joy of Footnotes                                                115
14  Clichés in the Psychology of Advertising                            122
15  Who's Framing Virginia Woolf?                                       132
16  Woolf's Working Window                                              143
17  Woolf in Scholarly Form                                             149
18  Ginny Whizz                                                         152
19  The Pinker Thinker                                                  155
20  Cultural Studies and the Literary                                   157
21  Derrida's 'Once and for All'                                        160
22  Derrida One Day                                                     164
23  Yale Theory                                                         168
24  The Future of Literary Thinking                                     170
25  *Passionate* about Literature!                                      172

**Interview**
26  Interview with David Jonathan Bayot and              181
    Jeremy De Chavez

*Acknowledgements*                                        239
*Index*                                                   240

# Preface

When something called theory first broke onto the seemingly stag-
nant scene of literary studies, it offered bright new ways and fields
for critical reading: new methods and subjects, and also new words
to speak them. The syllabus and the styles would never be the same,
and methods of reading inspired by theory were proudly claimed as
a mode of social critique. At a long remove and in different ways, the
essays and the interview in this book are all indebted to the sense of
critical openness and movement which began at that time: that really
learning to read in an active sense was a way of learning to think
about the cultural forms that surround us.

'Talking Walking' is, at one level, simply the name of one of the
chapters of this book, a talk about walking. But the title is also meant
to suggest broader questions that extend into the interview (at the
end of the book) and the different sections. To begin with, talking
and walking connect to the representations of movement and modernity that occupy the book's first chapters: between the urban and the
rural, or the car and the store. In a simple way, the two activities have
been used to suggest the authenticity of a natural culture unspoilt by
the artifice of technology and consumption, as when Aldous Huxley
has a mildly dissenting character invite a girlfriend to share in a
simple rural pleasure away from the usual world. Her response, with
the feminine complacency of Huxley's women: 'Walking and talking
– that seemed a very odd way of spending an afternoon'.[1] 'Readable
City' looks at how such clear codes of cultural meaning are both
present (and practically formative) and also, inevitably, provisional
and precarious. And in essays by Baudelaire and Woolf, the subject
of two further chapters, the fleeting and variable views of city walker
and rural motorist each, in quite different ways, provide a means of
thinking about new presentations of history and change. This section
also includes two short pieces on supermarkets which follow the
positioning of customers and cashiers in their respective subjective
places within this strange modern space in which people and trolleys
slowly process towards their passage through the checkout.

The second section is about changing conditions of parenthood.
Walking and talking are two of the fundamental skills acquired in

the humanwards development out of babyhood. In the charmingly antiquated language of present-day childcare books, they are 'milestones'; but all around these ancient boundaries, it is as if everything else in the parenting world is in flux. The family situation into which the baby is born may well be quite different from the one that its parent or parents found themselves in a generation before – as chosen single parenthood, or same-sex co-parenthood, for instance, become increasingly common. And even before she or he was born, the talking walker may have been subject to processes of creation unknown to any pre-baby until this present time, as new reproductive technologies have actually altered the seemingly natural and eternal 'facts of life'.

Talking and walking may stand together as solid stages of every child's growth, but like the words of a babbling beginner or the elements of a basic poem, they also go together because they rhyme – because they sound as if they belong together. And that brings me to the third section, which is about the languages of criticism. The pieces here engage with different arguments now and earlier about the uses and history of critical reading – of literature, and also of other cultural forms. There are short pieces on the changing styles of critical writing, and on the place of particular writers – Woolf or Derrida – in contemporary critical culture. There are essays on clichés, on footnotes, on the language of the university job interview, on the use of 'domestication' as a catch-all negative term.

In the development of the book, it was the interview, now at the end, that came first. David Jonathan Bayot is to be thanked for that: for the initial idea and for formulating the questions and putting the text together when it was published by LaSalle University Press in 2014. It was his idea too that the interview could be amplified for publication in the present form, with a selection of additional writings that would hopefully do several things. It could show in more detail the kind of work talked about in the interview, and it could also introduce further areas – like reproductive technologies – that didn't get mentioned much in that exchange. It could gather together pieces previously scattered in different kinds of publication – from newspapers to academic articles to, in one instance, a blog – or not previously published in any medium. And it could give a sense of changing preoccupations and changing writing styles over a fairly long period of time. So while I don't pretend that this particular mix of research interests is anyone's but mine, I also think that there may be something more recognisably representative in how I have gone about pursuing them in writing. This sort of likeness probably emerges much more clearly when, as is now the case, many of the pieces have passed some way beyond their initial present time. And sometimes, too, this question of contemporary styles and subjects is the topic I'm talking about ('*Passionate* about Literature!', for instance, or 'Woolf in Scholarly Form').

The book derives from several decades of working and writing and talking and walking within the changing contemporary landscape of literary and cultural studies. I hope that old and new arrivals into this world will find pleasures of reading and matter for thinking.

1 Aldous Huxley, *Brave New World* (1932; Harmondsworth: Penguin, 1970), 77.

# Modern Spaces

# 1
# Talking Walking

'Let your fingers do the walking': this was the famous 1980s slogan used to promote the use of the telephone by BT, the company that then had a monopoly of landlines in Britain. But in putting it like that, I'm already distorting the situation. The only phones were landlines: in other words, in order to make or receive a call, you had to be where the phone was, rather than the phone being where you were. The mobile phone would begin to come into view – an unaffordable, inefficient, and enormous piece of kit – at the very end of the decade, but no one was even dreaming, yet, of the twenty-first-century state of that particular art: that one day, in the not so distant future, we wouldn't so much be letting our fingers do the walking, as letting our walks do the phoning: that is to say, we would be walking and roaming, tapping and talking everywhere and anywhere, head down and eyes on the screen.

'Let your fingers do the walking' was specifically an ad for Yellow Pages, that huge directory of local businesses. If you wanted to find a bakery or a butcher's or a candlestick maker, a place to eat lunch or a person to unblock your drain, then Yellow Pages was where you went to 'look it up'. It had the addresses and phone numbers of companies small and large, and the idea was that instead of going on foot or by any other means of transport – instead of having to take your body physically to the destination – you simply stayed where you were and picked up the phone. This giant book of the stay-at-home search was the precursor to the internet: where once you sought in paper pages, now you seek online. We still, however, keep much of the language of the old form of search: we speak of webpages, even though we cannot turn them, and we speak of 'visiting' sites or pages, even though we are are not one step nearer to the physical location (if there is one) of the business concerned. In fact the point of Yellow Pages and letting your fingers do the walking was that you didn't have to visit at all: you could simply remain where you were, and use the phone to save yourself the trouble of displacement.

British Yellow Pages does still, just about, exist. It comes through your letterbox once a year, just as it always used to.[1] But it is a wholly different object, a fraction of its former bulky size. (In the US, Yellow Pages seems to have survived in a fatter form.) Before, it might well have been the heaviest book in the house.

'Let your fingers do the walking' implies that the walking is work, from which your phone will relieve you. The difference is really to do with time (the time that would have been taken to call round yourself to the place you can phone instead), but the comical overt suggestion is that it involves a minimisation of physical labour. Only your fingers need to move; the rest of you can stay sitting at home. But the point was also that fingers, in miniature, could look like legs, and could also be moved in childishly walklike ways. In a wonderful American TV ad from 1970 the bottom half of a frumpy woman is seen to stride purposefully across the screen, before she is replaced by a couple of vertical fingers occupying the same space and moving, one finger in front of the other, from left to right. They dance on top of the open book of Yellow Pages, and one of them sticks itself out to dial the number on what now, of course, looks like an antique piece of equipment with a circular dial like a rotatable clockface. Point taken: the fingers are doing the walking, and you and your legs aren't going anywhere: you are staying just where you are. It may not be quite true to say that you don't have to lift a finger; but a finger is the only thing you do have to lift, and the suggestion is that Yellow Pages, and your phone, are freeing you from the effort of having to exercise the larger limbs of your body.

But walking has not only been represented or experienced as a burden, not only as an annoying addition of energy and time which it would be desirable to eliminate or replace with something lighter. In fact just now, in the early (or not so early) twenty-first century, it might seem that a very different image of walking is everywhere – everywhere, that is, in the old-fashioned world of printed books, of which Yellow Pages, in its idiosyncratic way, remains a sort of example. Sometimes it seems as if you can hardly move without encountering some new book about the pleasures or, more grandly, the philosophy of two-legged locomotion. Often these books combine thoughts about thinking with thoughts about walking; usually they will involve, as a basic structure for the narrative, some sort of long-distance journey on foot – most often, it seems, between north and south in Great Britain, and preferably between Land's End, the furthest southern tip of England, and John O'Groats, the northernmost point of Scotland. Recently I wandered (on foot, not online) into a branch of Waterstone's bookshop, where they display about twenty current 'recommended' non-fictional books. Two titles jumped out at me – or perhaps I should say that they simply stood placidly on the shelves. One was called *Walking through Spring* and the other, *Walking with Plato*. The author of the first is Graham Hoyland, and of the second, Gary Hayden; so perhaps in order to write a contemporary walking book your initials have to be GH. The Spring book moves up northwards from Cornwall to the Scottish borders; its subtitle is *An English Journey*, and it doesn't venture all the way into that other country of Scotland. The Plato book goes the whole way, from the far north of Scotland down to tip of Cornwall. The subtitle modestly calls it *A Philosophical Hike through the British Isles*. The blurb informs us that 'In this humorous, inspiring and delightfully British tale, Gary finds solitude and weary limbs bring him closer to the wisdom of the world's greatest thinkers. Recalling Rousseau's reverie, Bertrand Russell's misery, Plato's love of beauty and Epicurus' joy in simplicity, *Walking with Plato* offers a breath of fresh country air and clarity for anyone craving an escape from the humdrum of daily life.' The book, in other words, is going to substitute for the walking it describes, just as the fingers once did the work of the legs. Once you avoided schlepping all the way to the store by using your phone, and now you can have your walkng 'escape' from the everyday by letting your fingers turn the philo-sophical pages.

Despite my tone, though, I don't in fact want to dismiss or damn this proliferation of walkbooks. Much as with The Great British Bake Off, or gardening programmes since TV time immemorial, it is no doubt true that the consumers of the books and programmes are more likely to spend their leisure time enjoying the story of the walk, than to embark on their own off-screen or out-of-book experience in the kitchen or the garden or on the road or footpath. (There have also been – of course – a couple of walking series on TV too, at least one of them with a spin-off book.) But that doesn't make them bad, and leaving aside the bodily and mental benefits of actual physical walking, it would be wrong – all the more for someone like me who's spent much of their life in books – to suggest that enjoying walks in words is a less beneficial or less desirable experience than enjoying walks on the ground. And in any case, the two alternatives can be so readily separated. When we walk – when we really walk, not reading-walk – our experience is shaped by ideas that are not derived only from our present sensations of movement and the sights and smells around us that we may or may not be taking in as we go. I would happily go along with some pop-philosophical credo such as I Walk, Therefore I Am – how you feel when you reach the top of the slope on a beautiful day – but I know as well that no such elementary surge of walking feeling or flat-footed sentiment would have entered my head, at least not in that form, if I hadn't been reading about walking, as well as walking real walks, for most of my life.

But it is time to take a step backwards – first one step, and then a great many. First, a single step, in the direction of the immediate precursors to the current talking of walking. The books in Waterstone's are part of a large population which, in recent times, has grown from a few dominant progenitors. Or in publishing language, these new volumes are mostly 'copycat' books that are placed in what's now an established market for walking literature. Rebecca Solnit's *Wanderlust: A History of Walking* was published in 2000. *Marcher, une philosophie* by Frédéric Gros, came out in French in 2009 and was swiftly translated into English, something that rarely happens with French philosophical books, as *A Philosophy of Walking*. Solnit's 'history' is more of a set of different strands or paths. As an American, she is full of wonder and praise for the traditional British system of public 'rights of way', which means that walkers have access to established paths on land that is privately owned: it is true that, together with the comprehensive mapping of the Ordnance Survey, this resource – quite apart from the variety of the landscapes in quite a small country – may well make Britain the country most hospitable to outdoor walking for pleasure. Robert Macfarlane, author of *The Old Ways*, is probably the most prominent contemporary walking writer: the one whose books were first noticeably displayed in large stacks when the topic was new. There are numerous others, the two GH's being simply a couple of the more recent. One of these, Geoff Nicholson, is the author of *The Lost Art of Walking*, which is subtitled *The History, Science, Philosophy, Literature, Theory and Practice of Pedestrianism*.

I hope that I've now said enough to suggest that all this philosophical walking and pedestrian pontificating is a striking feature of our present literary landscape.[2] But the most remarkable feature of it, to me, is the way that it looks like a kind of historical throwback, and this is the further stage of the historical retrospect. On the one hand, all these walkers are more or less consciously Romantic. They take their bearings from the great thinker-walkers from Rousseau to Wordsworth to Thoreau, the ones who set the pace and charted the territory for this particular practice. This is a return to the sense of walking as a solitary pursuit, as a means of appreciating the beauties of nature, and a means of meditation in motion. The old ways and the old walks evoke, just as much, the old wayfarers and the old walkers; and these are reflective, leisured walkers of a recognisable modern intellectual type. They were walker-thinkers at a time when walking was the default means of getting from one local place to another. Here is Rousseau, in the *Confessions*: 'Walking has something that animates and brings to life my ideas; I can barely think when I stay in one place; to put my mind in it, my body must be in motion.'[3] But while walking is essential to thinking, leg-movement to mind-movement, there is still an inherent and separate value in walking itself:

> The ambling life is the one for me. To travel on foot in beautiful weather in beautiful country, in no hurry, and to have a pleasant object as the end-point of my way [*course*]: that of all the modes of living is the one that is most to my taste.[4]

The tradition of walking-thinking is now being continued in a world in which walking's place among the means of transport is much more eccentric and exceptional. Rousseau's long-distance walking was a matter of not taking the stagecoach. For most of the nineteenth century, though, if you walked then you were implicitly choosing not to take the infinitely faster train. In the twentieth century it is the motor car that gathers the comparative force, and more directly so than the train. For a car, unlike a train, is a personal means of transport, just like your legs. You can leave when you want and go where you want; you are not bound by a collective timetable. I was not going to mention air transport, that other early twentieth-century transport innovation, because it didn't seem likely that any journey that might once have been walked would be long enough to be superseded by the plane. But of course, that's not strictly true. If there were a plane (there isn't), then it would have a perfectly respectable length of flight from the north of Scotland to the south-west end of England. (Or if you are Donald Trump, you could travel in your private machine.) And maybe walking can be imagined on an even larger scale. One of those contemporary philosophical walking books, Geoff Nicholson's *The Lost Art of Walking*, comes with the information (on its Amazon page) that its author 'divides his time between Los Angeles and London' – something that must certainly clock up the foot-miles, one way or another.

So it is noticeable, to begin with, that the present-day walking philosophers or philosophical walkers all consciously refer back to their eighteenth- and nineteenth-century forerunners – or rather, forewalkers. In fact, large swathes of the new books are taken up with going over the same grounds as did these earlier writers, as if we might find our own way as modern walkers only through their words, which give meaning to their walks and ours. But there is something still more intriguing about this present proliferation of walking books, and that is its firm turn away from a very different kind of walking history: I mean city walking, and the literature of the *flâneur*.

For more than a hundred years, it would be fair to say – more or less from the middle of the nineteenth to the very late twentieth century – *flânerie* was really the only walking game in town. The heyday of the *flâneur* overlapped with that of the rural walker (there were plenty of metropolitan strollers in the Romantic period), but country walking somewhat faded from representational visibility after the first decades of the nineteenth century. Instead, the *flâneur* was everywhere to be seen. *Flânerie* is walking, but it is walking of a very different kind from the kind of walking in natural spaces that was celebrated by Rousseau and the Romantics. The *flâneur* is a man with time to spare (he has no job to go to, he's probably quite well off) who is able to enjoy the random sights of the city as he walks. He is going nowhere in particular; he is open to distraction; in fact distraction, not destination, is the purpose of his movement around the streets. He is curious, and interested in what is new: a creature who follows the changes of style as seen on the street, and derives his daily pleasure from taking in this sense of the sighting of anything and everything that is of the moment.

The country rambler, on the other hand, loves the stability and constancy of the world he walks through. He will notice and appreciate the regular and relatively predictable changes, of the seasons or the weather, the light and the darkness at different times of the day and the year. But differences, whatever they are, should be natural, and man-made alterations (such as were brought about by the building of the railways) are most often experienced as a threat to the walking landscape. For the *flâneur*, nature is non-existent and human construction, human art, is all; the one natural limitation to his experience is the start and the end of the day, and in *The Painter of Modern Life* (*Le Peintre de la vie moderne*, 1863), Baudelaire reports on the über-*flâneur* who berates himself for getting up late – and thereby missing several hours of the sun's shining in which he could have been out and about. This wonderful essay of Baudelaire's may well be the high point of the *flâneur*'s literary existence. In it, the more than *flâneur*, not a philosopher but a painter, is someone who is compelled every day, all the time, not only to see and absorb the changing spectacle of the city, but also to set it down, to represent it. The ordinary *flâneur*, the common or garden (or main-street) *flâneur* just looks; he is not particularly energetic and has no particular task to fulfil, whether self-imposed or external.

Episodes of *flânerie* appear in many nineteenth-century Paris novels, minor and major (there is plenty of it in Balzac, for instance); and apart from fiction there are also manuals (or footbooks, perhaps we should say) in the first half of the century which guide the would-be *flâneur* in the sophisticated ways of this highly specialised practice. It was, in other words, a fairly mainstream activity (though definitely not a main road activity), between the bohemian and the gentlemanly; and it is something that you might enjoy in the representation of it just as much as you might enjoy it in reality. In this respect, it is exactly like the twenty-first-century crop of rural walking books, which are intended as narrative journeys in their own right, quite apart from whether you might ever embark on a personal rewalking of the route that has been described. Just as with rural walking, then, the pleasure of *flânerie* can be partly in thinking about it and reading (or writing) about it.

*Flânerie* is also, like rural walking, an activity that is usually done alone. There is even an explicit prohibition, in some of the guidebooks, on doing it in company. Anyone else is going to distract you from your (purposeless) purpose of being open to whatever appears on the way. And at all costs you should not think of *flân*ing with a woman. Not only will her presence prevent you from appreciating other passing members of the same sex, but she may well start forcing you to buy things for her. Bad idea, either way. This evident masculinity of nineteenth-century *flânerie*, both in the writing and in the reality, has itself been an important topic of argument in the past few decades of our own time – the period when, in the wake of Walter Benjamin's writings in the interwar period, the nineteenth-century *flânerie* epitomised by Paris and by Baudelaire was imported as a lost walking history to be rediscovered and remade. In a way, and paradoxical as it may sound, the nineteenth-century *flâneur* had his golden age in the late twentieth century, when Benjamin's writings, much read at that time in the English-speaking world, gave him a new lease of modern life as the figure *par excellence* of the critical, consuming man about town.

The *flâneur* is not really a philosopher or thinker, unlike his country counterpart; instead, he is out to experience whatever is offered by the city around him. He takes it in, and he may reflect on it and be conscious of his enjoyment of it, but his pleasure in his walk is not primarily intellectual. And whereas the philosopher-rambler will use the rhythmic action of walking as a spur to his thoughts or a way of bringing them out or working them through, the *flâneur* is not interested in the regularity of the physical movement, let alone in getting some exercise. On the contrary, he is much more likely to pause and stop *en route*; he has no particular destination in any case, and that indeterminacy is part of the very definition of his enterprise. The verb *flâner* is usually translated as something like stroll or wander; no English word quite captures the sense of being situated in the city – there is no other place for *flânerie* – but English does at least have these walking words that go against any idea of a set direction or purpose. Aimlessness and openness to stalling are the very essence of *flânerie*.

For the *flâneur*, in fact, the main advantage of walking is that it enables a constant pausing. If you notice something or someone you want to investigate further, you can; you can pause in front of shop windows, sit in a café, even take a short nap on a park bench, as the middle-aged Peter Walsh does in Woolf's novel *Mrs Dalloway*. Walking is also a sign that you are in no hurry. But rural and city walking have this much in common, that they are both undertaken for pleasure. To 'go for a walk' has that sense of taking the air and seeking enjoyment, wherever the location; in French, although there is no equivalent noun to 'a walk', the verb *se promener*, which is not confined to either town or country, has a similar sense of openness. If you go for a walk you are probably making a round trip of some kind, coming back to where you started rather than stopping at a destination: the walking itself, in other words, takes precedence. There is a perfect example of this in Woolf's essay 'Street Haunting', from the 1920s, in which the speaker declares her love of strolling around the local London streets at the end of the day, but gives herself, by way of excuse for going out, the trivial object of buying a pencil.

Another kind of walking from which *flânerie* must be distinguished is the sort that turns into a transitive verb in English. When you walk the dog, you do something which may very well resemble the motions of the *flâneur*, especially if your beloved creature is the sort who likes to dawdle here and there; or alternatively, if he or she is the sort who is let off the lead and runs around while you, the careful owner, do something else in the meantime. Walking the dog is a very British pastime (or duty); it has some resemblance to other kinds of accompanied walk in which human beings take other human beings, usually the young or the old, and generally anyone who is not able to to get about on their own. In some places walking dogs and walking babies or toddlers is so much seen as the natural reason for walking at all that a lone pedestrian can appear to be oddly out of place. 'Aren't you missing something?' a stranger once abruptly asked me – joking, I think (I hope) – on a semi-rural footpath on the outskirts of a town and much frequented by people with dogs. Further out in the country, the footpath demographic is very different. Pairs of people, groups of people you will find; but also many who are walking on their own. There will always be a friendly exchange of words, whether you are passing in opposite directions, or (a bit awkward, sometimes) going at different paces in the same direction, with one pair or person overtaking another. On country walks everyone is engaged in the same kind of leisure activity. In the city or town, on the other hand, there is no sure way of distinguishing between those who are out for a stroll and those who are definitely going to particular places. And often, as well, that distinction does not exist in the first place, as with Woolf's pencil-buying *flâneuse* – or with anyone who turns a necessary trip to the shops into a happy excuse to step outside.

The mention of stepping outside brings me to a different aspect of walking. So far I have taken it for granted that walking is something that goes on out of doors and in the open air – even if that air might be the more or less foggy or otherwise polluted atmosphere of a nineteenth-century capital city. This is true of anything that counts as 'going for' or 'taking' a walk, and even the *flâneur*, however unmindful of exercise, has to be outside, and moving his legs from time to time. But there is also, most basically, the walking that happens within a building: inside, indoors, upstairs, downstairs, from room to room or just a couple of steps across one. Because it is not continuous or prolonged, this walking does not figure as active exercise. But walking it is, all the same: the walking without which, as functional human animals, we would not get very far, as it were, with our daily lives. This ordinary all-the-time walking is now generically called 'mobility' – if you can't do it, or can no longer do it, then what you have is a mobility issue.

Mobility tends to become an issue towards the end of a long life, and it is one of the those so-called 'landmark' or 'milestone' achievements at the other end of it: the 'toddler', no longer the crawler, represents a distinctive transitional identity in the development of baby to fully-legged child, and the first momentous steps – giant steps, however tiny they may be – will be duly noted and remembered by an admiring adult entourage, just like a baby's first words. In English, the convenient rhyme of walking and talking makes these two early achievements, beginning to walk and beginning to talk, seem comparable to one another. Humans are animals that have *logos*, as Aristotle said – and that have two legs, as he possibly didn't say but could have: unlike other mammals, they stand upright and keep their other pair of limbs for activities other than walking.

The acquisition of speaking skills is a hazy and gradual process compared with learning to walk, with the first word (often a hopeful guess on the part of an adoring listener) being a long way off from the flexible invention of sentences and the more or less adequate understanding of everything everyone else is saying. Walking, as opposed to standing, or as opposed to crawling or shuffling, is much simpler to define and is a skill much more rapidly acquired. And it might seem that it's much less culturally specific than talking – after all, languages are infinitely nuanced and variable from one culture or subculture to another, whereas walking is just one foot in front of the other and everyone does it in much the same muscular way. But in fact there *are* differences, just as there are with most other features of physical comportment and movement. Most obviously, men and women tend to hold themselves and move themselves in different ways in different cultures and different social milieus; but there are also variations across the generations, or from one long century to another: variations that are minimal and imperceptible as they occur, but noticeable in the long term and nowadays through the documentary record of footage from many years ago of the way we walked then. Some time before that possibility, Baudelaire noted, again in *The Painter of Modern Life*, that each age has its distinctive way of holding the body, its way of looking, and its way of smiling; or more concisely, in French, '*chaque époque a son port, son regard et son sourire*';[5] these seemingly natural features of bodily behaviour are as mutable as anything else in human culture. And at the start of his *Lettres persanes*, a pseudo-ethnographic comparison of French and Persian culture in the early eighteenth century, Montesquieu, in the persona of an oriental visitor to Paris who is writing to a friend in Smyrna, says this:

> You wouldn't believe it, perhaps: in the month that I've been here, I haven't seen anyone walking. There are no people in the world who make better use of their machine than the French: they run, they fly. They would be stunned by the slow vehicles of Asia and the measured pace of our camels.[6]

In the nineteenth century, Europeans and Americans would cling to the idea of walking as a resistance against the machine speed of the the train, or else (on the other side) emphasise the effectiveness of modern transport as so much faster than horses' legs, let alone humans'. But with Montesquieu, long before anything faster than four-footed or two-footed locomotion of whatever kind is possible, there can still be a clear distinction between a culture of hurry and a culture of ambling, with the difference apparent in the contrast between the two.

Elsewhere in the book, another of Montesquieu's fictional correspondents speculates on the difficulty of imagining heavenly joys, as opposed to heavenly punishments:

> It is very confusing, in all religions, when it comes to giving an idea of the pleasures that are destined for those who have led a good life. It is easy to frighten the wicked with a long series of punishments you are threatening them with; but for virtuous people, you don't know what to promise them. It seems that it is in the nature of pleasures to be short-term; the imagaination has difficulty in imagining any others.
>
> I have seen descriptions of Paradise capable of making sensible people give up on it: some show these happy phantoms constantly playing the flute, and others condemn them to the punishment of eternal walking.[7]

This unstoppable walking, *se promener éternellement*, means leisurely walking, as opposed to the workaday movement of the verb *marcher* in the first passage I quoted. French makes this walking distinction, and also allows for non-pedestrian forms of the promenade: you can *se promener en voiture*, seated in your horsedrawn carriage, to see and be seen. The very endlessless of that outing, Montesquieu suggests, might as well be torture: as if stepping out and stepping along, even for pleasure, becomes, in the end, as mechanically monotonous as the repetitively incomplete works of Sisyphus with his boulder, or Ixion at his wheel. This is perhaps why Frédéric Gros ends his walking book *Marcher, une philosophie* not with some affirmation of the freshness of pedestrian movements of thought, but instead with the meaninglessness of the same steps repeated over and over again. For that too is walking, like the death drive – or death walk:

> Turning right, turning left: just to continue walking. The end of the world is not when everything stops but when everything continues, interminably: nothing else to do but to put one foot in front of the other, beneath the cold moons.[8]

Writing in the early eighteenth century, Montesquieu imagines how a pleasure prolonged might become indistinguishable from the opposite experience, of tedium. He could not have known that one day walking itself, his own example of an ordinary enjoyment, might take on the appearance of an everyday hellish compulsion. Minute after minute, step after step, and day after day, bodies in gyms put themselves through their self-appointed walking paces, never going anywhere and always continuing to walk and walk and walk, on the spot, and with no other object than the plan to keep going for a set amount of time in order to fulfil a given daily target of simulated distance. The activity has all the futility of one of the tasks in the classical underworld. It is a repeated physical action with no useful outcome; it mimics an act in which the body is moved from one location to another, but it keeps it exactly where it started. And finally, it takes place indoors, in an environment that has none of the chancy pleasures or other contingencies of the weather, the terrain, the different air we breathe or the different sights we see. It is a non-walk in a non-place.

Related to gym-walking is the way that now even real walking, outside or inside, can be represented and measured as if it were primarily to be understood as part of a daily quota. The pedometer straightforwardly counts your steps, wherever and whenever you make them. It takes its place alongside a growing number of devices under the category of wearable technology, which are designed to monitor many different kinds of bodily activity and expenditure of energy. Crossing the room or crossing the road; slowly making your way up and down the aisles of the supermarket; walking to work or (let's supppose) actually going 'for a walk': all these different types of leg motion come down to the same measure, to be triumphantly totalled up at the end of the day. What a life!

But at least, despite the common currency of paces or steps, when you move with a pedometer you are not confined to the gym. The gym scenario seems to be particularly unromantic in its refusal of any feature of walking beyond the bare physical use-value, as part of the regime required for maintaining a functional, well-tuned body. When this mode of walking is linked to the consumption of calories, as if that were a positive value in itself, it does not have even that limited use, since the maximisation of energy use is only a preoccupation of affluence: for those who have so much, potentially, to eat that their only worry is taking in more than they need.

Indoor walking might seem like a contradiction in terms: recreational movement needs open spaces, the street at the very least. But when walking is not (as it is in the gym) concentrated on an idea of physical benefits, then there is no particular reason for it to be restricted to the world beneath the sky. Benjamin made the Paris arcades, which do have a roof (though they are open at one end or both), the *locus classicus* for his *flâneur* to find himself in. He also said that the department store was something like the *flâneur*'s last shot.[9] The new stores were designed, above all, to appeal to women: to ladies of the the middle classes who were now provided with a space in the centre of the city where they could comfortably come and engage, for as long as they liked, in that indeterminate activity known as shopping. For one of the great innovations of the department stores was that they made possible casual browsing: the customers were free to come and go, to look and not necessarily to buy. The woman could be, in this way, an indoor, city *flâneur*.

So if it is not quite enough to say that department stores were the last stop for the *flâneur*, it could much more truly be said that they were the first port of call for the woman. They gave women their own distinctive form of *flânerie*, both respectable and enticing, a place where they could wander about for as long as they liked in a home from home that also had all the appeal of an elsewhere, full of exotic and interesting things.[10]

But we should not forget a much less romantic association of women and walking and shopping, and that is as part of a daily routine of travelling on foot to the market or shops every morning to purchase the food for the family meals. When supermarkets first arrived in the UK, in the 1960s, they were greeted with very mixed feelings, not least because they added to the burden of women already weighed down by too much shopping to carry home. In that context, a few small shops close to the street where you lived were more practical than a big store at a further distance. British households at that time mostly did not have cars. In the US the story is very different, with cheap cars available and the first supermarkets, in disused factories and warehouses out of town, relying on the people having the means to bring themselves to the place, with a vehicle that could also take home what they bought.[11] America ceased much sooner than other countries to be a walking culture, not least because of the rapid development of the suburbs, where houses were built without neighbourhood shops and the car was fundamental to the way of life. Today, in some places, there is a movement back to local shopping. with the supermarkets getting smaller not bigger and fewer but more frequent trips. .You buy what you can comfortably carry home, on foot. And it's no longer only women who are taking the things home.

At the end of this walking talk, I think it will be more invigorating to finish by coming out of the store and returning to the country air of the earlier history of walking without a purpose: walking with thoughts in your head and a spring in your step. As we saw at the beginning walking of the Rousseauesque and Wordsworthian kind can be matched by the post-Romantic walking of a walker who is acutely aware that this is a chosen means of movement, that there are other means of conveyance and that walking offers something that is now to be valued precisely because it is different from the faster and more efficient alternatives of mechanical locomotion: the railway first of all, but later also the car and the plane. In the middle of the twentieth century, here is the English memoirist Diana Athill giving a eulogy of walking that has much in common with Rousseau's:

> Such pleasure can only be enjoyed alone and on foot. Earth, stone, water, trees must be touched and smelt in order to be fully realized. I have seen landscapes more magnificent from cars, buses, trains, and boats, and have been pleased to see them; but the ones I have *learnt*, the ones which have become part of the fabric of my memory, are those which have made the muscles of my legs ache, have scratched my ankles and caused sweat to drip off my forehead. Why I should still consider the conscientious hiker slightly absurd I cannot conceive. He is undoubtedly gaining a more intense and enduring experience than any other traveller.[12]

Athill's lyrical praise of walking is dated in only one respect: her apology for mocking the character she calls the hiker. Today, with the walking guides running off the presses – 'rough guides' *par excellence* – that figure has been elevated to a superior status (and of course his or her equipment is high-tech and sophisticated in ways that could never have been envisaged in the 1960s, when he carried a paper map in his rucksack. But Athill is spot-on, I think, with her glorious celebration of the pleasures of walking and of sensing the local world you are in and the body you are in – the aching muscles and the sweat. Athill's hundredth birthday is in 2017; she had a new book out in 2016 so she is still writing. I don't know if she is still walking at all, but I hope so.

*Written for a talk at National Chiao Tung University, Hsinchu, Taiwan, 21 November 2016*

1  In September 2017, though, it was announced that the 2018 edition of Yellow Pages in the UK would be the last.
2  There are exceptions to the presently dominant country mode of book-walking, but they are often situated outside the familiarly flâneuresque metropolitan paths and practices. Matthew Beaumont's *Nightwalking: A Nocturnal History of London* (2015) changes the waking walking time, thereby reversing the mode of Baudelaire's artist-*flâneur* who berates

himself for getting up late and so missing some of the sun's new sights. This book is also goes against the leisurely perspective of most walking literature by dwelling on those who are moving about because there is no place to stay. In recent years there have also been various accounts of determined forays into modern spaces where no foot passenger was ever meant to go, and these are non-rural but also non-city walking books. The best known example is probably Iain Sinclair's *London Orbital* (2002), which documents a pedestrian circuit round the route of the M25 motorway that encircles London; its aim is to write about the places and histories that have been dislocated by the unrural lanes of that 1970s construction.

3 Jean-Jacques Rousseau, *Les Confessions* I, ed. J.-B. Pontalis (Paris: Gallimard, Folio, 1977), p. 215.

4 Rousseau, p. 227.

5 Charles Baudelaire, *Le Peintre de la vie moderne* (1863), in *Œuvres complètes*, ed. Marcel A. Ruff (Paris: Seuil, 1968), ch. IV, 'La Modernité', p. 554.

6 Montesquieu, *Lettres persanes* (1721; Paris: Garnier Flammarion, 1964), Lettre XXIV, p. 55.

7 Montesquieu, p. 199.

8 See Frédéric Gros, *Marcher, une philosophie* (2009; 2nd edn. Paris: Champs Essais, 2011), p. 300.

9 'Das Warenhaus ist der letzte Streich des Flaneurs', in Walter Benjamin, 'Paris, die Hauptstadt des XIX. Jahrhunderts', *Illuminationen* (Frankfurt: Suhrkamp, 1977), p. 179.

10 Some decades ago there was a lively literary discussion about the places of the woman city walker in the time of the flâneur. This developed in response to Janet Wolff's suggestive article, 'The Invisible Flâneuse', Theory, Culture and Society, 2:3 (1985), pp. 37–46. See for instance Rachel Bowlby, 'Walking, women and writing', in *Feminist Destinations and Further Essays on Virginia Woolf* (Edinburgh: Edinburgh University Press, 1997) and Deborah L. Parsons, *Streetwalking the Metropolis* (Oxford: Oxford University Press, 2000). A recent continuation is Lauren Elkin, *Flâneuse: Women Walk the City in Paris, New York, Tokyo, Venice and London* (London: Chatto & Windus, 2016).

11 This history is recounted in more detail in my book *Carried Away: The Invention of Modern Shopping* (London: Faber & Faber, 2000).

12 Diana Athill, *Instead of a Letter* (1963; 2nd edn. London: André Deutsch, 1976), p. 194.

# 2
## 'Half Art'
### Baudelaire's *The Painter of Modern Life*

In this piece, I look at an essay that I have probably read too often not to find in it the key to all matters aesthetic, historical, philosophical, and more. The essay is Charles Baudelaire's *Le Peintre de la vie moderne* (*The Painter of Modern Life*), first published in 1863 and written, most probably, around 1859 to 1860. Baudelaire's exhilarating innovation is to downplay the significance of eternal value in art, in favor of what he designates as its other half, the fleeting presentness that is modernity. My essay is unapologetically an appreciation – for the most part – of a text that, in focusing on another artist, itself appears to be just that. For Baudelaire develops his arguments through a mock-anonymous celebration of the artist Constantin Guys, referred to as M. G. (Monsieur G.), whose prolific sketches, done at speed, for rapid journal publication, chart the smallest of day-by-day changes and typical scenes in the appearances of the city. Guys's pictures – the art of modernity – give to the day a second life, and 'translate' into a different medium – from sight to (mental) impression to its 'rebirth' as a sketch – that which would otherwise be lost with its passing.

At one level, *The Painter of Modern Life* is a celebration of the work (and the lifestyle) of Constantin Guys, whose subjects ranged from fashion to war, and whose work was reproduced in widely circulated magazines such as the *Illustrated London News*.[1] Guys is not named directly by Baudelaire; there is a coy pretence of anonymity, on the grounds that this is what the mysterious M. G. himself would prefer, but he is readily and intentionally identifiable. The 'fiction', as Baudelaire calls it, of his subject's 'incognito' is essential to the elevation of a form of art that, in conventional terms, is not proper art at all. This 'painter of modern life' is pointedly not a singular, named genius whose work conforms to classical conventions and is confined for tasteful inspection within the precincts of a museum. Artists, in the usual sense, are debunked as 'village minds [*des intelligences de village*]', or, just to make the point quite plain, 'hamlet heads [*des cervelles de hameau*]';[2] whereas M. G. is 'cosmopolitan', a 'man of the world', someone who spends his time in 'the capital cities of the modern world' (VIII, 558).

Guys makes his appearance in the essay not exactly in his own right, but in the role of illustration or elaboration of a manifesto. Starting on aesthetic and art-historical, as opposed to urban or modern grounds, Baudelaire rejects art's confinement to established, and would-be permanent, media and modes of display:

> This is a perfect opportunity, in truth, to establish a rational and historical theory of the beautiful, in opposition to the theory of a unique and absolute beautiful; to show that the beautiful is always, necessarily of a double composition, even though the impression it produces is unified. . . . The beautiful is made of an eternal, invariable element, whose quantity is excessively difficult to determine, and of a relative, circumstantial element that will be, if we want, in turn or all together, the period, fashion, morality, passion. . . . I challenge anyone to discover some sample of beauty that does not contain these two elements. (I, 549–50)

Later on, this grand theory is stated from the other direction, starting from the historical rather than from the eternal, in what may well be the most famous sentence of Baudelaire's essay:

> Modernity is the transitory, the fleeting [*le fugitif*], the contingent, *half of art* [*la moitié de l'art*], the other half of which is the eternal and the unchangeable. (IV, 553; emphasis added)

At a stroke, or a couple of strokes, Baudelaire transforms, or claims to, both the likely subject matter and the evaluative criteria for art. The whole field of contemporary life and manners is opened up as worth representing, worth making into art–as having its own beauty. But Baudelaire is not simply making a claim for a new art that will do justice to the beauties of the present–the mid-nineteenth-century present in particular. He is also affirming that all art, always, has 'contain[ed] these two elements'; and that there is a pleasure in the art of the present *as such*. The art of past times can be seen, in this light, to have been representing its own present; one polemical thrust of the essay is Baudelaire's contempt for artists who insist on draping their subjects in 'historical' costumes, rather than showing them in the fashions of their own moment: 'The pleasure we take from the representation of the present derives not only from the beauty that may clothe it, but also from its essential quality of presentness [*sa qualité essentielle de présent*]' (I, 547).[3]

'The pleasure we take' draws everyone into an appreciation of a world out there now that is already and always half art, awaiting its completion or visibility in the form of the artist's representation. It is also perpetually changing, with the observer or artist enjoying and noting what Baudelaire calls, in a lovely phrase, *la métamorphose journalière des choses extérieures*, 'the daily metamorphosis of external things' (II, 550) – a formulation that seems to be poised halfway, mythically and historically, between Ovidian transformations and the tiny but perpetual changes of *The Origin of Species*, which is exactly contemporary.[4] The scene is set far from the natural variations of seasons, landscapes, or living things; nature is neither an image of stability against the confusions of social change, nor in itself a model of constant growth and change. Unlike either of these, though, Baudelaire's changing world is proudly urban and man-made--and woman-made: his paradigm of daily change and proto-art is fashion. Woman may be the first spectacle, inseparable, says Baudelaire, from her costume, her *toilette*; she is also, by implication, the primary artist, who knows that nature stands in need of embellishment.

The chapter entitled 'Eloge du maquillage' ('In Praise of Make-Up') draws Baudelaire's most scathing remarks against the idealisation of nature in both an aesthetic and a moral sense. This leads him to yoke together two seemingly quite disparate halves. Fashion and make-up, emblematised by the woman, are joined to the civilising necessity of collective morality that has to be added on. Just as nature is to be improved, or beautified, by makeup and dress, so morality is founded not on following but in departing from a nature which, if left to itself, would be violent: 'Crime is originally natural; the human animal drank in the taste for it in its mother's womb. Virtue, in contrast, is *artificial*, supernatural, because in all times and for all nations there have had to be gods and prophets to teach it to brutish humanity and because *on his own*, man would have been powerless to discover it' (XI, 562). This is how Baudelaire slips an ethical half in alongside his theory of art: morality is like art, in that both of them seek to improve on a nature that is originally flawed.

Baudelaire's half-and-half theory of art is not itself presented as belonging to any particular time. Implicitly, it is transhistorical or even quasi-eternal. For any given work of art–and the earliest example he offers is pretty early: primitive religious art–there is and was a circumstantial, cultural present, discernible in retrospect as distinctive and often now as ancient. Some past presents, though, are evidently more worthwhile than others. Baudelaire has little time for what he sees as the falsely historicising or pseudo-simple self-representations of the eighteenth century – just as early-twentieth-century modernists would routinely debunk the benighted aesthetics and values of the nineteenth century. But it might also seem that the idea Baudelaire is promoting about both the significance and the perpetual change of the present could only have come up in the modern period in which he was writing: in other words, in a world conscious in a new way of change, rapid change, as the normal condition of life. This does not invalidate the theory; but it might suggest that only in the modern period, the period in which both the constancy and the rapidity of visible change are taken for granted, could artistic images come to be viewed in this way: as the remains of modernities past.

In this connection, we might also wonder about the almost arithmetical division of art into two halves – with nothing apparently in between these mutually defining, separate-but-united extremes of historical time, the eternal and the momentary. It makes for a neat dialectic and for a perhaps too easy complementarity of form and content: 'Without this second element' – that is, the second element of the present age – 'which is like the amusing, titillating, apéritif envelope of the divine gateau, the first element would be indigestible, unappreciable, unadapted and not appropriate to human nature' (I, 550). For the consumer of art, this sounds like a way of having your cake and eating it – of doubling, not halving, a pleasure which, in perfectly Baudelairean fashion, is both digestive and divine.

Guys, as the exemplary observer and reporter of daily changes, appears in various guises, all of them associated with a post-Romantic protean self. He is said to be like a child: curious, and seeking and finding everywhere evidence of novelty. Or, like a convalescent, he is an adult whose childish curiosity is revived, so that he always sees the world as new. Here Baudelaire appeals to Edgar Allan Poe's short story 'The man of the crowd' (1840), but omits the tyrannous fascination exercised by the figure whom the narrator cannot help but pursue. In this Baudelairean world are no mysteries, no threats or unreadable signs; the pleasure is all in a visible image that is its own present, given to the curious eye. Following this line, Guys is also a casual *flâneur*, one quite unthreatened by any imagined enemy or alien figure within the crowd. On the contrary, he plunges into it, becoming a 'mirror' or a 'kaleidoscope endowed with consciousness' (III, 552); he is even a self who can't get enough of non-self – a '*moi* insatiable du *non-moi*' (III, 552).

Alongside this immersion a countermovement makes M. G. the artist into a restless, tireless worker whose job is never done. Things are changing all the time, new sights coming into view, and M. G.'s task, by definition impossible and endless, is to get them all down, all represented, before it is too late. But first, his day job is to see: when he wakes in the morning he rushes off in regret that he's already missed so many hours of the light and of '*lit-up* things I could have seen and I haven't seen!' (III, 552). Baudelaire's highlights of Guys's typical day show him swooping down from the panoramic 'landscapes of the big city', all the way to the details of a minutely modified way of buckling a belt or tying a bonnet. 'All this enters into him, jumbled up; and in a few minutes, the poem that results from it will be virtually composed' (III, 553). Until finally: 'But evening has come!' Everyone else is in bed, the gaslights are out, but M. G. is at his work, 'fighting it out with his pencil, his pen, his paintbrush, making the water spurt up from the glass to the ceiling, wiping his pen dry on his shirt, in a hurry, violent, active, as if he was afraid of the images escaping him. . . . And the things are reborn on the paper, natural and more than natural, beautiful and more than beautiful' (III, 553). There is real work here, part of an idiosyncratic daily pattern, involving excesses of energy and haste – there is no time to lose but somehow, from the material mess of the workshop, the magical rebirth occurs. The fleeting present, temporarily stored as mental images, must and can be saved, re-presented, rematerialised, to give it a second life.

The notion of rebirth is crucial here: 'And the things are reborn [*renaissent*] on the paper.' Phrases like 'the representation of the present' or 'the memory of the present' highlight the disjunction inherent in this present that is always moving past, that is separated from itself the second it is seen and registered as such. But the painter can bring about a miracle of resurrection, through what Baudelaire calls 'a memory that says to each thing, "Lazarus, arise!"' which is all the time contending with 'a fire, a pencil-drunkenness, almost like a madness. It is the fear of not going fast enough, of letting the phantom escape before the synthesis has been extracted and seized' (V, 555).[5] The stress is not on something that must be lost in the change of form, the movement away from reality, but on the energy and passion that brings about a new or a transformed life. And the life belongs not to the subject, the artist-observer, but to the things themselves. This is not, in other words, an elegiac version of *carpe diem*, mourning the predicament of a subject condemned to make the most of his transitory existence before it is too late *for him*; rather, it is the external, contingent things of the world that must be grasped and revived in a form in which they can begin and continue to matter.

Baudelaire more than once uses the image of fencing, the 'duel' that is set up between 'the will to see everything, to forget nothing, and the faculty of memory', which takes in the general contours of what is seen (V, 555). But he also has another metaphor for Guys's working practice: translation. For the most part, Baudelaire insists, Guys does not and should not draw from nature; he gains or takes *impressions*, which are then, in a subsequent stage, set down. In all there are three image-stages: the image first seen, then the image in the memory, and finally the image that is actually drawn on the paper. Baudelaire calls what Guys does 'translating his own impressions', the impressions – much more plainly a printing term in French – being the image in the mind of the image out there. Spelling it out a few sentences later, he says: 'The spectator is here the translator of a translation' (V, 555). In the choice of this word, we can glimpse the first hints of some other kinds of translation that may be taking place, more or less surreptitiously, throughout the essay. Any art criticism must, by definition, put pictures into words, must represent the image in a different, verbal medium. Baudelaire takes this process right back to the artist's own practice, so that a visual representation of what is seen is already being conceptualised in the destination medium of its present representation in words: as a series of translations.

In other ways, too, Baudelaire's transposition of Guys's art into the terms of his own theory of modernity clinches or subtly affirms its own argument. At various points, Guys's work is actually described as a 'poem' – as in, 'the poem that results from it will be virtually composed' (III, 553). The effect is to make it seem as if Guys's art was from the outset awaiting this final translation in and into words; his consecration is granted by, and also entirely dependent on the words of the critic. Baudelaire emphasizes, and praises, the provisional, half-art condition of Guys's works. His method 'has this incomparable advantage, that at any point in its progress, every drawing looks finished enough; you may call that a sketch [*ébauche*] if you like, but a perfect sketch' (V, 555). Baudelaire admires Guys's casual, dispersed and dispersing, attitude. He works on several pictures at once; now and then he goes through them and picks out a few to touch up a bit more; he is always giving them away or throwing them out. In its very practice, Guys's work illustrates the perpetually ongoing external changes that are the ephemeral side of art's subject. But it needs the writer to finish off the image of Guys himself as the artist of modern life. So Guys himself is brought alive or reborn in a new, Baudelairean way: raised up to embody that role.

Over the years, critics of Baudelaire have often speculated about alternative artists who might have been chosen instead to take Guys's exalted place. Why this minor figure, little known at the time – and today, ironically, known best as the artist who figures in Baudelaire's *Le Peintre de la vie moderne*? But I think this misses the point of the essay, which positively requires a half-artist to exemplify the uneternal, uncanonical half of art that is said to be excluded by traditional aesthetic values. Guys's type of art is not to be found in museums, or not primarily; instead it is scattered in modern media that are themselves both actual – of today – and ephemeral. Guys was not a poster artist, but that would have been an equally pertinent choice, since posters at the time were themselves a ubiquitous feature of the always changing street views of big cities. Half art *par excellence*, they were part of the present reality that the art of the modern should represent.[6]

But still, there is a sense in which Baudelaire's radical add-on to the paradigm of art can be seen as a device for having it both ways. The second, new half of art is supposed to differ from the first by its transitoriness of both subject matter and artistic medium. The art of modern life is characterised by its impermanence, valued as such. And yet a wish for continuance is present, too, from the start. The present is present, says Baudelaire, in all art, not just the art which is avowedly the art of the everyday, ephemeral in its subjects and its media. But the present thereby hitches a ride to eternity, which has the effect of downgrading its own opposite value – as fleeting, as passing – that the essay is promoting. Guys is differentiated from an ordinary *flâneur* because he is not interested only in 'the fleeting pleasure of circumstance', of what's around. Rather, Baudelaire goes on, 'it is a matter of disengaging from fashion the poetical in the historical that it may contain, of pulling out [*tirer*] the eternal from the transitory' (IV, 553). In this and other formulations, the value of the transitory lies in its having an extractable element of the other half, the eternal, which continues to predominate or to be the ultimate form or matter of art.

It is striking, with regard to the representation of the transitory, that Baudelaire was not interested in the artistic and representational possibilities of the then new medium of photography; in fact, he loved to hate it, describing what he called 'the photographic industry' as 'the refuge of all the would-be painters too little gifted or too lazy to finish their studies.' The incompleteness of the sketch is not a virtue here, nor does photography appear as a means of capturing the momentary or infinitesimal modifications of the day that are his focus in *Le Peintre de la vie moderne*.[7] And yet, in speaking of Guys's visual dispatches from the Crimea, Baudelaire singles out one image to which the artist has added, in English, the words 'Taken on the spot' (VI, 556). What could be more of an advertisement for photography as a mode of eye-witness reporting?[8]

In one way, it is ironic that this essay about the importance of the ephemeral should have acquired an extended history and thus a kind of proto-immortality. In one of its recent reincarnations, it finds a place in the monumental *Norton Anthology of Theory and Criticism*.[9] Several brief extracts are distilled as the portions fit for a place in the canons of criticism; the longest are the chapters on modernity and make-up. From all the passages chosen, but the one on make-up in particular, Baudelaire's essay emerges as a manifesto for the postmodern – as celebrating the images and surfaces of everyday fashions and beauties without the backing of a substantive, foundational authenticity, and as insisting on the necessity but also the contingency of ethics. It is a selection and slanting that is designed to highlight Baudelaire's continuing modernity – and to show him as a precursor of contemporary philosophical theories. In its new digest, Baudelaire's essay on modern life and art is brought back to life for new readers – with half, or less than half, picked out to represent the whole of it in the terms of a primarily playful and pleasurable postmodernity.

This new weighting, or selection, in new present times, may also suggest a different kind of absence in the original text. For while the essay on Guys stresses the historicity of both art and daily life, it is not concerned with how future cultural changes might bring about new versions or new understandings of past times, in such a way that the art of the past would be constantly made to matter in new ways by being reinterpreted or re-presented in relation to altered norms or possibilities of engagement. Yet Baudelaire's essay itself, like any enduring work of art or criticism, has continued to be retranslated or transplanted into new contexts and idioms. Such retranslation, it could be argued, is the very condition of the survival or perpetual renaissance of any work of art or criticism; it is how, if not why, art comes or continues to matter.

*An expanded version of a paper written for a one-day conference on 'Why Art Matters', in honour of Malcolm Bowie, Cambridge, December 2005*

1   The weekly *Illustrated London News* had a circulation of 300,000 in 1863; the figure for the (daily) *Times*, which was the dominant serious British newspaper, was just 70,000.

2   Charles Baudelaire, *Le Peintre de la vie moderne* (1863), in *Oeuvres complètes*, ed. Marcel A. Ruff (Paris: Seuil, 1968), ch. III, p. 551. Further citations will be included in the main text.

3   There is a related complaint against a false historicism in art in Henry Fielding's 1749 novel *Tom Jones*: 'Vanbrugh and Congreve copied nature; but they who copy them draw as unlike the present age as Hogarth would do if he was to paint a rout or a drum in the dresses of Titian and of Vandyke. In short, imitation here will not do the business. The picture must be after nature herself. A true knowledge of the world is gained only by conversation, and the manners of every rank must be seen in order to be known'; quoted from John Bender and Simon Stern's edition (Oxford: Oxford University Press, 1996), 648–9. Unlike Baudelaire, however, Fielding's primary target is not those who consider the present an unfit subject for art, but those who write about the upper classes without having any personal familiarity with them; from this he makes the analogy with a hypothetical picture of a fashionable contemporary social event in the costume of a previous age. That art should be open to the authentic representation of present-day scenes, à la Hogarth, is here taken for granted; it is not the subject of special advocacy.

    More directly in the French literary line as a precursor to Baudelaire is Stendhal's argument for a literature suited to its own time in *Racine et Shakespeare* (1823). Shakespeare, for Stendhal, stands for a responsiveness to contemporary culture that is absent from the French persistence in following literary models and rules that have long ceased to have any vitality in the present. One style may be the right one for the time it emerges, but dated and quite inappropriate for a later period or society. Stendhal uses the terms *classicism* and *romanticism* to differentiate between the two attitudes to literary production:

> Sophocles and Euripides were eminently romantic; they gave the Greeks assembled in the theatre at Athens the tragedies which were bound to procure the greatest possible pleasure for this people, based on their moral habits, their religion, and their prejudices.
>
>     To imitate Sophocles and Euripides today, and to make out that these imitations will not produce yawns in a nineteenth-century French person, is classicism.

See Stendhal, 'Racine et Shakespeare', in *Racine et Shakespeare (1818–1825) et autres texets de théorie romantique*, ed. Michel Crouzet (Paris: Honoré Champion, 2006), p. 295.

    Whereas Baudelaire insists that the eternal and the present are two sides or halves of the same artistic coin, Stendhal makes a much clearer demarcation such that works will fall into one or the other category, unequivocally. But the binary mode of manifesto argument is the same, as is the emphasis on the value of presently relevant artistic practice (and the mocking dismissal of the perpetuation, in contemporary work, of modes of writing whose time has long since passed).

There is also in Stendhal, as in Baudelaire, an appeal to the speed of change–which Stendhal specifically associates with recent history: 'In historical memory, no people has ever experienced a more rapid or total change in its customs and its pleasures than the change from 1780 to 1823; and they want to give us still the same literature!' (p. 302).

4  The first edition of Darwin's book was published in 1859. Its running evolutionary argument is directed against the idea of natural history proceeding by means of sudden leaps or shifts or obliterations, and in favour of a countermodel of constant, infinitesimal change, without a clear teleology of development – what Darwin calls 'a slowly changing drama'. Without large or decisive events, this drama is anti-tragic: 'The old notion of all the inhabitants of the earth having been swept away at successive periods by catastrophes is very generally given up. . . . On the contrary, we have every reason to believe . . . that species and groups of species gradually disappear, one after another, first from one spot, then from another, and finally from the world.' See Charles Darwin, *The Origin of Species*, ed. Gillian Beer (Oxford: Oxford University Press, 1996), 254, 256.

5  Another reference to Lazarus's resurrection occurs in Baudelaire's poem 'Le Flacon'. In his moment of reemergence into life, Lazarus appears with the stench of a corpse several days old, 'Lazare odorant déchirant son suaire'. In this poem concentrated on a power of smell that is stronger than either matter or death, the odorous Lazarus comes over very differently from the Lazarus of *Le Peintre de la vie moderne*. The reawakening of 'Lazare, lève-toi' is clean by comparison; it is aural and visual, to do with response and recognition. (In the analogy, the dead man hears the words; the figure who rises again can be seen to be the image of Lazarus.)

6  At the time of Baudelaire's writing, posters were far more prominent on city streets than they are now: this was their heyday, before the regulation that kept and keeps them off the external surfaces of public buildings. In Paris, the words 'Défense d'Afficher: Loi du 29 juillet 1881' ('No Bill Posting: Law of 29 July 1881') may still be read, inscribed into the walls of many buildings around the city: as though ephemeral images and writing could only be prevented by permanent writing in the very place from which they have been prohibited.

7  Baudelaire, 'Le Public moderne et la photographie' (from 'Salon de 1859'), in *Œuvres complètes*, ed. Ruff, pp. 395–6.

8  In this connection it is also noteworthy that Roger Fenton, one of the first war photographers, was commissioned to document the conflict in the Crimea.

9  See *The Norton Anthology of Theory and Criticism*, ed. Vincent B. Leitch et al. (New York: W.W. Norton, 2001), pp. 792–802.

# 3
# Readable City

'Reading' the city is so commonplace a metaphor that we tend not to see or hear it as such: it is an indifferent feature in the lexico-graphical landscape, something we see and pass by every day without giving it a second look. Geographers, sociologists and architects, as well as literary critics, all speak of – and write about, and design courses on – the 'legibility' of the city, usually taking the phrase for granted – taking 'read' as read. But why should it seem so obvious to speak of reading in relation to urban experience? (Or, to put this from another direction, why does 'reading the village' sounds like a contradiction in terms?) And what kind of reading is being evoked when we go about reading the city?

Reading city-reading, the first meaning we come to is something relatively simple, suggesting a process of orientation. If you can read the city, or bits of it – this landmark, this person, this street – that means that 'you know where you are'. The city that is read in this way is like a map of itself, with repeated signs that have meanings that are readily supplied. 'Readers' decode what they see, smell or hear, with differing capacities to do this – according to their own general skills in city literacy, or in the signs of this particular city or neighborhood, or according to the variable legibility of the signs out there to be read.

In Book VII of *The Prelude* (1805), city reading appears in sev-eral guises, beginning with this simple sort that suits a process of gradual familiarisation with what is initially strange. Wordsworth evokes the contrast between the fantastic travellers' tales of the city that he heard in his Lake District childhood and his own experience of the place itself in adult life, and he uses a reading metaphor: 'And now I looked upon the real scene;/ Familiarly perused it day by day.'[1] The speaker teaches himself to read the city 'scene'. Later, referring to the infinity of urban spectacles 'that do each . . . / Look out for admiration' (lines 567, 571), he says that he did not '[make] unto myself a secret boast/ Of reading them with quick and curious eye' (lines 579–80).

But against and alongside the readable Wordsworthian city is something else, an unreadable London of 'blank confusion!' (line 695) where nothing and no one is known: 'How often, in the over-flowing streets,/ Have I gone forwards with the crowd, and said/ Unto myself, "The face of every one/ That passes by me is a mystery!"' (lines 594–8). Uninterpretability, multipled *ad infinitum* – the crowd, the overflowing, 'every one' – is at the other extreme from the sameness and comparability that is presumed for a practice of decoding, in which sights and persons are read according to known classifications and there is no 'mystery', nothing hidden or incomprehensible. From this endless series of unknowable passers-by Wordsworth chooses one, the 'blind Beggar, who, with upright face,/ Stood, propped against a wall, upon his chest/ Wearing a written paper, to explain/ The story of the man and who he was" (lines 611–14). The description brings into the picture of the city a piece of real writing whose superficial legibility – the speaker can see what it says – only points to another kind of unreadability, through the sense of an irrevocable separation of the man himself (unable to read it) from the 'paper' that supposedly tells his story and 'who he was'. Whereas the metaphorical perusal of the city brought things closer, made them 'familiarly' everyday, the actual 'written paper' here marks a distance. Literal legibility – the identifiability of sequences of letters and their meaning – is the sign of a more fundamental absence of human understanding, in which the impossible connection between two men appears as the inability of one really to 'read' the other.

Poe's 'The Man of the Crowd' (1839) invokes versions of the same three kinds of city reading. In the story's opening scene in a London coffee house, the convalescently curious narrator has 'a cigar in my mouth and a newspaper in my lap', in which he has been intermittently 'poring over advertisements' (84).[2] This actual reading then gives way to a study of the rush-hour crowd of pedestrians passing the window, in which 'I descended to details, and regarded with minute interest the innumerable varieties of figure, dress, air, gait, visage, and expression of countenance' (85); some of these varieties he then systematically proceeds to separate out and list, together with their identifying features. This urban observation is displayed as a form of classificatory comprehensiveness. The omnivident narrator calls it reading: 'it seemed that . . . I could frequently read, even in that brief interval of a glance, the history of long years' (87). Finally, the third kind of reading appears in the shape of the 'absolute idiosyncrasy' of a figure who cannot be classified and whose hidden and therefore unreadable story spurs the narrator to the futile pursuit that occupies him for the rest of the tale: '"How wild a history," I said to myself, "is written within that bosom!"' (88). Poe's story is framed at both ends by a declaration of unreadability that is itself cast, unreadably, in a foreign language: '"*er lässt sich nicht lesen*"' (84). But the words are then immediately translated – 'It does not permit itself to be read' – as if to make utter unreadability at least readable as such. At the beginning of the story the sentence is referred to "a certain German book"; at the end the subject is the elusively unknowable 'man of the crowd' himself.

The two metaphorical senses of reading in both Wordsworth and Poe point to opposite types of interpretation. On the one hand, reading is a fairly straightforward, learned skill in which urban details are understood as signs with common meanings. On the other, there is the profound, in-depth 'reading' that is inexhaustible and ultimately impossible, descending beyond evidentiary detail to the absolutely idiosyncratic for which there is no shared code or language. This non-reading is prompted by the confrontation with someone or something that cannot be assimilated to a recognisable, known pattern. In the absence of the codes or keys that would make this possible, there is 'blank confusion' and dislocation: Poe rushes out of the café to follow his man, and Wordsworth's 'mind did at this spectacle turn round/ As with the might of waters' (lines 615–16). Feasible, practical reading produces or enables the comfortable relationship that gives the urban subject his imagined familiarity in and with his surroundings, while unreadability marks the breakdown of that settlement, as if exposing it as merely provisional. But the strangeness of *reading* as the term for either experience, either mode of relation to the city, remains.

Wordsworth's and Poe's texts provide clues to one possible explanation for why it might be that we 'read' the city. Both include real reading and writing as part of their descriptions of London. Poe's narrator is initially absorbed by newspaper advertisements, among other things. In Book VII of *The Prelude*, apart from the blind beggar's written paper, there is mention of other forms of street lettering, as 'files of ballads dangle from dead walls;/ Advertisements, of giant-size, from high/ Press forward, in all colours, on the sight;/ These, bold in conscious merit, lower down/ That, fronted with a most imposing word,/ Is, peradventure, one in masquerade' (lines 209-14). Words and images compete for the passer-by's attention, demanding to be read – and Wordsworth and Poe themselves take note of these forms of urban writing as prominent, 'in-your-face' aspects of everyday urban reality.

Thus the readable city in the nineteenth century is not only a metaphor. This city is readable – literally, whatever 'literal' reading might mean, in this or any other context. Experiencing the city, where posters and newspapers are concerned, is also, plainly, a matter of reading. As something to do, by choice or by chance, whether glancing at a poster or stuck into a newspaper, and as involving a material 'written paper' to touch or see, reading is really and unmetaphorically a part of everyday urban life. Long before Walkmans, let alone iPods, it can also take on the role of providing the reader with his or her own semi-private space within a public place. Like daydreamers, readers are in a world of their own, 'poring' or perusing or just browsing; but their partial absence from this one, unlike that of daydreamers, is visibly marked by the presence of the book or newspaper.

There is a further way that actual reading is highlighted in the nineteenth-century city. In both metaphorical models of city-reading, decoding and 'depth', there are no actual letters, and the role of the signs that are 'read' is only that of the means to the meaning, simple in one case and unfindable in the other. But in the case of advertisements, in newspapers and on walls, the letters stand out, not only if they are 'giant-size' on the scale of the poster, but because they are part of a design that is meant to be visually attractive. Seeing the letters aesthetically is another kind of 'literal' – letterly – reading.

In the early part of the nineteenth century, there was more and more urban reading going on – more of it crossing the daily path of the city-dweller. There was an increasing number of daily newspapers, with rising circulations. New printing technologies, especially lithography, greatly expanded the production of posters, as well as offering more sophisticated design possibilities, with the result that posters were everywhere you looked – or would have seemed so to twenty-first-century eyes. The nineteenth century was the multi-coloured age of the postered city – until, in its final decades, their siting began to be regulated by legislation both in European countries and in the United States. (The phrase 'Défense d'afficher' – 'No billposting' – can still be seen etched into Paris buildings, marking this historical turning point, as these words are always followed by the exact date of the 1881 law which put them where they are. (Ironically, the wall can only be secured as an image- and writing-free zone by imprinting it, forever, with words: no longer just a wall, it is now a wall that has to be read as being just a wall.) Newspapers, too, had a Victorian high point, before the cinema and the radio and then TV cut into the primacy of this written news medium. And with the extension of education, people who lived in cities were themselves now mainly literate, seeing their urban world through reading eyes.

We may have forgotten the details of this nineteenth-century back-story but it may begin to explain how it is that in the twenty-first century, texting or not as we go, we are still, automatically, 'reading' the city.

*Written for a Forum on the city in the journal* PMLA, 2007

1   William Wordsworth, *The Prelude* (1805), Book VII, lines 139-40, ed. J. C. Maxwell (Harmondsworth: Penguin, 1971). Further references will be given in the main text.
2   Edgar Allan Poe, 'The Man of the Crowd', in *Selected Tales*, ed. David Van Leer (Oxford: Oxford University Press, 1998), p. 84. Further references will be given within the main text.

# 4
# Motoring through History
## Woolf's 'Evening over Sussex'

A tiny essay with the longest of titles, 'Evening over Sussex: Reflections in a Motor Car', is described by Andrew Thacker as 'a mysterious yet inconclusive piece of writing'.[1] It is true: the piece gets stranger every time you read it, and that strangeness drives you to repeat the journey – and then again. What may have seemed relatively straightforward – a meditation on motoring late in the day through a still just visible landscape – starts to shift in all directions and between all dimensions. In spatial scope and scale it ranges from the close-up of a hedge to the vision of a fairly distant shore. In terms of time there is a grand historical spectrum, backwards and forwards, that goes all the way from the Norman invasion, past the present, to come to the picture of some semi-utopian future five hundred years away – only then to end up at in anticipation of the everyday cosiness of supper tonight back home.

There is also a generic movement from what starts out as seemingly a picture of a landscape seen from a historically new perspective – the moving motor car – and then becomes something much more like a staged philosophical debate between competing existential possibilites or ways of seeing. It is a sort of dialogue of self and soul – 'these two selves then held a colloquy'[2] – except that here the initial sparring halves of the self-divided passenger become three, then four. And eventually even six or seven, depending on how you count them. After the four have had their say in turn, a further character is wheeled on, or pulled into the car, to bring them together and summarise the discussion. Along with this chairperson yet another creature then appears who is some sort of hybrid or composite figure for all the things that been severally said up till then; but who, or which, at the same time is seen to be separately visible: 'Look at him; there on my knee' (455) Is he cute or grotesque? Not clear. (But the car must be thoroughly overloaded by now.) Finally, seventhly, out of the blue is 'the body', who gets a speech or chant that is a list of its favourite foods, and that is wanting the journey to end so that it can enjoy them – though the last sentence (and last paragraph) also suggests a kind of solipsistic fusion of this physical being with the multiple mind that has previously held sway: 'And the rest of the journey was performed in the delicious society of my own body' (456).

From this summary – I'm not sure whether it's a retrospect or an approach, a distillation or an interpretation – you can see that it is not really possible to speak of 'Evening over Sussex' apart from its secondary title, 'Reflections in a Motor Car'. Both Sussex and the evening rapidly give way to the several conflicting chattering viewpoints that emanate from within the travelling motor car. Once past the colon, as it were, there is no going back, no way to turn round: it is as if we were leaving behind the here and now of the time and the place, to enter instead into an enclosure where various competing arguments are voiced, one after the other. The travelling car, in turn (but it doesn't turn, as far as we know) is momentarily the emblem of a modernity that enlightens the visible world rather than darkening it into night.

The essay begins in a way that suggests something like a piece of eccentric travel writing. It is really odd :

> Evening is kind to Sussex, for Sussex is no longer young, and she is grateful for the veil of evening as an elderly woman is glad when a shade is drawn over a lamp, and only the outline of her face remains. The outline of Sussex is still very fine. The cliffs stand out to sea, one behind another. (453)

The disorientation of this view is many-layered. First of all, someone whose looks have been enhanced by a flattering light-shade is not in a position to see the improved image. This fanciful personification is literally a prosopopaiea, as the worn skin on the face of an aged female disappears from view in the more favourable lighting of dusk. From the beginning, Sussex is presented aesthetically, as a kind of sketch of itself, or herself, with this outline on the one hand masking the wrinkled reality it does not reveal, and on the other showing itself as the picture that accurately represents a certain time of day. Late in the day, a rejuvenation takes place that is both natural (evening shows Sussex at its best, 'still very fine') and dissimulating (it hides old age).

Woolf's writing does manifest, from time to time, an old-fashioned, not to say patriarchal tendency to feminine personifications. With this old lady Sussex, we aren't far from feminised ships or hurricanes or countries. In various of Woolf's essays of the 1920s, we find a generalised 'literature' being given the form of a protean female through the ages: in 'Mr Bennett and Mrs Brown', for instance, literature is an old woman who has been violently treated of late. But let us note in passing that there is something else quite strange about the use of the woman-as-landscape assimilation here. Growing old is represented as a process of disfigurement and deterioration; the original outlines can be seen or restored in the forgiving evening light. These are the premises, conventional enough. But following that thought, the cause of Sussex's appearance of ageing is everything modern or recent: the new is the old and the old – the Norman Sussex – is when Sussex was young and beautiful and unmarked.

So that is the beginning. The next sentence of the essay develops this complicated landscape thought by adding the detailed imprint of particular place-names and a bright listing of likely seaside paraphernalia. But there is a sting at the end of the sentence:

> All Eastbourne, all Bexhill, all St Leonards, their parades and their lodging houses, their bead shops and their sweet shops and their placards and their invalids and chars-à-bancs, are all obliterated. (453)

At first you might think that these are listings of Sussex's modern beauties. They are not, as the last words show: this is not a continuation of the passing view, but a description of everything that is not now visible in the fading light – or, in the more violent language of the essay, of what is 'obliterated', invalids and all. The following sentences go on to amplify this perspective, including a signature Woolfian reference to eyesore 'red villas' normally cluttering the coastline, but happily hidden from the evening eye:

> What remains is what there was when William came over from France ten centuries ago: a line of cliffs running out to sea. Also the fields are redeemed. The freckle of red villas on the coast is washed over by a thin lucid lake of brown air, in which they and their redness are drowned. (453–4)

Leaving aside the fact that William did not, at Woolf's time of writing, come over ten centuries ago (*966 and All That?*), what this does is to make the Norman conquest into an image of ancient stability (and strength, presumably): 'What remains is what there was when William came over'. The fields are 'redeemed', no less. Those nasty little villas, or are they bungalows maybe (can't tell the difference in this light) have vanished beneath the waters; while 'drowned' suggests that this might be an aesthetically fortunate extinction of their inhabitants too, as with the wiping out of the Eastbourne invalids.

But the evening eradication of the offensively modern 'red villas' and, generally, 'redness' does not put an end to their presence in the essay. The ugly accretions, the surface tat, may have been chucked out into the sea, but the next paragraph brings in the subject or source of the reflections as someone who isn't at peace; who can themselves be represented as a complex geological formation, evidently less clear-cut than the lines of the cliffs:

> But, I thought, there is always some sediment of irritation when the moment is as beautiful as it is now. The psychologists must explain. (454)

And there follows an elaboration of the subjective frustration of not being able to master or put into words an experience of 'beauty and beauty and beauty' (454) that is blown up like a balloon but then somehow bursts:

> But what is the pin? So far as I could tell, the pin had something to do with one's own impotency. I cannot hold this – I cannot express this – I am overcome by it – I am mastered. Somewhere in that region one's discontent lay; and it was allied with the idea that one's nature demands mastery over all that it receives; and mastery here meant the power to convey what one saw now over Sussex so that another person could share it. (454)

Note that already at this stage there are no fewer than four iterations of 'I', disjoined by their dashes into semi-separate sentences, and held apart from the other self that was basking in the endlessly added beauty. The writing has departed from description of what is seen, or its allegorical cover, into description of how it cannot be described, via a new personification of a semi-articulate split-up self who is defined by thwarted communication. To see and to say and to say to you (to an other) would be the continuous tranquillity that the first late Sussex sighting, the 'beauty and beauty and beauty' of the outline, is pushing towards. But that is precisely what is sharply deflated as not possible, as if the pleasure in the view were to vanish with the perceived impossibility of representing it, of 'the power to convey': there is no sublime transcendence of that impossibility.

This tension and snapping in the experience of the overmastered spectator then leads to further spin-offs of the self, together with the first hint, apart from the title, that the scene of reporting is located inside a moving car:

> And further, there was another prick of the pin: one was wasting one's chance; for beauty spread at one's right hand, at one's left; at one's back too; it was escaping all the time; one could only offer a thimble to a torrent that could fill baths, lakes.
>
> But relinquish, I said (it is well known how in circumstances like these the self splits up and one self is eager and dissatisfied and the other stern and philosophical), relinquish these impossible aspirations, be content with the view in front of us; and believe me when I tell you that it is better to sit and soak; to be passive; to accept. (454)

The multiplication of selves is now taken as a conversational commonplace ('it is well known'), rather than a specialised research problem beyond the reach of the non-expert ('The psychologists must explain').

What is seen by the series of selves is mostly quite unspecific to Sussex. In one case, the third self, it is barely even a view. Or rather, it is a view at one remove, what the third self imagines the other two to be looking at:

> I (a third party now declared itself) said to myself, how happy they were to enjoy so simple an occupation. There they sat as the car sped along, noticing everything: a hay stack; a rust red roof; a pond; an old man coming home with his sack on his back; they they sat, matching every colour in the sky and earth from their colour box, rigging up little models of Sussex barns and farmhouses in the red light that would serve in the January gloom. (454)

In fact 'they' – the first two selves – are not just looking, in this view, but reconstructing, painting the picture before them to store it for future use. The sequence of things they see includes the only real whole person in the essay, the old man on his way home. These disparate bits of 'everything' can be fitted together as parts of a pastoral working economy, just as the observing 'they' are seen by their co-self as actively doing something, 'so simple an occupation'. This self no. 3 defines itself through an incapacity for such engagement:

> But I, being somewhat different, sat aloof and melancholy. While they are thus busied, I said to myself: gone, gone; over, over; past and done with, past and done with. I feel life left behind, even as the road is left behind. We have been over that stretch, and are already forgotten.

There, windows were lit by our lamps for a second; the light is out now. Others come behind us. (454)

This allegorising self will be glossed by the chairperson self at the end as having spoken of 'the death of the individual. The vanishing road and the window lit for a second and then dark' (455). And then, in an even briefer summary of the summary, it is simply 'death'. Here the car represents a kind of technological upgrade on the established analogical language for brief mortal lives: in the quick shining of a headlight, the person passes (though the implication is that the watcher inside the cottage – I'm sure it is not a villa – will remain). The minimalisation of human life, whether personal or collective, is suggested by the passing of the car's momentary headlights.

But this is not the end. Death itself passes, is only a middle stage or a present fleeting moment that then makes way for the final self to appear, which is described as 'the economical, powerful and efficient future' (455). To long-standing readers of Woolf, past and present, this last self is quite unexpected. The fuller description seems to be without irony, at most with a touch of end-of-essay autopilot or self-drive:

I think of Sussex in five hundred years to come. I think much grossness will have evaporated. Things will have been scorched up, eliminated. There will be magic gates. Draughts fan-blown by electric power will cleanse houses. Lights intense and firmly directed will go over the earth, doing the work. (455)

Apart from the early twentieth-century emphasis on electricity, and the equally dated mention of the 'elimination' of excess – a preoccupation to be found in in much interwar discourse, from literary criticism to shop design – this could be a present-day promotion of smart technology for home maintenance at a distance. But in Woolf this sort of fantasy is usually presented as a caricature – as when Arnold Bennett's novels are said, in another essay, to be populated by characters in a first-class railway carriage, `pressing bells and buttons innumerable` while *en route* for 'an eternity of bliss in the very best hotel in Brighton'.[3]

It could be said that the playful-serious multiplication of selves while the body is away from home becomes almost a Woolfian signature structure around the time that 'Evening over Sussex' was written (it was drafted in 1930). Not long before, there is *A Room of One's Own* with its many I's or Marys thinking their way around Oxbridge and London. There is 'Street Haunting', set at the same twilight time of day as 'Evening over Sussex', in which the self is free to be what it likes – any other self – as it walks about in the centre of London. There is *Orlando* which, apart from the sequential male-female duo with their differently gendered views of the world, allots a couple of thousand selves to its heroine by the time of its early twentieth-century concluding day.

It is notable that these four texts all involve ongoing movement on the part of the various selves, and are all located away from home (with a home, nonetheless, on the horizon). *A Room of One's Own* and 'Street Haunting' have urban walkers who are happy to be out and about. *A Room* never goes into the enclosed private space that its title claims and honours, while 'Street Haunting' is presented as a liberation from home, whose circumscription signifies a broader constraint of the possibilities of the self. But in the other two instances, *Orlando* and 'Evening over Sussex', the setting is rural and home is the ultimate destination, not the vague point of departure. (Although to be truthful here I do need to say that the aristocratic Orlando has two homes; she's come from the one in the city and is travelling down to the one in the country.) Home is where Orlando is headed and where, as we have seen, the multiple person of 'Evening over Sussex' eventually longs to curl up. And both these rural home-bound multi-selves are also travelling in a car.

Orlando is very much the solo driver of her own car, but in 'Evening over Sussex' it is difficult to know who is at the wheel; and if it is not the proliferously conflicted speaker – for safety's sake, one hopes not – then the driver, a further presence next to the surrounding talk of the chattering passenger, is never mentioned at all. It is also difficult to know if any particular journey is envisaged. In his notes to the essay, Stuart Clarke maps out a round trip that starts from Rodmell and passes through Eastbourne, Bexhill and St Leonards.[4] But although it is true that Woolf lists these three towns in the right geographical order, they are not so much separate places as a generic red blot or blur on the outlined landscape; the only other distinguishing mark of a would-be specific Sussex location is 'pink clouds over Battle' further on.

But at this final juncture I would like as it were to park the squabbling family of selves – the backseat philosophers – to look instead at their mode of transport. The car of the essay appears to travel in almost splendid isolation. Just once, there is the momentary identification of 'the moving light in that hill' as the lights of another car – to be taken not as a fellow traveller, but rather as part of the image of the future:

it is the headlight of a car. By day and by night Sussex in five centuries will be full of charming thoughts, quick, effective beams. (455)

This reads like a curiously positive preview of the 24/7 media flashes of early twenty-first-century culture. At any rate, it's clear that the roads being driven in 1930, the roads taken and not taken, are not exactly congested. *Pace* the wish to eradicate Eastbourne and the rest, the only overcrowding to be found on these roads is within the car itself.

Here I can't resist quoting Woolf's innocent diary driving boast. Less than two weeks after mentioning that she is about to have a first lesson, she states: 'Since writing the last entry I have learnt enough to drive a car in the country alone`. Those were the days! We notice not just the speedy and testless learning time, but also the independence: on her own not just inside the car but also, it would appear, on the road. 'The world gave me this for writing *To the Lighthouse*`, she goes on (its strong sales had enabled the Woolfs to buy a second-hand car).[5] That 'this' is, specifically, 'a nice little shut up car in which we can travel thousands of miles'. For instance, in another entry during this first fine flush of the motoring expansion:

> Yes, the motor is turning out the joy of our lives, an additional life, free & mobile & airy to live alongside our usual stationary industry. We spin off to Falmer, ride over the Downs, drop into Rottingdean, then sweep over to Seaford, call, in pouring rain at Charleston, pass the time of day with Clive – Nessa is at Bodiam – return for tea, all as light & easy as a hawk in the air.[6]

This begins to sound like a jolly children's book from a few decades later – or like copy for *Country Life*; but the concluding car reflection, in a different mode entirely, is a boringly plain statement of gender equality: 'After a week here [in Rodmell, in Sussex], Leonard has become perfectly efficient; I am held back by insufficient lessons, but shall be expert before September is half through.'[7]

And in the previous diary entry, just before this would-be matter-of-fact little plea (just as good as him!), there is this:

> We have motored most days. We opened one window when we bought the gramophone; now another opens with the motor.[8]

At such moments that highlight new ways forward, it does look as if the future in front of 'us' is one that is getting better–getting better in ways that have to do with a private and personal experience. We are safe in the enclosure of our own home or vehicle, into which a world elsewhere, of sound or sight, music or landscape, is selectively and virtually filtered for critical discussion. This future is purchasable (if not necessarily affordable to all) and it involves the latest technologies. Already, new windows can be opened at the touch of a button. The twenty-first century has already arrived in Sussex.

*Paper given at a conference on 'Sussex Modernists and Transformations in the Twentieth-Century Landscape', organised by Alistair Davies and Hope Wolf, at the University of Sussex, June 2017*

1   Andrew Thacker, *Moving through Modernity: Space and Geography in Modernism* (Manchester: Manchester University Press, 2003), p. 182.
2   Virginia Woolf, 'Evening over Sussex: Reflections in a Motor Car', in *The Essays of Virginia Woolf*, vol. 6, ed. Stuart N. Clarke (London: Hogarth Press, 2011), p. 454. Further references will be given within the main text.
3   Woolf, 'Character in Fiction' (1924), *Essays*, vol. 4, ed. Andrew McNeillie, p. 155.
4   See Woolf, *Essays*, vol. 6, p. 456n2.
5   Woolf, *The Diary of Virginia Woolf*, vol. 3, ed. Anne Olivier Bell (1980; Harmondsworth: Penguin, 1982), Saturday 23 July 1927, p. 147.
6   *Diary*, vol. 3, Wednesday 10 August 1927, p. 131.
7   *Diary*, vol. 3, loc. cit.
8   *Diary*, vol. 3, Monday 8 August, p. 13; the last six words belong with the following entry, for 10 August.

# 5
# Shopping for Christmas

It was the afternoon, if not the night, before Christmas. There were only two supermarket shopping hours left in the world before the beginning of that unreal time out of time, two days of total shoppinglessness. Every good citizen, and especially every good mother, had long since filled fridge, freezer and every available household cavity with turkey, pudding, crackers, brussels sprouts peeled in advance, and everything else required or desired to survive or enjoy the interval. Or so it seemed if, like me, you were wandering around along aisles that seemed suddenly empty. Gone were those tailback queues, the trolleys stockpiled with festive fortifications as though to last out the whole winter. Now there were just a few people merrily scurrying about with baskets, air of a job long done, picking up one or two last things. It was all as jolly as could be. My two-year-old daughter, as yet unimpressed by the packets on the shelves, was grabbing all she could of the unaccustomed space in the aisles. I was thinking we might as well go and see what there was in the way of, say, turkeys, and also sprouts, and especially smoked salmon, when the first of the announcements came up. All items in the bakery department reduced to 10p. Extensive selection remaining, you are invited to come and look. A short pause. Then it was turkeys down to a pound, or was it 50p. Then it was maybe the puddings or the cream or the sausages. Anything you ever wanted for Christmas day you could have for next to nothing. We drifted about with the prices dropping audibly at every turn. Big yellow REDUCED stickers beckoned with offers you couldn't refuse. We could have had Christmas every day for the next year and still had change from... In fact, why not stop off on the way home for a couple of cut-price freezers and stock up now for fifty convenient Christmases to come? This, perhaps, would be a form of just appreciation for our undeserved good fortune.

For of course the scandal now was that we, the ungodly, the non-planners, the last-minute dissolute, were the ones who were being so magnificently rewarded. We had failed to attend regularly through

December, carefully laying up our stores and buying always more than we meant. Imagine if all the others had known, the faithful of the full trolleys, the list-makers and impulse-buyers of all shades, all those who had filled and fulfilled the lures and demands of super-market orthodoxy. For them Christmas had been a long-term, long-month project, one which requires – and start in November, by all means! – that you spend as much in four weeks as you would in four months of ordinary mistletoelessness.

Now naturally when we went up and asked the people energetically unloading the loaves and the fruit cakes it turned out that no such dramatic drop of price or convention had been intended to gladden the hearts of the last shoppers – not even the cheery top-up crowd, let alone the feckless unturkeyed few. There had been, it appeared, some almighty *error of judgement*, that was certainly *never to be repeated*. Calculations in high places and on far-off computer screens had gone wrong. Over-ordering based on mistaken predictions of levels of demand in the final days, not to say the final hours, had regrettably taken place. But the proof that the mistake was at least honest, and even in some sense *not* a mistake, because accurately based on the available evidence and premises, was that not coincidentally *the same thing was happening right now in East Grinstead*. However, lessons would be learned. Next year it would not be like this year.

And nor would I, not daring a second time to risk the possible effects of a supply swing in the opposite direction. A year on I was a reformed consumer. Planning and preparation had occurred. A bird awaited stuffing. A stocking awaited filling. And I was not the only one to have grown up. The former two-year-old was picking up things that appealed to her off every reachable bit of shelf, and chucking them adeptly into the trolley. Supermarket shopping had become a newly dangerous business, not to be undertaken on a whim, still less without a plan.

But drawn back as though to the scene of a crime, I couldn't resist having a look, same time, same place, to see if history or fairy tale would repeat itself on the afternoon of Christmas Eve. No such luck. This time there seemed to be very little fresh food left on the shelves, and nothing that was reduced beyond a half-hearted 20p or so. Maybe that wonderworld last year had all been a fig of the over-heated Christmas imagination, a tale told to gullible toddlers and listless grown-ups to indulge and correct their misbehaviour for one magic and final moment.

Shopping at Christmas is pictured as a joyful, impulsive experience, at the same time as it is also meant to be meticulously planned.

In this respect, it is like a magnified version of other kinds of shopping, striking an uneasy or intriguing balance between images of work and pleasure.Get a list! Prepare in advance! Christmas shopping has to be done, and the sooner the better, to get it over with, all ticked off and ready. First the plan, then the purchase, then the event, in a straightforward, ordered sequence. A crucial prop is the sacred List, which in this once-a-year form oddly involves a mixture of people and commodities. An aunt is one kind of thing, a box of chocolates another, but here they bump up as potentially compatible matches between those in the category of the to-be-bought-for and those in the category of the to-be-bought. At the same time, have fun! Be spontaneous, open to inspirations of the moment. Christmas buying is now, but it is also a time of nostalgic echo and hopeful anticipation, recalling and remaking imagined Christmases past when the snow is always just starting to fall in soft white flakes and the presents have yet to be opened. Christmas shopping makes magical providers, finding the very thing for the very person, creating a surprise.

This double face of a commercial Christmas is nothing new. In two famous English novels from the first half of the twentieth century, both sides appear in sharp relief, in the women who act out their roles. Jan Struther's Mrs Miniver, the subject of sketches in the *Times* in the late 1930s, became a cult figure of middle-class Englishness. First becoming a novel, in 1942 she was made into a Hollywood film that was instrumental in swaying American public opinion in favour of entering the war. And the thing about Mrs Miniver is that she does it all effortlessly. In the book version, we see her returning from a successful day of Christmas shopping. All her Christmas shopping is gift shopping (she has servants to take care of the food), and no war is yet interfering with her whimsical meditations on her not very but just planned enough attitude to buying presents, and her pleasure in the actual experience of finding just the right thing. However much she might try to, persuade herself to get it done early, she ponders, by pretending Christmas was on another date or that all her friends lived abroad, 'Mrs Miniver knew very well that Christmas was not until the 25th of December, and that all the people on her list lived in England':[1]

> Besides, successful present-choosing depends very largely on finding the right atmosphere, upon the contagious zest of crowds, upon sudden inspirations and perceptions, heightened rather than otherwise by a certain sense of pressure in space and time. To do it

cold-bloodedly, in a half-empty shop, without any difficulty or competition, is as joyless as a *mariage de convenance*.[2]

Hence, there is no point or pleasure in shopping before the middle of December, when the 'pressure' of people and time has mounted up. Mrs Miniver's self-congratulatory consummation is meant to convey the happiness of her matches. Pressure engenders not stress but a positive urge. Atmosphere, zest and inspirations far outweigh any sense of duty or necesssity in what still remain as 'all the people on her list'. Mrs Miniver is effortlessly munificent, passionately punctilious, everybody's attractive mother.

At the other extreme, and thirty years earlier, it would be difficult to find a more dreary scene of Christmas shopping than the one in *Howards End* (1910). Forster writes:

> The crisis opened with a message: would Miss Schlegel come shopping? Christmas was nearing, and Mrs Wilcox felt behindhand with the presents. . . . Margaret accepted, and at eleven o-clock one cheerless morning they started out in a brougham.
>
> 'First of all,' began Margaret, 'we must make a list and tick off the people's names. My aunt always does, and the fog may thicken up at any moment.'[3]

Then Mrs Wilcox tells Margaret to put her own name down first. '"Oh, hooray!" said Margaret, writing it' (76). That is about as jolly as things get, as fogs of seasonal depression and annoyance duly drift between the two of them:

> They drove from shop to shop. . . . At times they passed through a clot of grey. Mrs Wilcox's vitality was low that morning, and it was Margaret who decided on a horse for this little girl, a golliwog for that, for the rector's wife a copper warming-tray. 'We always give the servants money.' 'Yes, do you? yes, much easier,' replied Margaret, but . . . saw issuing from a forgotten manger at Bethlehem this torrent of coins and toys. Vulgarity reigned. . . . A poster of a woman in tights heralded the Christmas pantomime, and little red devils, who had come in again that year, were prevalent upon the Christmas cards. . . . How many of these vacillating shoppers and tired shop assistants realized that it was a divine event that drewthem together? (77)

Unfortunately Mrs Wilcox ends up 'overtired by her shopping' and indeed 'inclined to hysteria'. Apparently Margaret has kept her critical thoughts to herself, but readers, who have no choice but to share them, are not likely to be cheered any more than her companion would have been by her dismal pronouncements on the commercialisation and vulgarity of Christmas.

Nearly a century later (*Howards End* was published in 1910) there may be some distraction to be found in the transformation of the golliwogs and copper warming-trays into items of historical curiosity rather than purchasing potential. They figure as fall-back gift possibilities at the time, while there is also a sense of changing Christmas fashions in other areas, like greetings cards; though little red devils, in or out of style, have not been seen for some time.

Mrs Wilcox's depressive Christmas spirit and Margaret Schlegel's censorious one get a necessary job done with a certain morbid efficiency, making the world appear a slightly less tolerable place in the process. No Mrs Miniver sparks here. Margaret's 'hordes of purchasers' are in a different world altogether from Mrs Miniver's 'contagious zest of crowds'. Mrs Miniver manages to embody a remarkable mixture of blissful maternal generosity with multiple varieties of self-satisfaction: in the moment of shopping, in herself as inspired shopper, in her brilliant reflections on both. What a satisfying image, in its turn, of adorable femininity.

No supermarkets are yet in existence to require of these fictional ladies the food-buying work that servants, somewhere off-page, are no doubt performing on their behalf while they go to buy their presents. But change the scene, and set them all down in a supermarket on Christmas Eve at the end of the century. Mrs Miniver's eyes light up as she starts to formulate some excited and pointed thoughts on the automatic pricing scales or the end-of-aisle display. Mrs Wilcox, sadly, becomes faint at the very first whiff of store-baked bread, leaving Margaret to go round resolutely locating every item on the list. Perhaps out loud this time (she is getting old), inviting strange looks from knowing toddlers, she delivers a fierce complaint at the contemporary conflation of commerce and spirituality, text slightly amended from 1910 version to allow for changes in detail. A REDUCED sticker on an Advent calendar containing chocolates elicits her particular condemnation. Meanwhile Mrs Miniver sails smugly by again, basket on arm, and picks up a luxury assortment of nuts.'Vacillating shoppers and tired shop assistants' continue to circulate for the remaining hour, vaguely looking for yellow labels or mechanically sticking them on.

Perhaps it is time to get out of here. A solitary Santa Claus, as though unsure whether this is the place he should be, is hovering at the top of the aisle like a ghost of department stores past. There are things to be done at home and it is, after all, getting late. Mrs Wilcox needs to have her early night, and Mrs Miniver and Margaret will want to collect their consumerly thoughts together and wrap them up once more for rumination over the course of next year. Never before could so much be seen, to despise or desire, under a single Christmas shopping roof. Christmas has come again and again, with its repetitions and its surprises, its pressures of pleasure and planning. But next year – and the thought gives Margaret a pang she did not expect to feel – will be different, and even final. For better or worse, it will be the last twentieth-century Christmas.

*Published in the* Independent, *12 December 1998*

1   Jan Struther, *Mrs. Miniver* (New York: Grosset & Dunlap, 1942), 38.
2   Struther, 38.
3   E.M. Forster, *Howards End* (1910; Harmondsworth: Penguin, 1953), 76. Further page references will be given within the main text.

# 6

# Please Enter Your Pin

Sometimes alone, sometimes in pairs or family groups, the people walk up to the top of the aisles and wait their turn for the service. They push their carts, into which they have carefully placed, one at a time, all the bright things that will be theirs. One at a time, once more, the things are then taken out of the cart and set down on the moving surface of the altar. One at a time, once more, now the priest – most often a woman – takes hold of each of the things with her hands. Her blessing is marked by a special sound when they are gently brought up to a brightly lit object above the altar. After that they are passed to the other side where they will be picked up – one at a time, once more – by the people, then put into bags, and then returned to the cart. Certain words are spoken. At the end, a shiny card is put into a little slot and taken out again, and a small slip of paper is given to the people by the priest. The people depart into the world outside with their things.

The anthropologist has come from afar – from another planet or another time, perhaps the time when Zola described the department store, new in his day, as 'the cathedral of modern commerce'. No continent on earth is now without supermarkets, the least remarked yet most on-the-ground ubiquitous American cultural export of the twentieth century. Supermarkets began in the Depression of the 1930s, taking advantage of an already car-borne population who could travel for miles to the makeshift outlets set up in disused factories and warehouses, happy to 'wait on themselves' in return for the bargains they then drove home themselves. Within a few years, supermarkets had become the normal mode of food shopping in the United States; 'self-service' was the great shopping revolution of the century.

A commentator on retail trends called M.M. Zimmerman set himself up as worldwide promoter of the big new idea but it was several decades before other countries, each initially in their own idiosyncratic ways, began to feel its effects. In Britain the first self-service stores, after the war, were about the size of a large front room, and even when they started to grow they stayed where the shops always had been, on the high street, until planning restrictions on edge-of-town sites were modified in the 1980s. At that point the trip to the supermarket, in the car, became for many a weekly ritual – and often, after 1993, on Sundays, when that ancient restriction was lifted too. France outsupermarketed all its neighbours, and America too, by spawning vast *hypermarchés* from the 1960s, but it has also, much more so than Britain, maintained a culture of local shopping and small stores along with the mega-sized new ones. In recent decades, British and French chains like Tesco and Carrefour have been among the biggest players in a rush to colonise newly capitalist countries across the world with this particular feature of Western lifestyle.

The crucial change brought about by self-service is that it takes away the one-on-one exchange between the customer and the seller. In the traditional over-the-counter situation, a woman comes into a shop, waits her turn, produces her list, and asks the assistant for what she wants. He fetches and weighs it and bags it up for her, and perhaps he gives her advice about which or how much or a newly stocked product this week. When self-service came along, this supplanted scene looked different depending on how you regarded the new practice. For one side it became a spectacle of old-fashioned dirt, disorder, and rip-offs. Now, thankfully, the customer was in control and could pick out the things she wanted, in her own time: no shoddy goods slipped in, no waiting about, no grubby hands on her potatoes and no intrusively personal attention to what exactly she was buying. For defenders of the old way, the same story simply spun itself the other way round. Self-service meant the blandness of plastic packaging and the loss of human familiarity and warmth, of the shopkeeper who knew and cared about his stock and his customers. It also meant that you were doing the work yourself.

These alternative pictures of the selling scene can be linked to a history of ways of thinking about shopping that reaches far back. The pedlar coming to the rural cottage, his store on his back, is a romantic figure, the bringer of new things and stories from distant places; the door-to-door salesman is his crude twentieth-century descendant, foot over the threshold, pushing his way in where neither he nor his tacky wares are wanted. With another small shift of the viewfinder, the salesman becomes, in Arthur Miller's famous play, the very image of the unhappiness and failure of the ordinary twentieth-century man. Moving further back again, the shopgirl in the nineteenth-century department store has both innocence and a moderate glamour; she is working in a classy new metropolitan environment but probably comes from a provincial place, just like many of the ladies she serves. This woman works very long hours for very small wages, but her customer may not be well off either: both, as they perform their two roles, can share the fantasy of the beautiful shop and the grand life in which they are taking part.

When it comes to the supermarket, the mystique and the variability of the selling encounter have seemingly gone. The human salesperson is no more, his or her role discontinued and substituted only by whatever forms of persuasion or plain information the product package supplies. Salesmanship manuals in the early part of the twentieth century had attended with pride and delight to the nuances of the exchange between seller and buyer, described in terms of identifiable stages that might or might not result in a completed sale. But writers at that time were also beginning to refer to a figure called the silent salesman, the non-human replacement or successor to the talking version.

The silent salesman could take the form of anything from a poster to a package to a window display – or, for that matter, a cardboard dummy. The good thing about this neutral figure was that it didn't interfere with you; the bad thing – usually a bad thing – was that it didn't utter a word to you. Later on, the shelves of the supermarket would be seen as one long array of silent salesmen, with all the products visually vying to proceed through the four classic phases: to attract the customer's attention, then interest, then desire, and finally sale. How that appeal was supposed to happen depended on whether the customer was imagined (as she often was, especially in the postwar decades) as a 'mindless' machine responding automatically to scientifically measurable features of colour and layout; or whether, on the contrary – there was little in the way of middle ground – she was imagined as a model of informed rationality, sensibly comparing prices and quality to the best of her knowledge.

And imagined was what the customer was – imagined obsessively and fantastically, in endless, compendious American surveys which tracked her movements through the store, silently following her solitary passage along the aisles. But on the other side, the selling side, there seemed to be nobody left to imagine – no salesperson whose skills or whose own dispositions might have some significant part to play. Which is then what makes the checkout operator, present and active at the point of sale but not at the point of choice, such an interestingly neglected figure, until now written out of the supermarket story.

The checkout itself, far from being ignored, has always been a focus of anxious attention for supermarket chains. It is the point at which every customer, however darting or drifting their time in the store up till then, just wants to get on and get out; the point at which freedom of movement is suddenly brought to a halt; the point at which casually picking up whatever you think you might want becomes basically having to pay. The single great event in the history of the checkout was the improvement in speed and accuracy enabled by the invention of the barcode (the till receipt from the first ever barcode transaction, at a Marsh supermarket in Troy, Ohio, in 1974, is now on display at the Smithsonian). At the checkout, unlike anywhere else in the store, efficiency is all; a given task must be completed as fast as possible. Yet this, the one stage in the super-market shopping sequence which really is mechanical, is also the only point at which another person is necessarily involved along with the customer.

From this point of view, the checkout might look like the last supermarket survival of the old scene in the shop: there is a counter and on the other side of it there is a human being. But the formal resemblance conceals the great difference. The cashier, unlike the shop assistant, has no role to play in the customer's choice of what to buy, no words to say beyond formulaic instructions and questions; the job is just to get the given things scanned and paid for. There is nothing else for her to do; apart from speed, the only possible achievement is negative, not to have made a mistake.

It is not a promising position. The supermarket cashier joins a long line of sales personnel in history, but her presence and her predica-ment have been unrepresented in manuals or novels or plays or films like those in which shopgirls – and sales clerks – have sometimes appeared as figures of interest and complexity, to themselves as well as to their customers. Just as supermarkets, unlike other kinds of shop, have been largely passed over in literature despite their pres-ence, today, in most people's weekly lives, so supermarket workers have not inspired the sort of curiosity that emerged so readily in rela-tion to the department store assistant. Zola's novel *Au Bonheur des Dames*, for instance, energetically documents the social and economic world of a late nineteenth-century Paris department store, and lights its informational load with the fantasy story of a special shopgirl who ends up marrying the owner – and also sharing the running of the store.

Possibly the nearest novelistic equivalent to the checkout girl appeared in a story of more than a hundred years ago, 'In the Cage', in which Henry James imagines the imagining life of his young 'heroine' (his word; she has no name) who works behind the post office counter of a grocery store in an affluent part of London. Her main job is to take and transmit the words of the telegrams which, like expensive emails, her customers are constantly dispatching. Like the till operator who sees and handles all the things that her customers are buying, she is privy to the most intimate details of these people's lives; she knows or guesses their stories while they, on the other side, have no curiosity about her. As an interested intermediary who has no role of her own, she is free to observe them, unnoticed herself. Like an omniscient narrator she knows more about them than they know about each other – and, as she also knows, she is sharper than them all.

James for his part offers a specific source for the girl's picturings of the high life from which, behind her social and actual bars, she is cut off. He makes her a regular reader of 'ha'penny novels';[1] and when briefly she does have a real encounter, beyond the shop, with the male object of her outwardly mobile desires, her immediate concern is to dispel what she assumes is his stereotypical image of her. This is 'her thoroughly successful deprecation, though conveyed without pride or sound or touch, of the idea that she might be, out of the cage, the very shopgirl at large that she hugged the theory she was not'.[2]

In the end James returns his heroine to the social place from which her fantasies and her novels had removed her; in the parallel case of a female friend who has also failed to break into the other world, she sees 'the vivid reflection of her own dreams and delusions and her own return to reality. Reality, for the poor things they both were, could only be ugliness and obscurity, could never be the escape, the rise'.[3]

Yet in fact her reality, waiting patiently in the virile form of an enterprising and conscientious grocer who wants to marry her, has more prospects than for many.

With James there is no stated mission to raise his readers' consciousnesses about the inner life or the actual work of the unregarded shopgirl. But Anna Sam's *Checkout* really is an account of what it is like to work in the contemporary equivalent of the grocer's, and it was a surprise bestseller in France.[4] Sam worked behind the tills for eight years at a large supermarket in Rennes. Her book is written in the guise of a mock survival manual for the novice checkout worker. No frills – no plot or romance. (What not to say when you are asked at the interview why you want the job? Because my mother was a till operator and it's always been my dream.) Just the small incidents and frustrations of any likely day, told in a series of tiny themed chapters. Once hired, there is a mentor to guide you through the first few shifts, but after a month you will be used to the beeping, used to the exhaustion. You will be like a machine; more lovingly put, it will be 'as if you and your till are one'. Just you and it, a match made in supermarket heaven ('*Mes caisses, mes amours*', 'My till, my love'). There is also the friendly conveyor belt – more softly and magically, the *tapis*. With a sudden lurch forward or finely timed breakdown it is ready to join with you in upsetting the carefully stacked goods of a quibbling customer.

With these fragile intimacies of screen and button, it is a strangely isolated job, performed out of eye-contact reach of your colleagues in the line (thirty checkouts in Sam's store), but right in front of the people who pass before you as you physically move their purchases along. Most of the time the customers are occupied with each other, or with their own small moment of manual labour, unloading the trolley and filling the bags, and they do not even look at the person to whom they hand their card (half seriously, half not, Sam is grateful to the man who bothers to say hello in the middle of a conversation on his mobile). But they are quick to speak up when there is any kind of delay ('this always happens to *me*'). There is even a woman who shuts up a child with the thought that you'll end up like that lady, working behind a checkout, if you don't try harder at school.

Sam evokes 'your solitude and powerlessness' when faced with difficult customers. She describes moments of drifting off into a kind of computer-game reverie, suspended somewhere above the blinking screen and the moving belt, beyond the muzak and the beeps. Or, in the mode of pseudo-advice, she proposes that once your ever repeated movements and words have become automatic, as so soon they will, you should put your thinking mind on standby, thereby saving your brain cells for your old age. She manages to steer a delicate course between showing the (sometimes) comic variety of the people ('the full extent of human stupidity, and you will be thrilled to find that it has no limits'), and showing the sheer monotony and relentlessness of the work. Anecdotes about the crazy characters you have to deal with are snapped off with a few unforgettable customers, from the repulsive to the astonishing. There is the one who dumps down for scanning a half-eaten sandwich dripping with tuna mayo; the one with the CD smoothly sequestered inside the Camembert box, a perfect fit; and there is the obliviously snogging couple with four small children in tow.

At the same time, details of what the job actually consists of are magnified into cartoon-like absurdity by the simple tactic – it's what the cashier does after all – of counting. Sam weighs up just how many tons of goods she lifts per hour, per shift, per year (she recommends the job as a breast-enhancing workout). She figures out the average number of times a day she says hello goodbye are you all right for bags today do you have a loyalty card please enter your pin. She notes exactly the time used up in walking to the toilets, walking to the staff rest room, queueing, eating, and then walking back to the checkout, during the eighteen-minute break that is allowed during a six-hour shift. She watches how long it takes for the last customers of the evening, while she waits to get home, to pause and pick and pause and pick again at the end of the aisle. Minute by minute, she notes the movements of their opposite number, the couple who turn up half an hour before opening time to get the best parking place, angrily tap at their watches as they wait to be let in, whizz round the store, and then – she imagines – find themselves back at home with only an empty day before them. This is the one time that Sam ventures into the world away from the store, and she gets her own back by seeing these people enjoying a life as futureless in its way as that of the checkout girl they have just barged past.

Anna Sam's till-bound cashier is in no way a supermarket equivalent of Zola's rising heroine, but the true story of her and her book really has been 'a bit like a modern fairy tale', as she says in an afterword to its new French edition. Sam had begun working on the checkout when she was a student, and stayed put when she did not find the kind of job she wanted after finishing her literature degree. Later she started a blog, *caissierenofutur*, to share stories with fellow checkout workers. On the very day that she finally did quit, but with nothing particular in prospect, a local newspaper ran a story about the blog which was quickly picked up by national media. The next thing was publishers fighting for the book contract, and soon *caissierenofutur* had been transformed into *Les tribulations d'une caissière*. The book is now translated into numerous languages, and a movie version, directed by Pierre Rambaldi, appeared in 2011.

In the final chapter of the book, after describing her last day in the supermarket, Sam says farewell to her readers in her sweet sardonic voice:

> So, do you still want to be a checkout girl? Is it still your dream job? No? I didn't think so! But do you have a choice? No, I didn't think so. Good luck anyway. And then, if it's really terrible, do what I did and write a book.
>
> If only!

A piece about Anna Sam's book Checkout, published in the *London Review of Books*, 2009

1 Henry James, 'In the Cage' (1898), in *In the Cage and Other Stories* (Harmondsworth: Penguin, 1972), 45. Further quotations will be included within the main text.

2 James, 52.

3 James, 96.

4 Anna Sam, *Les tribulations d'une caissière* (Paris: Stock, Livre de Poche, 2009); first published in 2008; trans. Morag Young, *Checkout: A Life on the Tills* (London: Gallic, 2009).

# Family Mutations

# 7
## Œdipus Today
### Changing Family Stories

### 1. The Last Generation

It was when I was asked to present a paper for a conference panel on 'Feminism, sexuality and gender' that something about generations and changing stories started to intrigue me.[1] This, as it happened, was a psychoanalytic conference, to mark the 150th anniversary of the birth of Freud. But it struck me that the rubric could have been exactly the same for a conference twenty or twenty-five years ago – a generation ago, let's say – in a number of different fields, from literature to film studies to sociology. Fifty years ago, on the other hand, it would have made no sense. Feminism, sexuality and gender in the 1950s? I don't think so. It is unlikely that any of these words would have been up for discussion then, unless possibly sexuality in some specialised contexts – such as psychoanalysis. Gender did not even exist; it was a purely grammatical term, which had yet to be extended to suggest the socially sexed being of every human him and her.

By the 1980s, though, gender and sexuality had become common terms of academic and political argument – as had feminism, which had a long, intermittent history of its own. There was some suspicion of 'gender' as falsely equalising and neutralising, especially in comparison with the older term 'sex' – as in 'Sex: male or female?'. Twenty or twenty-five years ago, you might also, or instead, have had the more exotic and psychoanalytical-sounding term 'sexual difference' in place of the 'gender and sexuality' combination.[2] 'Sexual difference' does have the advantage that it can or should keep open questions that that odd couple of gender and sexuality tends to treat as settled, as if gender's social issues of masculine and feminine are in a category that can be clearly separated from another, more bodily category of sexuality.

But even if the type of conference and the panel title could have been identical in say the late 1970s or early 1980s, the issues those words addressed, I think, would have been very different from those that interest us now. A generation ago feminism was a strong force politically, and especially within universities, where courses in women's studies were being set up in all sorts of disciplines within the humanities; in many ways feminism appeared as *the* interdisciplinary subject, and the history and theory of women and womanhood – always 'femininity' in the French-inspired theoretical language – was increasingly visible and prominent as a question across every field. Psychoanalysis had a crucial cross-disciplinary place of its own in these initiatives and debates, because of its special relationship with feminism – frequently if not usually an antagonistic one. In Britain, Juliet Mitchell's book *Psychoanalysis and Feminism* had been crucial in bringing psychoanalysis onto the agenda of serious feminist debate.[3]

This theoretical focus on women did not mean that feminism in Britain was indifferent to other categories or commitments: class and, to a lesser extent, race, were also, at times, brought into the frame.[4] As in previous moments of women's history, 1960s feminism had partly developed out of an existing radical political movement which, to begin with, took no account of sex (sex that was not yet gender). Psychoanalysis was particularly useful here because it offered a theory of the structural primacy of sexual difference as preceding any and every other kind. But the characteristic form taken by political demands, both those that were and those that were not influenced by psychoanalysis, was a refusal of everything that tied women to the place allotted to them by an overarching patriarchal (or 'phallocentric') order. This included an idea of sexual freedom which had much to do with the availability of contraception. The emphasis was on the right for women *not* to have children – on pregnancy and motherhood as burdens, if not the key to all female oppression. This in turn implied the longer-standing feminist claim to the right to a life in some other sphere than the family. Motherhood, at this time, was really not much of an issue in feminist debate – at least the debates I remember, from my neck of the feminist forests – other than negatively, as what not to do or to be. Theoretically, it was either the reproduction of patriarchy (just as, in Marxist theory, it had been the reproduction of the proletariat for capitalism);[5] or else, in Freudian terms, it was a compensation for not being a man (and what kind of a 'choice' was that?).[6]

## 2. The Present

So gender, sexuality and feminism were all conceptually alive and argued over, in relation to one another, twenty-five years ago. But if the *terms* of debate appear to have mutated very little in the past generation, then what they talk about, the personal or collective issues that they do or might evoke, have altered out of almost all recognition, and far more than they changed over the previous quarter-century. The social and also the biological conditions for thinking about sexual identities have undergone radical changes in just a single generation – probably far more so than across the previous two or three, back to Freud's own time. To say 'a single generation' in this context is ambiguous, of course, since the length of a generation is one of those seemingly semi-natural categories that is actually subject to huge variations in history and culture – and even from one generation to the next, as we might question-beggingly say. While differences in generational length are necessarily constrained by the limits of biology and mortality, they also involve a combination of both personal and social factors.[7] Even in modern societies in which, to an increasing extent, having a child is a choosable option, not a social and familial expectation, the currently typical ages for doing so are not a matter of indifference to women's decisions (or couples' decisions) about when to begin the process. But that decision or choice is also, at another level, a personal one, just as the arrival or not of the child that is 'planned' or wished for is also a matter, at least in part, of biological (and sometimes technological) chance.

'Generations' have themselves changed quite a lot since say thirty years ago, with a significant rise in the average age of first maternity, and this is not unrelated to many other changes in Western family forms and norms and in reproductive possibilities and desires. For the sake of description, I'll separate these changes into the social and the biological, but the overlaps and mutual influences between them will be obvious.

First, then, social changes. The kinds of parenting regarded as possible or ordinary have gone forth and multiplied, to the point that the previously normative and usual unit of a married heterosexual couple, both first-time partnered, who raise two or three children to adulthood may now seem not just not assumed but not even particularly common. Parents may be single by choice, or gay, or cohabiting but not married. The stigma of illegitimacy has all but gone, with the term 'single parent' – a man or a woman, and often post-married – bearing almost no ideological relation to the now obsolete and culturally meaningless 'unmarried mother'. And where previously the new cultural focus was on the right not to have babies, it is now, and not only for women, much more on the right and the positive wish to be a parent. The question of where that wish might come from, or how it might differ between women, or between men and women, is rarely mentioned in any kind of discourse: where before it might have been seen by many as a normative ideological imposition on women, now it is almost always presented as a natural desire, sometimes bordering on a right, and not only for women. More broadly, in place of the old sexual division of labour – men as breadwinners, women as homemakers – the assumption has been shifting towards regarding all men and women as both workers and parents, potentially, whose needs in performing both of these roles should be met as far as possible with the help of various kinds of enabling legislation, from longer maternity (and paternity) leave to flexible work-time.[8] All these developments are related to another, equally prominent social change, which is the dramatic rise in serial families and, concomitantly, in the break-up of co-parenting relationships. No permanence in the parental couple is to be assumed – as it was before, when marriage was the parenting norm, and divorce was unusual.

On the biological side, the changes are equally striking. Alongside the proliferation of new family forms are the new reproductive technologies. There could be no more spectacular illustration of the difference of emphasis from a few decades ago, when the technological and medical news was all about reliable birth control, about how you didn't have to have children, as opposed to now, when it is about how you might be helped to do so. In general, the new reproductive technologies have the effect of separating sex from reproduction, just as contraception did in a different way: in IVF, as with artificial insemination, there is no two-body sexual act prior to conception. Conception outside the female body also undermines one essential difference between the two sexes as parents, bringing the contribution of each down to a neutrally named 'gamete'.

In other ways too, that difference between mothers and fathers is seen to diminish. Previously, it rested upon a fundamental dissymmetry, mentioned by Freud in his 'Family Romances' paper and elsewhere, whereby the identity of the father is always open to doubt – *pater semper incertus est*, in the Latin legal tag, which Freud quotes – whereas the mother visibly and palpably isn't uncertain in this way: from her the baby is seen to be born.[9] Now, DNA testing has made it possible for the first time in human history to know a biological father with scientifically proven certainty. Yet at the same time, biological motherhood has taken on an equally unprecedented degree of potential doubtfulness. A child now may have two 'biological' mothers, the one who provides the egg and the one who is pregnant and gives birth. This is true of some cases of surrogacy (where the future mother provides the egg for a child gestated in another woman's womb) and in all cases of egg donation. There is additionally a new process which even splits genetic motherhood into two, as one woman provides the chromosomal material and another something like the shell or outer substance of the ovum.

In a recent case that was front-paged in the *Daily Mail* in November 2005, a baby girl was born to a woman in her fifties who was thereby both her (surrogate) mother and her (biological) grandmother. She had been implanted with an embryo produced from the gametes of her son-in-law and her adult daughter (who was unable, because of a medical condition, to sustain a pregnancy herself), and the baby had been given the (middle) name Trinity. Intra-familial scenarios of this kind, blurring identities either within or between generations and sometimes involving quasi-incestuous combinations, are not uncommon in surrogacy arrangements or egg or sperm donation. The oddities of the situation tend to be unspoken even though the printing of the story in the first place suggests otherwise.[10] For such stories seem to verge on the fantastic, as if coming from the realm of myth, monstrosity or science fiction – which is why they feature in the *Daily Mail*.[11] 'Still' seem, I was going to say – they probably won't seem so sensational for long. We should remember that IVF, at its inception in the late 1970s, was regarded in just the same way: the extraordinary sci-fi case of the 'test-tube baby'. But in the space of, yes, a generation, IVF has come to be seen as a routine medical procedure.

Such rapid transformations in the norms and possibilities of chosen reproduction may take us back to the strangeness of all and any process of conception and birth – a tale of secret seedings and metamorphoses whose astonishing improbability fades away in the light of grown-up and responsible familiarity with 'the facts of life'. The mutability, at present, of those supposedly given conditions or 'facts' of reproduction also reveals the contingency in a part of the old reproductive story so well engrained as rarely to be spelled out: that a child is assumed to be the child of two parents and two only, one of each of two sexes. Here technological invention is amplifying and reinforcing the changes that are going on in the social forms of parenting. Now, biologically as well as socially, it is possible to have two parents of the same sex; socially, it is also common to have three or more active parents – when the first parental couple has split up and one or both of them has a new partner.

The multiplication of parents and family forms is inseparable from other changes, of incalculable significance: the loosening of social constraints on acceptable forms of sexual relationship, and a lessening of the social divisions between the sexes such that women, who may well positively choose to have children, are no longer seen as primarily meant for a maternal and domestic role (so that that's no longer the argument that feminism needs to be having). Looking positively at these changes, it might seem that today, it is possible to live out and choose identities and behaviours that the first Freudian patients could only dream of. At one level, that's true. At another, of course, there's no evidence to suggest that the limits and conflicts in people's lives, in their identities as parents or offspring or lovers or anything else, have diminished – or that the surrounding ideologies of sexual and family identities are progressive in some absolute sense.

Consider this recent statement on the part of a well-meaning fertility consultant speaking in relation to the legal change that has deprived sperm donors in Britain of the right to anonymity; this has led to a dramatic fall in the number of volunteers. He is concerned that the facility should be available, because of the cases when women have no male partner; if necessary, women will have to turn to the internet, which bypasses the constraints on anonymity. 'Using these services', he said, 'has got to be a step better than asking some half-drunk man to have unprotected sex, which is presumably what happens otherwise.'[12] Poor women! In order to have a baby, they might actually have to have sex – caricatured here in its most binge-unappealing form of the 'half-drunk' pick-up. (Why *half*-drunk, by the way? Perhaps this is no casually vulgarising adjective, but rather a precisely measured calculation on the part of the unfortunate maiden, because fully drunk he would be unable to deliver, and without a glass or two he might be unwilling to.) And poor men too! – now to find themselves pursued by women who are literally only interested in them for one thing. The ideological shifts and continuities are fascinating here. First, the attitude on the part of the consultant is one of the chivalrous protection of girls and ladies that would formerly have been offered to those in danger from the unwelcome and pregnancy-risking onslaughts of crude male lusts. Male and female sexuality are still what they always were, and why should women have to resort to bodily involvement with a live and present man, rather than one who can arrive hygienically in a sober brown envelope? Second – and this is the crucial change, to which the old idea of protecting the lady has been readjusted – the woman without a partner, whether straight or gay, is deemed not just not unsuitable for motherhood, but having a positive right to choose and achieve it.

## 3. A Hundred Years Ago

Freud's 'nuclear' complex, concentrating on the basic trio of mother, father and son, may now seem questionable in its focus, at a time when that particular arrangement has lost its normative moral force as well as its predominance in reality. Juliet Mitchell's recent work has drawn attention to the way that the inter-generational Oedipal model obscures the significance of siblings – always assumed in Freud, in fact often assumed to make up a virtually endless succession; sometimes given quite big parts in the case histories, but always, at the end, subordinated to the parent-child stories that are seen as the primary ones.[13] Yet in terms of demographic history, the curious thing is that Freud's minimalist family of father, mother and child projected a social reality that, in his own time – at least in his youth and middle life – was yet to be. The theory anticipates a specifically twentieth-century historical moment in which for a few decades, for the first and perhaps the last time in history, the typical reproductive pattern in Western industrialized societies involved a lifelong parental couple with a limited number of children, and no additional family members living with them. In this mid-twentieth-century world, 'family planning' was acceptable and available; divorce had not yet become ordinary; life expectancy was rapidly increasing. The tendency today is to think of second marriages and serial families as characteristically contemporary phenomena. But prior to this twentieth-century nuclear moment of both marital and spousal longevity, the frequency of early death, particularly as a result of childbirth, meant that more than one marriage, and more than one family, were commonplace, as they are now. There were the accompanying complexities, again as today, of step-parents and half- and step-sibling relationships. The one crucial difference between the periods before and after the heyday of the nuclear family is that children then acquired step-parents only, or almost always, after the death of a birth parent.

Freud's theories involved another prescient projection of a future lived reality. His separation of sexuality from reproduction, in the *Three Essays on the Theory of Sexuality* (1905), became a social norm with the increasing use of contraception in the course of the twentieth century; and this development is bound up, of course, with the changing possibilities in women's lives and identities over the same period. And as I've already suggested, reproductive technologies go one stage further: here not only is sex separated from procreation, but procreation can happen without sex.

Freud's isolation of the 'starter unit' nuclear family is interesting in another way from the point of view of his own family history. He was the son of his father's second wife, the first having died in child-birth, and had two elder half-brothers who were around twenty years his senior; his mother, twenty-one when he was born, was the same age as the half-brothers, her stepsons. When Freud was born, the first son of his younger half-brother was a year old: the two generations were on a level, horizontalised. And this was a lived actuality for little Sigmund: the other child, technically his own nephew (or rather half-nephew), was a near neighbour and a regular playmate for the first years of his life. So the generational conflation was not just some piece of family knowledge he might only have acquired at a much later stage; it was there as his own given world from the very beginning. In Freud's own case the core intergenerational Oedipal unit is bordered at home by the evidence of other possibilities which, like the presence or arrival of siblings, challenge its stability and complicate the identity of the child. Generational blurring makes it impossible to separate out the siblings from the parents as the 'vertical' from the 'horizontal': the two can no longer be set either alongside or at different levels from one another, as clearly distinguishable levels or categories.

Yet as so often in Freudian connections, it is the extreme cases which show up the confusions that may exist within the apparently normal. Even without the pluralisation of parents, whether from death or divorce, the division between the generations is often not simple. Parents may be widely separate in age even without there being previous marriages – though almost invariably, for both reproductive and social reasons, with the father being the older one. Siblings may be widely separated in age for reasons other than parents' new partners: not just when there is a large number of them, but often through the phenomenon of the late baby, the 'surprise' born some years after the rest, who may be 'mothered' by older siblings more than by its real mother, and for whom these big brothers and sisters may figure very differently from siblings of nearby age. By the same token – and Freud's female homosexuality case history is an example of this – the age-gap baby may have the effect of confusing the older children's ongoing arrival at the next, would-be adult and potentially procreative stage of their own lives.[14]

## 4. Oedipus Again

I have been stressing how much has changed since Freud's time, and especially in the shorter term since a few decades ago, but also suggesting how these changes can point us towards hitherto unnoticed aspects of earlier or continuing family formations. Taking this in another direction, I'd like now to go right back to Sophocles' *Oedipus the King,* Freud's source-text for the Oedipus complex, which, read in the light of recent changes in the social and biological conditions of identity, can I think seem surprisingly contemporary – and surprisingly un-Oedipal. At the surface level of the story – before the revelations of incest and parricide – the play involves a second family, a problem of infertility and an adoption – and a transnational adoption at that. None of these features is mentioned by Freud. Baby Oedipus, born in Thebes to Jocasta and Laius and abandoned to die because of the oracle saying he will kill his father, is adopted across the borders to parents in Corinth, Polybus and Merope; linked to this is their situation of childlessness. The second family is Jocasta's four children with Oedipus, following the death of the husband with whom she had had one child. In addition to these open data of the legend, the buried story also concerns more than the classic Oedipal – Freudian Oedipal – double parental violations of incest and parricide. A further point, and also unspecified by Freud though it is close to his concerns, is that the incestuous children bring about a blurring of the generations and of relational categories. Sophocles, though not Freud, lays stress on the intolerable confusion of identity that this entails, and he makes the point like a structural anthropologist, by way of the unbearable impossibility of naming that ensues when incompatible relational terms overlay one another, mixing fathers, brothers and children, and brides, wives and mothers.[15]

It has often been said that Oedipus cannot himself be thought to have had an Oedipus complex, for the simple reason that the Jocasta he married and the Laius he killed meant nothing to him emotionally; they were not the parents with whom he grew up, and he had no idea, when he murdered and married, that these were his birth parents. That Freud never mentions the fact of Oedipus' adoption is all the more bizarre in the light of his own claim, in another context (the 'Family Romances' paper, again), that every child at some point fantasises that they were adopted, thereby 'replacing' their existing or present parents with better ones, and perhaps also displacing a sibling or two along the way – if they alone derive from the superior source. What happens to Sophocles' Oedipus in fact bears a striking resemblance to some contemporary practices of transnational adoption which may involve an interim period of fostering after a baby's abandonment; in Britain, 'local' adoptions too are regularly preceded by a period of fostering. The baby Oedipus is cared for initially by two shepherds, the first of whom, Laius' servant, does not leave him to die as instructed, but gives him to a second one who then in turn gives him to the childless Corinthian royal couple. The 'giving' is highlighted in both cases, and defended by the first shepherd against the adult Oedipus's angry accusation that he might have 'sold' the baby.

The legendary Oedipus does in one way exemplify the Freudian Oedipal scenario, since he grows up as the only child of two parents. But there the comparison ends, and in any case those adoptive parents are not the ones in relation to whom Oedipus commits his 'Oedipal' crimes. Another significant feature of the Freudian interpretation is that it ignores those aspects of Sophocles' tragedy which concern not the son's emotions but those of the parents – all four of them, plus the shepherd foster-fathers who take the baby from Thebes to Corinth. In Freud's account, the Oedipus complex is generated as if by nature; it comes from the child. To have let the parents have a hand in it (as Freud does occasionally allow, only to pull back and reassert the other perspective) would have let in too much scope for the intervention of contingent historical factors: only infancy guarantees (or at any rate suggests) innateness and inevitability. But in Sophocles' *Oedipus*, the baby's parents, or at least Laius (it is not clear what part Jocasta played) had determined to have their baby boy killed: the violence began with them, if not just with him. The adoptive parents, on the other hand, give their son love that is said, at least in Polybus's case (Merope, the adopting mother, remains in shadow in the same way that Jocasta does) to be all the stronger because of the childlessness they had endured until they had him. 'Did he still love him a lot even though he had received him from someone else?' asks Oedipus. 'He was convinced by his former childlessness [*apaidia*]', says the Corinthian shepherd, directly (lines 1023-4). Infertility and childlessness are significant issues in the play. Polybus and Merope are childless before they gain Oedipus, and childless once again after he abruptly leaves home; Laius and Jocasta have understood the oracle to mean that they should remain without children.

Childlessness is also a theme in many other Greek tragedies, but is not one explored by Freud in this connection, and rarely in others. In terms of tragedy, there is a brief, unelaborated mention of childlessness in relation to *Macbeth,* right after the crucial passage on *Oedipus* and *Hamlet* in *The Interpretation of Dreams.*[16] Generally, Freud stays with the hypothetical fantasies of the child, or the childhood-derived fantasies of the adult. A woman's wish to be a mother is a secondary formation; it is the normal way of finding something to make up for the lack of a penis, which is her lifelong unconscious preoccupation. As for men, Freud never analyses their wish (or not) to be fathers; it does not figure in his discussions of masculine development. Yet on the other hand, it can be seen as radical on Freud's part, in his time, to have seen maternity as a problem for women, not something to be taken as a natural instinct, and this is the positive reading of his myth of maternal desire as a secondary formation, and a compensation for non-masculinity. It could be argued that fatherhood in Freud's time impinged much less on men in its psychical and practical demands and pleasures than it usually does today, whereas for mothers, even more than now, it was at the centre of their lives. But it is still intriguing that Freud did not turn his attention to the meanings of fatherhood for men; here, it is as if he did take the socially normal masculine-paternal development for granted, if not for natural.

Sophocles' *Oedipus*, then, is much concerned with parental, or pre-parental, desires and fears in relation to possible children; it is not at all about the desires or hatreds of a small child in relation to its parents. It is, however, about an older or grown child's need to know his origins. It is often pointed out that Oedipus fulfils the oracle's warnings only as a result of the evasive action taken against them – first by his birth parents, who try to kill him, and later by Oedipus himself, at the point when he leaves his home in Corinth, or rather fails to return there, after he has himself heard the oracle's bad news: he decides he must stay away from his mother and father in case he should accidentally murder one and have sex – and children – with the other. But behind Oedipus's departure lies a story of parental withholding which has nothing to do with avoiding the oracle. A drunken – or maybe half-drunk – man had insulted young Oedipus at a dinner, by saying that Polybus was not his real father. This gets to Oedipus, who then goes and questions his parents; they are angry at what has been said; Oedipus is relieved, but then still, he finds, disturbed. It is at that point, in his later retelling of this turning point in his life, that he goes off to consult the oracle – crucially, without telling his parents, 'λαθραι'(line 787), 'in secret', as if picking up on the parents' own secretiveness as well as, overtly, feeling the need to get information for himself. The oracle's extreme and seemingly unrelated response relating to a destiny of incest, incestuous children and parricide then implicitly does away with the earlier doubt about who his father is; in fear of the future foretold, he runs away from those he knows as his parents. But if those parents had communicated what they knew of his origins from the beginning, and all the more at the point when Oedipus questions them, then once again, as with the acts that were meant to evade the oracle, the 'Oedipal' events would never have come about. From this point of view, Oedipus' downfall arises from what we could perhaps call, in a currently popular understatement, a parental 'error of judgement'. And the parents' denial of there being anything to tell – their failure to say that Oedipus' origins are not only the ones he knows – then has its counterpart in Oedipus' own secrecy and his clinging to a fantasy of knowing, without any possible doubt, where he comes from: his country and his parents.

Oedipus' birth parents do what they do, in abandoning him, out of fear (of the oracle); no motive is given for Polybus and Merope's failure to tell Oedipus that he is adopted. But the episode now speaks to discussions about the disclosure of origins in relation not so much to adoption – where that is usually now taken for granted – as in cases of sperm or egg donation or both, where it is a highly contested issue. In most cases, a donor parent will never have known that they engendered this particular child, who may well, in addition, have unknown biological half-siblings, perhaps many of them, all raised by different parents. What we might call the proto-parent is a different kind of parent for the child to know of or come to terms with, and all the more so when the eventual, postnatal parent or parents wish to forget this other origin, as used to happen in most cases of adoption. The donor parent is someone who, again in most cases, has never had a sexual or other relationship with the eventual parent of the other sex (the one with whose second gamete the baby is conceived) and who may, as in the so-called 'reproductive tourism' of those who seek IVF treatment abroad, have a different cultural origin from the future parents. Or else, at the other extreme, the donor may be confusingly close to home, a friend or someone who is already part of the family, but whose position in relation to the new baby is to be understood as other than that of a parent. The peculiar status of donors also raises the question of just how many parents a child can imagine or seek, now that both biologically and socially the old assumption has broken down that in the beginning there must have been two, who once had sex, and to whom the baby was born.

In the wake of the radical changes to the social and scientific modes of reproduction, a further question arises about what differences remain between mothers and fathers. I mentioned as shadowy the figures of Jocasta and Merope. Jocasta's account of the exposure of her baby is icily controlled, and ostensibly designed only to prove the uselessness of oracles rather than to express any feelings of hers about having, or losing, let alone killing babies – and in her case for a reason which, she believes, turned out to be mistaken. She assumes that that baby did die, and that it was not he who murdered Laius; she doesn't mention a prophecy of mother-marrying and incestuous children. On the Corinthian side, Merope is only represented as an obstacle to peace of mind: when the shepherd reports that Polybus is dead, Oedipus points out that even if the father-murdering issue is out of the way, what he crudely calls 'the one alive' or 'the living woman' (της ζωσης, line 988) is still a source of fear. It is Polybus who is given some psychological interest: in the shepherd's report, he loved his son to bits because that was the lesson of his childlessness. And Oedipus wonders, when told of his death, whether the oracle might not have been fulfilled after all, if Polybus died from grief at his son's departure, out of 'longing for me' (τωμωι ποθωι, line 969). For Sophocles, it is only ever the fathers' emotions that are marked.

In our own time, perhaps the seeming neutralisation of parental difference as the contribution of two separate but equal gametes, together with the new ascertainability of paternity and vagueness of biological maternity, have taken attention away from the dissymmetries that remain or that now appear in new forms. At the basic biological level, women have just a few hundred eggs, men an infinity of sperm; egg donation is a complicated and protracted process, while sperm donation, comparatively, is not. Pregnancy, whichever mother is doing it, is quite different from biological fathering – 'It only takes ten seconds, Dad', I was told of a six-year-old pleading, who very much wanted a sibling (and got one). It is perfectly possible for a man to be unaware of being a father (and until DNA, arguably, it was impossible for him to be sure that he *was* one); it is virtually impossible for a woman not to know that she has given birth.

Sophocles' *Oedipus* touches on yet another issue in relation to the new ways of begetting, and getting, children in which, once again, some given differences between the sexes appear to be reaffirmed. I mentioned Oedipus' rush to surmise that the discarded baby must have been used for profit. After the Corinthian messenger has spoken of the baby as a 'gift' to the childless Polybus (line 1022), Oedipus suspiciously asks whether he had bought him (line 1025). Indignantly, the shepherd denies this and points out that he was 'your rescuer, child, at that time' (line 1030).

The new forms of transnational adoption and the new reproductive technologies almost always involve issues of money: babies, or the ingredients to make them, or the means of gestating them, can be bought. Private IVF clinics, as Sarah Franklin has argued, trade on the purchasability of an indefinite 'hope' that in reality is not usually fulfilled.[17] In the past ten years, the internet has greatly facilitated processes of personal selection and research; surrogacy services, eggs and sperm, as well as ready-made babies, can be sought and found and paid for. Sophocles' dialogue between the shepherd and Oedipus is on the same ideological side as the standard modern revulsion against the mixing of babies with profit, but the (equally traditional) image of the woman or couple 'desperate' for a baby tends to override the monetary issue: the internet has had the effect of bringing down moral as well as national boundaries in this connection. Apart from the specifically financial aspect, some of the new practices, some of the time, involve new forms of exploitation of women's labour (in both senses).[18] As in sexual tourism, so-called, so in reproductive toursim, so-called: here the differences of women's bodies from men's determine what they can be used for or paid for; the technologisation and depersonalisation of baby production at one (scientific) level is matched at another by an age-old reliance on the bodily contributions of individual women's often painful work.[19]

Payment for reproductive services also makes them into an area of consumer choice. Potential parents can shop online for possible donors or surrogates, with different qualities emphasised or visible in each case: the donor's education and attractiveness, the surrogate's health and sturdiness. Here the newly separable bits of the mothering process may be divided not just between two individuals, but along class lines too (professional, educated women are not normally the ones who do surrogacy). While the argument about 'designer babies' has focused on the selection of embryos in IVF and the kinds of preference or requirement that should or should not be considered, such selection is seen as quite natural for the purpose of choosing donor parents, part of the process of 'sourcing' suitable pre-mothers.

Oedipus's situation as one who was adopted from one country to another has the further effect of blurring his origins geographically, as well as parentally. The two are given equal weight in the characteristic ancient Greek identity question, put to every new arrival, every stranger who turns up, in tragedy or epic: τις και πόθεν; 'Who are you and where do you come from?' With four parents and two countries of origin, this is another aspect of the confusions and multiplications of identity to which Oedipus is involuntarily subject. Today, the growth of transnational adoption has made this once unusual situation seem characteristically modern and even ordinary. It occurs in another form when IVF babies are conceived abroad using sperm and eggs from local donors, and then born in the mother's home country; in this case the place of birth is set apart from the place of genetic origins.

Yet we should also remember that origin has always been – at least – double: two parents, and sometimes two places of origin. When Oedipus gives his own life-story – as he knows it – he begins: 'My father was a Corinthian, Polybus; my mother Merope, a Dorian': no single origin even in the simple story. Similarly, a baby's parents always have two separate lives prior to their becoming that unit that 'had' him or her.

As I hope to have shown, Sophocles' *Oedipus* continues to speak to issues of contemporary identity, just as it did for Freud. The play, like Freud's own theories, becomes like a buried source or origin, but one whose meanings change all the time, in each generation, as it is unearthed and reinterpreted in the light of our new day – so like and so unlike the old days.[20]

1　This essay is an extended version of the talk I gave. The conference, 'Freud Yesterday, Freud Today', organised by the Freud Museum and the British Psychoanalytical Society, took place on 28–29 January 2006. Juliet Mitchell was the other speaker for the session on 'Feminism, sexuality and gender', which was chaired by Felicity Dirmeik. A slightly different version of the essay was published as 'Generations' in *Textual Practice* 21: 1 (2007), pp. 1–16.

2　A big conference on the topic of Sexual Difference, under the aegis of the theory journal *Oxford Literary Review* was held at the University of Southampton in 1985. 'Sexual difference' is still flourishing, though frequently undermined or abetted by 'gender': Juliet Mitchell's own paper at the 2006 Freud conference was entitled 'Psychoanalysis and Feminism/Feminism and Psychoanalysis: From Sexual Difference to Gender Diversity'.

3　*Psychoanalysis and Feminism* was published in 1973 and reissued as a Pelican (i.e. Penguin) paperback the following year – a sign of its widespread influence. This was well before psychoanalysis and feminism, often in the context of the new feminist literary criticism, had started to become established features of university courses in arts and humanities subjects.

4　I am speaking here of the British context; in the United States, for instance, race and class in this formulation would be the other way around.

5　Nancy Chodorow's book *The Reproduction of Mothering* (1978) made mothers essential to this process in their (unconscious) inculcation of the gender-differentiated dispositions that would then, in turn, produce the next generation of mothers and men. A related argument about maternal forces was made at the same time by another American, Dorothy Dinnerstein, in *The Mermaid and the Minotaur* (1976).

6　Freud's argument for the roundabout route to female normality in the form of heterosexuality and motherhood was useful to anti-maternal feminists at the time not only because it emphasised the difficulties of getting to this seemingly obvious point, but also because it denaturalised female reproductive desire. Feminism was thus not against nature, but simply against patriarchal values and conditions, in which motherhood was the best substitute for women's lack of any other kind of life.

7　These 'natural limits' are themselves subject to wide variation, through cultural differences in health and life expectancy, and depending on whether the generation is measured from the maternal or paternal point of view. Menopause, not death, puts an end to women's natural reproductive capacities, so that maternally measured generations are on average shorter. But new reproductive technologies may well abolish this difference, as post-menopausal women are enabled to become pregnant via IVF with donor eggs. In July 2006, a British woman aged 62 who had had treatment abroad gave birth to a child.

8 In the United States, while the dual-income couple has become the norm as elsewhere, there has been a marked absence of the parent-friendly legislation, starting with state-supported maternity leave, that has been enacted to varying degrees in most other Western countries.

9 See Freud, 'Family Romances' (1909), *Standard Edition of the Complete Works of Sigmund Freud*, trans. James Strachey, vol. IX (London: Hogarth Press, 1959), 239.

10 'I'm not a smoker,' the newly delivered granny was quoted as saying, or prompted to stress – as if that was the issue.

11 The story also featured positively in the *Guardian,* in the context of an article about the donation of body parts (such as kidneys) between family members: see Emma Cook, 'Our Flesh and Blood', *Guardian* 'Family' section, 25 March 2006, 1–2. Incidentally, the fact that the *Guardian* now has a 'Family' section rather than a women's page is symptomatic of the ideological and social changes I have been invoking: the new assumption that parenting is not an exclusively female concern; and concomitantly, the end to the assumption that an interest in family matters detracts from 'broader' social or political interests.

12 Bill Ledger, quoted in Ian Sample, '"Severe shortage" of sperm donors', *The Guardian*, Monday August 15 2005, 10.

13 See Juliet Mitchell, *Mad Men and Medusas: Reclaiming Hysteria and the Effects of Sibling Relations on the Human Condition* (London: Allen Lane, 2000); and *Siblings* (Cambridge: Polity Press, 2003).

14 See Freud, 'The Psychogenesis of a Case of Homosexuality in a Woman' (1920), in *Standard Edition,* vol. XVIII (London: Hogarth Press, 1955), 147–72. The eighteen-year-old girl who is the subject of the study has a young brother who was born when she was sixteen.

15 See Sophocles, *Oedipus the King*, ll. 1405–6. Oedipus is both father and (half-)brother to his four children, and son of their mother; Jocasta is bride, wife and mother – all three – to Oedipus. Oedipus speaks of the *haima emphulion*, intra-family or incestuous 'blood' or kinship, produced by these crossed relationships, which represent 'the most shameful things for people' (l. 1408). Throughout the play, the horror of producing incestuous children is the most prominent fear in Oedipus's utterances about the oracle pronouncing his incestuous and parricidal future.

16 'Just as *Hamlet* deals with the relation of a son to his parents, so *Macbeth* (written at approximately the same period) is concerned with the subject of childlessness [*auf dem Thema der Kinderlosigkeit*]', Freud, *The*

*Interpretation of Dreams, Standard Edition,* vol. IV (London: Hogarth Press, 1953), 266.

17 See Sarah Franklin, *Embodied Progress: A Cultural Account of Assisted Conception* (London: Routledge, 1997).

18 I say 'women' because in sperm donation, the oldest and simplest repro-ductive technology, which occurs in another form in IVF, there is no long-term labour involved. Egg donation, on the other hand, requires disuptive hormone injections and a potentially painful process of extrac-tion; while surrogacy takes pregnancy's full nine months and involves the woman in all its risks but few of its pleasures: she must consciously avoid the emotional bonding of a mother-to-be with the growing baby. In this regard, it is striking that many women are willing to offer their services as egg donors or surrogates as a gift; in some countries, including the UK, surrogacy, for instance, is not permitted other than on an 'expenses only' basis.

19 Wet-nursing – whereby ladies' babies were given to lower-class women to be breast-fed – is an earlier, postnatal version of surrogate mothering; but in that case the practice occurred not because the mother's own body could not do the job, but because the too bodily job was not thought to be socially appropriate for her.

20 Many of the topics of this article are further discussed in my book *Freudian Mythologies: Greek Tragedy and Modern Identities* (Oxford: Oxford University Press, 2007); see also Rachel Bowlby, 'Family Realisms: Freud and Greek Tragedy', *Essays in Criticism* 56:2 (April 2006): 111–38.

# 8

# The Third Parent

The news that Britain is set to become the first country to authorise IVF using genetic material from three people – the so-called 'three-parent baby' – has given rise to (very predictable) divisions of opinion. On the one hand are those who celebrate a national 'first', just as happened when Louise Brown, the first ever 'test-tube baby', was born in Oldham in 1978. In the same way as with IVF more broadly, the possibility for people who otherwise couldn't become parents of healthy children is something to be welcomed. On the other side, the cry goes up that this is a slippery slope, the thin end of the wedge, or any other cliché that you care to click on: at any rate, it is not a happy event, and it takes us one step further towards the spectre of 'designer babies'. The issue here is about meddling with nature for the sake of hubristic human desires: seeking to ensure the production of a 'perfect' baby, and in the process creating the new monstrosity of triple parenthood.

The negative line about the new baby-making procedure is most often countered in these arguments by pointing out how negligible, in reality, is the contribution of the shadow third party. All that happens is that a dysfunctional aspect of the (principal) mother's DNA is, as it were, written over by the provision of healthy mitochondrial matter from the donor; this means that the resulting baby will not go on to develop debilitating hereditary diseases that might otherwise have been passed on. The handy household metaphor of 'changing a battery' is much in use for this positive line: the process should be seen as just an everyday upgrade. But the way that the argument is made – presenting the new input as a simple enabling device – reveals a need to switch off any suggestion that this hypothetical extra parent has any fundamental importance. The real identity of the future child must be seen to come from a mother and a father, and from them alone.

According to the established facts of life, it might seem obvious enough that a baby has two biological parents, and that the contribution of each is distributed with the god-given genetic equality of exactly twenty-three chromosomes each. But that is to forget a third biological element, the female body in which the new baby grows from conception (or just after, in the case of IVF) to birth. This used to be elided in the obvious certainty of maternal identity: if a woman gives birth, then the baby is 'biologically' hers: she was pregnant, and the ovum came from her. (Whereas a father, until DNA testing, was always uncertain – *pater semper incertus est*, in the legal phrase – in the sense that there was no bodily evidence of any particular man having engendered any particular child.) But modern medical science has brought about the practical as well as the theoretical separation of egg and womb, breaking up what had previously appeared as – and still usually is – the one biological mother. With this not uncommon doubling of motherhood through IVF, three-parent babies have been with us for quite some time.

Twofold motherhood plays out in various possible scenarios. Conception outside the womb – *in vitro* fertilization – leads to the possibility of a woman giving birth to a baby of which she is not the genetic mother. Depending on whether that baby is going to become the (postnatal) child of the birth mother or else of the woman whose body provided the egg, this pregnant woman will be referred to as either the mother or the surrogate. Or, to tell the same story from the genetic point of view: IVF leads to the possibility of one woman's egg making an embryo which develops in another woman's womb. Depending on which of them is to raise the child, she will be regarded as either the egg donor or the mother (who used a surrogate).

In all these scenarios – two in reality, four in story – biological motherhood is already divided between two women, with one or other element – the egg or the pregnancy – emphasized, depending on which of them is to become, in practice, the baby's mother. In other words, biologically three-parent babies are nothing new (or only as new as IVF). But the drive is always towards the subordination of one maternal biological contribution so as to validate the other (and to remove the risk that the discounted proto-parent, the donor or the 'gestational carrier', might have any postnatal responsibilities or rights). This is what is happening again with the latest controversy over the additional mitochondrial 'mother'. Biological parenthood is what is sought; but the biological element can have more than one definition, and more than one physical manifestation.

The invention of reproductive technologies has had the odd effect of reinforcing – if it did not generate – a belief that the child of one's own, that object of desire, should be above all the 'biological' child of those who seek to 'have' it. In one way this contemporary valorisation marks a bizarre departure from earlier modern times when the bodily part of parenthood was something that women more often sought to be free from. In *A Vindication of the Rights of Woman*, at the end of the eighteenth century, Mary Wollstonecraft urged her fellow women to think of themselves as something above mere reproductive organisms, 'born only to procreate and rot'.[1] Wollstonecraft considered motherhood to be one of the privileges of being a woman, and she was also a passionate advocate of maternal breastfeeding at a time when women regularly paid other women to take on that physical aspect of motherhood; wet-nurses are another example, this time an ancient one, of supplementary mothers. But even so, she vehemently rejected the notion that having babies should be thought of as the be-all of human female lives. Purely biological parenthood is what plants and animals do: to procreate and rot.

*Written for an Oxford University Press blog in 2013*

1   Mary Wollstonecraft, *A Vindication of the Rights of Woman* (1792), ed. Janet Todd (Oxford: Oxford University Press, 1999), 133.

# 9
# Woolf and Childhood Abuse

Since the publication of her autobiographical writings in *Moments of Being* (1976), the fact that Virginia Woolf suffered from sexual abuse at the hands of her two half-brothers has been publicly known, supplying new material and questions for those interested in the complex relations between Woolf's life, her writing, her episodes of madness and her eventual suicide. Louise DeSalvo's book is a reading of Woolf's life and work as directly related to forms of abuse – ranging from active molestation to an everyday lack of parental care – which she sees as endemic to Woolf's 'pathologically dysfunctional family'),[1] including the previous and following generations. In this light, Woolf's political and feminist views can be read as conscious attempts to think through the social order within which such injustices were fostered, and argue for changes in it; her creative writing, for DeSalvo, should now be seen as involving more or less direct transpositions of childhood and adolescent experiences in families as wayward as Woolf's own. DeSalvo devotes a great deal of space to readings of childhood stories and diaries written by Woolf, which are all presented as ways of dealing with or trying to 'speak out' about what had been done to her.

Throughout the book, DeSalvo stresses that Woolf was an almost self-made survivor – 'these adolescent diaries and journals record the difficult yet exhilarating process through which Woolf created herself as an adolescent, and as a writer' (p. 261). She also measures the writing in terms of its adequacy in dealing with the real circumstances or the real memories of Woolf's life, speaking, for instance, of 'a mature and completely appropriate assessment of the situation in which she found herself' (p. 254). There is frequent reference, in relation both to Woolf and to all victims of abuse, to 'appropriate responses', implying that events ultimately are both unambiguous and able to be negotiated in ways that can be normatively codified.

Running through the book are two powerfully propounded arguments, one about history and the other about Freud. In relation to the first, DeSalvo wants to maintain that all child abuse, including incest, is an effect of cultural malaise (not, for instance, a natural potential, which cultures would find ways of controlling). The peculiarities of the Stephen family in which Woolf grew up were an extreme but not qualitatively exceptional illustration of the failings of British Victorian society in general, which inculcated a false belief in the irrepressibility of male lust. It was cultural indoctrination that led 'J.K.', Virginia's much older male cousin, to rampant physical excesses in pursuit of her half-sister Stella Duckworth. When he 'acted out that Victorian belief in male sexuality as pure aggression' (p.34) he was not so much being anti-social, as taking his social training all too literally. This sort of formation going on in nineteenth-century homes and schools needs to be seen as directly linked to the wider oppressions of the culture of that time, with its deleterious effects on men and women alike.

Against this Victorian view, DeSalvo sets her modern one, in which sexuality and violence are fully separable, and from which all these forms of aggressive misogyny arfe absent; and it is Woolf's achievement to have succeeded, in spite of and through her own harrowing experiences, in 'anticipating' this possibility. In her first novel, *The Voyage Out* (1916), 'Woolf demonstrates that the greates threat to an imperialist state is a warm, loving, intact family, in which parents share equally in child rearing, in which contact between parents and their children are [*sic*] maximized' (pp. 165–6). Looking at this with less of an eye for the lurking subtext than DeSalvo does when she reads Woolf's texts as covert verbalisations of histories of abuse, the reader supposes that this maximised contact will exclude anything sexual or violent. For what it significant here is that this other characterisation has completely reversed the features attributed to the Victorian family, setting up as a realistic goal a healthy, 'intact' norm that is as free from its ills as the Stephen family was saturated with them. At this point, the historical argument fades into a noble-willed assertion that current ideals are both superior and attainable, with the use of a rhetoric of common-sense, transhistorical truth – '*we now know* how essential it is to hold infants' (p. 116, italics mine). In effect, the nineteenth century is now pathologised in relation to a naturalised norm associated with contemporary wisdom.

The turnabout in the historical argument – from a model of cultural relativity to the assertion of a good nature identified with present knowledge – is related, I think, to the other major argument, centring on DeSalvo's objections to psychoanalysis. Freud claimed – against his initial beliefs – that hysterics' stories of childhood seduction were significant as fantasy but usually not related to actual occurences. Following other critics of the past ten years (she mentions

Alice Miller in particular), DeSalvo regards this as a betrayal of his patients and, by extension, of all victims of abuse. In terms of Woolf's own life, DeSalvo sees her final depression as having been exacerbated by her belated reading of Freud and subsequent doubt of the truth of what happened to her as a child. Woolf's believing Freud would mean both that she had been mistaken about her own memories and that she was mad, which for DeSalvo would count as a negative judgement. This is the most paradoxical feature of the book, which argues both that Woolf had appalling experiences in her childhood, which must have affected her for life, and that she was entirely rational (an attainable and praiseworthy characteristic) in her subsequent life and writing.

In these terms, the fit of words to what they attempt to record is taken as being potentially faultless – the 'mature and completely appropriate assessment'; 'one rational, cool, carefully considered analytical argument after another' (p. 291) – and DeSalvo reads the tendency in Woolf's writing to question the adequacy of language and the full accessibility of memory as merely quirky, related to histories of abuse. If the past of a character 'whose father is suspected of abusing her . . . is not availabale to her, because she has blocked off her memories' (p. 167), then by implication the past would be wholly available to someone who had not suffered in this way. But if we go back to DeSalvo's own form of argument in relation to the Stephen family – and exception but not unrelated to the ordinary Victorian case – then it might seem more appropriate to suggest that the ambiguities of language and memories to which stories of all kinds bear witness are not contingent errors, prompted only as a response to instances of exceptional injury, but (to varying degrees) a common condition of human 'interaction', to use DeSalvo's word. This might go some way towards explaining how it is that Woolf's writing is intriguing not only to those who recognise in it specific signs of childhood violationsn; and also why, as DeSalvo's book shows, someone who had suffered as Woolf had might have been especially drawn to explore and elucidate these uncertain conditions of individual and collective life.

1   Louise DeSalvo, *Virginia Woolf: The Impact of Childhood Sexual Abuse on Her Life and Work* (Boston: Beacon Press, 1989), 2. Further references will be given within the main text. The present review was published in *Journal of the History of Sexuality*.

# 10
## Kinship Under All

What are the *constancies* of kinship? To what extent are there universals in this aspect of the human condition, and are there forms of devotion to another, in life or death, which constitute a kind of kinship beyond or above the laws of the land? Judith Butler's Wellek Library Lectures, given at Irvine in 1998, use the figure of Antigone as a focus for a densely written, wide-ranging discussion of kinship and mourning.[1] Sophocles' heroine offers a possible approach to contemporary questions of changing familial relationships, such as gay parenting, which challenge established norms and force the emergence of a debate about what exactly those norms are supposed to ensure, for society or for the child. Related to this, Butler is interested in mourning and in the melancholic half-life of those whose connections of solidarity and love are not socially recognised, an issue which Aids has brought into focus.

To explore such questions, Butler takes us through some of the chief appropriations of Antigone from Hegel onwards. For many, Antigone's defiance of Creon's edict by her insistence on seeing her brother Polyneices properly buried has represented an opposition of the claims of kinship to those of the state, sometimes glossed as a feminine protest against masculine or patriarchal authority. Hegel, as often, is where Butler's heart is, and she enlarges upon his slightly contradictory versions of Antigone's role. Most famously, the Hegelian Antigone is the (feminine) 'eternal irony of the community', the familial domain with which she is associated being at once its support and its subversion.

Commentators have often read the conflict of this play, like that of some other Greek tragedies, as emblematic of a transition to democratic or at least to established state power, with some form of matriarchal or familial order preceding and countering it. This fits with a certain nineteenth-century version of historical anthropology, followed by Engels among others (and later, vestigially, by Freud). Butler counterposes her Hegelian Antigone with twentieth-century structuralist anthropology, looking at Lévi-Strauss's version of kinship and Lacan's psychoanalytic deployment of that. Lévi-Strauss made the prohibition of incest the one cultural invariant, whatever the specific exclusions that may operate in any given culture; it is that which produces the transition from nature to (human) culture. Lacan cast this theory in linguistic terms. The laws and regularities of kinship are constituted and reinforced in the language we speak all the time, that places us, verbally and pronominally, in relation to others. Lacan's 'symbolic' order, established in language and based on the kinship system that it also maintains, is prior to the variations of the social. But, as Butler stresses, this has the effect of making kinship appear as an unchanging and unchangeable ground.

Butler's claim, against this, is that however Antigone is to be understood it is difficult to argue that she is representative of any kind of stable order, whether familial or feminine or symbolic. She is, after all, the child of an incestuous relationship (between Oedipus and Jocasta); the relationships in her family are everywhere confused and conflated, with a father-brother (Oedipus' relation to his four children with Jocasta), mother-grandmother (Jocasta's relation to them), daughter-sisters (Antigone and Ismene's relation to Oedipus), and so on. She is is devoted to Polyneices to the point of following him to her own death, declaring in a famous (and famously contested) passage that a brother is more than either a husband or a child because the latter two can be replaced whereas a brother, if the parents are dead, cannot. But Eteocles (killed by Polyneices) is also her brother, and so was her father Oedipus (he too is Jocasta's son). The point could also be made that the opposition between the state and the family is itself blurred when the ruler is part of the family in question: Creon, Jocasta's brother, is Antigone's uncle (and, for that matter, Polyneices').

Butler emphasises the specifically linguistic nature of Antigone's acts of defiance and fidelity, not just a matter of throwing earth over flesh but of using words to lay claim to that action in its significance as a violation of one law (and observation of another). She also shows how Creon and Antigone, insofar as they are indeed speaking the same language about what has happened, are not radically different, but 'mirror images' of one another. Unlike Oedipus when he murders his father and marries his mother, Antigone does what she does with full knowledge of its meaning, claiming to base her action on 'unwritten' religious laws that override the recently promulgated edict.

Given the weight that she gives to the effectivities of language, there is a direction that Butler does not pursue which might have contributed to her own sceptical argument in relation to fixity of a

(Lacanian) symbolic order linking kinship and language. Throughout the book, she refers to Antigone's predicament as the object of the curses that have been uttered against her family, using the formulation 'the words are upon her'. By this Butler means to suggest both the constrictions on Antigone's power to act and the force of words, and words alone, in curtailing her possible life; more generally, she points to the way that words 'curse' us with their shaping of what and how we think, of who we can think we are. One of her illustrations is taken from *Oedipus at Colonus*, when Oedipus is on the point of dying: 'From none did you have love more than from this man, without whom you will now spend the remainder of your life'. Butler characterises these lines as one of 'several utterances' by the dying Oedipus 'that assume the status of a curse'. She comments:

> His words exert a force in time that exceeds the temporality of their enunciation: they demand that for all time she have no man except for the man who is dead, and though this is a demand, a curse, made *by* Oedipus, who positions himself as her only one, it is clear that she both honors and disobeys this curse as she displaces her love for her father onto her brother. (60)

Yet even in the translation quoted, it is not clear that this is in fact a curse. 'Will now spend' is a straight future, in the English as in the Greek: Oedipus is simply stating that he is not going to be around much longer for Antigone.

And not only for Antigone. For the words are spoken not to Antigone alone, but to her and her sister, Ismene, and they are addressed distinctly as a pair. Greek, unlike English, has available a 'dual' form between the singular and the (indefinite) plural which has the effect, not least because it is only rarely used, of making a unit out of the couple doubled out in this way. When there are two that form a pair, 'they' or 'we' or 'you' become not indeterminately several, but an indivisible one plus one. English can speak of 'the two of them', say, or 'you two'; but it can do that equally well for 'the four of you', for instance. The closest that English gets to a dual is 'both' – but unlike Greek it doesn't have the full array of special grammatical forms to match.

Butler wants to argue against the fixity of a symbolic order linked to kinship and to language: it is not so and it should not be wished or cursed upon us. Her challenge proceeds from the evident mutations of familial and sexual relationships at the present time; in her account language is left out of the picture, not obviously open to movement. But the example of the Greek dual, buried beneath the English translation, shows how the grammatical building blocks of a language, never noticed as such as we speak, are intimately cemented to its normal constructions of subjectivity.

The pairing of Antigone and Ismene suggests other gaps in Butler's reading. Antigone's fiancé Haemon, Creon's son and her cousin twice over (both in the same generation and once removed), is mentioned only in passing, although he ends up defying his father and dying for and with Antigone. And the bond and the tension between the sisters is a dominant theme in the play. The opening scene is their falling out over how to respond to Creon's edict; later, Ismene attempts to be reunited with Antigone. This sister-sister pair is further linked and contrasted to the brother-brother duo, Polyneices and Eteocles, who have just killed each other in battle. Yet despite the insistent force of these same-sex sibling couples, Butler attends only to Antigone's hypothetical 'desire' for Polyneices: a strange choice for someone who is (self-mockingly) disappointed to find Antigone 'not quite a queer heroine' (72).

Butler is right to point to the need for thinking about new forms of relatedness and commitment in the light of changing norms and practices. She is mistaken, though, in implying a history of relative (in both senses) stability until recently. Until the mid-twentieth century's nuclear moment of marital stability and spousal longevity, the frequency of early death made second marriages a commonplace – swith their accompanying complexities, as now, of step-parents and half- and step-sibling relationships. Kinship has always, or almost always, been muddled. But Butler also fails to mention the recent radical changes in the conditions of kinship: the new reproductive technologies. As well as socially (via adoption or step-parenting), it is now biologically possible to have more than one mother (the egg-bearer and the one who carries the child); while it is also now possible to identify positively a biological father. Paternity is no longer unprovable, while maternity has acquired a new vagueness. Along with the many new kinds of couple and family grouping, of dual and multiple connections and cohabitations, what will the new technologies of childbearing do to the way we imagine our ties and our origins?

1   Judith Butler, *Antigone's Claim: Kinship between Life and Death* (New York: Columbia University Press, 2000). Page references will be given within the main text. The present review was published in *Cambridge Quarterly*.

# 11
# James's *Maisie* in Manhattan

Not far into Henry James's novel *What Maisie Knew* (1897), the young heroine, daughter in an acrimonious divorce, learns that one of her parents has married again. She finds herself 'vaguely puzzled to suppose herself now with two fathers at once. Her researches had hitherto indicated that to incur a second parent of the same sex you had usually to lose the first'.[1] Maisie's bemusement here fits with James's brilliant portrayal throughout the novel of the way that a child – any child – grapples with and grows into some sort of under-standing of an adult order of things, which must be learned and fathomed in all the intricacies and contradictions of its local mani-festations at home, and in the wider world in which that home is situated. Taken as a given, the 'researches' wittily qualify Maisie, like any new person on the planet, as a sort of private investigator, trying to make sense of all the strange goings-on. Freud used the same figure in essays a few years later about the 'sexual researches' of the cynical and curious small child.

In the 1890s, Maisie's two-father (and shortly, two-mother) situ-ation really is out of kilter. Supplementary parents were common enough at the time, but the cause was not death rather than divorce; 'you usually had to lose the first', in Maisie's semi-Wildean phrasing. But ironically, *What Maisie Knew*, which is all about ignorance, unknowingly antipicates a family set-up that a century later is anything but exceptional. A twenty-first-century Maisie might be as puzzled, and upset, or fascinated as her nineteenth-century precursor by the prospect of a new father, but nothing in her contemporary researches would have suggested his arrival on the scene as going against the usual conditions of parental possibility. Modern Maisies may get numbers of new parents of more or less exclusivity or longevity (as parents).

Given this difference, the decision to set a new film version of *Maisie* in present-day Manhattan seems quite bizarre. What is socially extraordinary in the late nineteenth century is now a commonplace scenario, and the story might seem to have lots its edge or scandal. But in fact, apart from the passing puzzlement, James never himself makes a point of the rareness of Maisie's daughterly story. Instead, he is concerned with how she finds a way among the various predicaments, and interpretations of them, that are foisted upon her. When her third and fourth parents – her birth parents' new spouses – themselves get together and form a fourth couple, transgressing the two transgressions of the original marital pair, the social disapproval comes not from a world at large but from yet another surrogate parent, a governess called Mrs Wix. It's with her, not with the newly formed step-parental couple, let alone with one of the long ago birth parents, that Maisie, at the end of the novel, makes an agonised choice to live: agonised because her love (and her sense of being loved or not) is torn between all three of the prospective future parents.

Scott McGehee and David Siegel's 2012 movie makes one cheeky nod to the momentous changes in family norms. In a sort of impromptu 'show and tell', Maisie has proudly introduced 'my new stepfather' to her school class, and a boy sticks his hand up to outdo that one: 'I have two stepfathers, but one is almost dead!' The story unravels and rebinds in many of the same ways as the original novel, as Maisie is shunted (in endless yellow cabs) between the residences of her irreducibly inimical parents, who are less and less seen and heard as their replacements come to the fore. Maisie's blurred awareness of the meanings of everything occurring around and beyond her is brilliantly translated into a cinematic medium of obscure or fragmentary or frightening sounds and sights.

The absence and preoccupation of the Victorian first parents are deftly updated into characters who are always seen attached to their mobiles, their passionate embrace of a returning or departing daughter like a distracted add-on to a primary connection which is always somewhere else. The film's off-on mother (Julianne Moore), alternately smotheringly manipulative and neglectful, is matched by a portly English father (Steve Coogan) who is given – when he bothers to formulate a full sentence – to laboured cliché ('Your grandmother isn't getting any younger', as a reason for returning to London), or to would-be pastiche of Marx. So, to his ex-wife's new husband: 'I'd do you a couple of pointers, but I doubt that the Jacobean tragedy that our relationship was would apply to the farce that you two guys are playing out'.

In contrast, the second spouses of Maisie's parents are unequivocally nice – to Maisie herself, and to one another – except for a couple of small glitches, one on each side, whose smoothing only confirms their devotion and decency. Their relationship develops first, in this case, through their shared love and concern for their new spouses' little girl; but otherwise, and setting aside the fact that they're married to other people, their story is like that of any romcom. The end of the film finds all three – Maisie and those who are now, in effect, her parents – installed in a beachhouse idyll, where they play Monopoly of an evening and go for a long-awaited boat trip. In this situation, Maisie's refusal to leave when her mother turns up without warning to take her away appears obvious and satisfying – both for Maisie herself and for the narrative logic of the film.

Recent films have begun to explore a modern scenario in which, for various new kinds of reason, having children may come before, not after, the parents' falling in love: in Lisa Cholodenko's *The Kids Are All Right* (2010), another Julianne Moore character, a lesbian mother, has a fling with her now teenage children's sperm donor. In this context, what's radical about the new *Maisie* is that the parents who finally get together are not the original ones, and the film firmly endorses the rightness of that outcome (and the rejection of the feckless originals). In that sense, it is progressive – all the more so in that the eventual parents are much less affluent or well connected than their predecessors – a point rubbed in with post-9/11 consciousness when the 'bartender' stepdad gently introduces Maisie to the notion that some people – such as teachers, nurses or firefighters – find it worthwhile to do things for motives other than money.

But by the same token, the film comes over as morally clear and simple in a way that James's novel is absolutely not. In the first *What Maisie Knew*, Mrs Wix's sense of propriety is signified by her wearing of a pair of spectacles known as her 'straighteners'. She sees how things should be seen, and worries about the skewed example of the inappropriate liaison between the step-parents; she is also herself, like Maisie, and like the stepmother, in love with Sir Claude, the step-father. The movie dispenses with Mrs Wix's morals, her distracting affections, and her addition of a further would-be parental party; and it makes sure the stepmother (unlike the novel's Miss Overmore) is as straightforwardly sweet and nice (a Scottish lass!) as the selfish mother is not. She and Maisie initially go away as a pair, and the stepfather/lover comes later.

In other words, the film – even though it is rooting for the once questionable couple – takes over the place of moral Mrs Wix by presenting an unambiguous view of who is deserving and who is not, and where Maisie should rightfully end up. We may have come a long way in the loosening of sexual and marital ties since the first Maisie's time, but the wish for moral certainty is often firmer than ever.

*A review in 2013 for* Times Higher Education *of the film* What Maisie Knew, *directed by Scott McGehee and David Siegel*

1  Henry James, *What Maisie Knew* (1897; Harmondsworth: Penguin, 1982), 46.

# Critical Languages

# 12
# Domestication

In collections of essays on topics of current theoretical interest, it's becoming quite common, if not yet a fully established part of the genre, to start off the piece with a little story about the final stages of its genesis. Such a story typically mentions the last-minute influence of a suggestion or critique by someone whose position, in terms of their gender or race or sexual orientation, might be thought to give their opinion a a legitimacy of a kind which the writer, by his or her own position, might be thought to lack. 'I was discussing this article over breakfast with a lesbian friend, and she said . . . ', writes someone who will thereby be identifying themselves as either a man, or straight, or both.

This type of gesture serves a number of functions. It seems to apologise for writers' disqualifications to speak about what they are going to speak about, marking an awareness that what they say will be open to modification. And it also does the opposite, making up for the disqualifications through the medium of the qualified friend who puts things right, and supplying the text with a provisional certificate of political, or even general, correctness: with an input from every possible position, the chances are that you can add up all the elements into a complete account.

A third element is the setting of the little story, which is regularly given a context of domestic intimacy: this is the sort of friend I have breakfast with. This aspect contributes to the legitimation effect ('some of my best friends . . . '), but it also provides a bit of human interest and narrative enigma by hinting, through the provision of tbe homely detail, at the possibility of a personal story. In this instance, domestication functions in an odd kind of way. It supplements and disrupts the abstract theoretical scenario, taking us somewhere else. Yet it also harmonises, calming down the possible disjunctions between the positions, theoretical and social, of the writer and his interrogator over the soothing influence of the shared bagels and cream cheese.

In these instances, an image of domestication serves as a hidden support to a theoretical argument which appears to be coming from somewhere else, from a would-be neutral, overview position which, for purposes of narrative and political plausibility, needs to be brought down to earth – into the kitchen. And this, it seems to me, is one of many diverse ways in which domestication, as a concept and as a theme, functions in relation to contemporary theoretical arguments, deconstructive and feminist in particular. In a minute, I will be starting to look at some of these; but first, let me just throw in one or two autobiographical nuggets, which you can believe or not. They certainly have something to do with the writing of this paper, though I'm probably in no subject-position to say what.

In the summer of 1992, Gillian Beer asked me if I would like to give a lecture in a series that was being organised at Cambridge in the wake of a controversy over Derrida's election there to an honorary doctorate. I suggested the topic of domestication, and then noticed that this had happened in the week when I unexpectedly acquired a kitchen table, having thought that the room wasn't big enough to take one. My pleasure at the transformation of this domestic space was both mitigated and reinforced by the events of the following two weeks, when I went to Paris – a place where I like to think I feel at home – and had my wallet snatched, twice within the space of one week. For the first time, I felt a strong sense of urban paranoia, if that's the phrase, huddling inside the cosy familiar interior of the place where I was staying – and wondering how I was ever going to sit down and write this paper on, of all things, domestication.

The other story goes back a bit further, to earlier that year, when I woke up one morning to the sounds of two voices which turned out to be those of Gillian Beer and George Steiner soundly and roundly in their different ways defending the importance of Derrida's work on the BBC Radio 4 *Today* programme. As I drank my coffee and started to wake up, I reflected that thanks to the Cambridge controversy, here was deconstruction apparently reaching, or being pushed, beyond the books and the seminar rooms, out onto the airwaves and the headlines and into the kitchens and bedrooms of the daily life of the supposed British nation – an ambivalent passage between hypothetical insides and outsides, crossing, erasing and reinforcing innumerable imaginary and symbolic borders. In some sense, it all seemed to suggest that Derrida was beginning to personify a particularly curious specimen of the proper noun: he was becoming what is called a 'household' name.

It seemed to me that this process was at the very least a strange and unpredictable one, aligning Derrida with a hitherto unfamiliar and probably unwelcome peer-group. Not so much Heidegger, Kant, Descartes and the rest; or, in another connection, not so much Lacan and Kristeva and Foucault. Instead, this new grouping would include, I suppose – if you are British – the likes of Brian Redhead, Domestos, Bruce Forsyth, Boot's, Fergie, Chanel no. 5 and Jeffrey Archer. (On the other side of the Atlantic, perhaps this near-meaningless Anglo-domestic list should be rewritten to something like David Letterman, Mr Clean, Hillary Clinton, Chanel no. 5, Tylenol and Judith Krantz.) It can't be an easy or straightforward transition to find yourself sharing the household name status and facilities with such a heterogeneous community, one whose capacities for comfortable cohabitation, whether with each other or with their new associate, might seem anything but assured.

And yet the related notion of domestication is generally regarded as being the most obvious thing in the world – so obvious, in fact, that once someone or some idea is deemed to have been sent home in this public way, it is as if there is no more to be said: the front door closes definitively on a place removed and retired from the open air of its previous existence – and even though the movement implied is also one of extension, moving out. If a theory gets domesticated, that's the end of it: it becomes like everything else.

The term domestication is used in this way all the time in relation to deconstruction, and to 'theory' in general, including feminist theory. But it does not usually feature the specificity or concreteness of any recognisably domestic location, 'Dunroamin' or wherever. Instead, 'domestication' is used to signal something unproblematically negative which happens to a theory, when – what? Well, when it loses its radical edge, gets tamed, is co-opted or institutionalised (these last two words are often used virtually as synonyms of domestication). The 'domestication' of deconstruction or other theories implies something which may include the kind of mediatisation that occurred with the 'Cambridge and Derrida' story, but refers generally to processes of simplification, assimilation and distortion – any or all of these – to which the theory in question falls victim, or which it is powerless to resist. And it will already be becoming clear that domestication, in this sense, involves a very undeconstructive story: of a wild and natural identity, a full presence, subsequently, and only subsequently, succumbing to forces that deprive it of an original wholeness.

Here is one particularly clear example of how the term is invoked, from Judith Butler's *Gender Trouble*, one of the most significant deployments of deconstruction in a feminist context:

The complexity of gender requires an interdisciplinary and postdisci-
plinary set of discourses in order to resist the domestication of gender
studies or women's studies within the academy and to radicalize the
notion of feminist critique.

And later on, she says:

Parody by itself is not subversive, and there must be a way to understand what makes certain kinds of parodic repetitions effectively
disruptive, truly troubling, and which repetitions become domesticated and recirculated as instruments of cultural hegemony.[1]

What gets domesticated – in this case, a form of feminist theory – is
something defined as being subversive of what will thereby attempt
to take it over, settle it down, suppress its difference.

What interests me in this use of domestication in connection with
theory as something radical and subversive is the way in which the
word itself, and the implied narrative that it brings with it, can go
unexamined within an argument which is deconstructively on the
look-out all the time for the subtle simplifications and assumptions
that discourses of every kind install and seek to maintain. In the
opposition played out between radical critique and domesticating
cultural hegemony, the qualifications of the two forces are not at
issue: the first gets its value from the very fact that it is a challenge
to the second, which is identified largely in terms of its superior force.
In an inevitable movement, the latter then brings the former under
its sway.

Butler's argument does not attribute anything inherently good or
natural to the radical theory which succumbs to domestication: this
is not a case of a hypothetical full presence or genuine content then
becoming contaminated by something else. Rather, the narrative
proceeds in terms of power, with the oppositional, positive force
inevitably succumbing to the stronger, negative one which prompted
its protesting existence in the first place. Implicitly, then, there are
three stages to the story: initial homogeneity or harmony of the hege-
monising force, then the breakaway of the wild radical critique, to
be followed by its reintegration or re-assimilation into the dominant
culture, accompanied by the loss of its critical impetus.

At this point, we might take a first step back indoors to look at
one of the stories implied by the word domestication in its more
homely, extra-theoretical, everyday existence. Within the word itself,
home does not appear as the first place or the natural place: it is a
secondary development, *becoming* domestic. In one French usage,

*domestiquer* means quite simply the subjugation of a tribe to a colonising power. To 'domesticate' is to bring the foreign or primitive or alien into line with the 'domestic' civilisation and power, just as a 'domesticated' animal is one that has been tamed into home life. Something wild, pre-civilised, and verging on the non-human, gets brought into line with an existing order represented in this case as more complex and sophisticated, but also as less natural.

In anthropology, too, the concept of domestication has had an unexpectedly dynamic, if less imperialistic, existence. The word is used to mark a turning point which is supposed to represent not so much a takeover, a 'home' civilisation absorbing and thereby abolishing the difference of one that lies outside its domain, as a transition from what are thereby recognisable as two distinct states of culture. 'The domestication of the savage mind', in Jack Goody's recapitulation of a categorisation adopted for instance by Lévi-Strauss in *The Savage Mind* [*La Pensée sauvage*] links together a whole series of two-term oppositions which have been deployed in accounts of the history of humanity in general, and also in relation to the changes affecting what came to be called 'developing' countries in the later twentieth century. Domestication in these connections is associated with a move from oral to literate culture; from collective life to individualism and private families; from myth to history; and from concrete to abstract thinking.[2]

The reliance on the two-term division and the set order of events – or rather the set position of the one event, which can somehow only be pointed to retrospectively as a boundary which a collectivity is seen to have passed – is of a type which deconstruction, even garden-variety or kitchen-variety deconstruction, would be quick to point out. Goody implicitly answers in another way: yes, there are narratable changes, but historically and culturally they by no means fall into these easily superimposable parallels. This line is different from, but not I think necessarily incompatible with deconstruction, despite what kitsch deconstruction might think or be thought to think. To say that this is a pre-deconstructive mode of argument would be to restore just that narrative logic of identifiable progressions and demarcations which deconstruction seeks to make problematic: it is to operate, in fact, with an already 'domesticated' version of deconstruction which would assert its own logics as superior to and clearly distinguishable from the others.

But there is still a further layer to this, which is indicated by the concentration on domestication as a process of civilisation or taming. For insofar as domestication has to do with home, it would seem to elide the starting point. Home is the place of origin, the place that has always been left; domestication, then, would be a return to or reinvention of the home that you left or lost. This three-part story has its standard modern forms in relation both to daily life – wake up, go to work, return home – and to the process of growing up: from home, out into the world, and then on or back to some form of domestic 'settling down'. In this narrative of nostalgia, home is imagined as a place of peace, stability and satisfaction which has subsequently ceased to be; but also as a withdrawal or seclusion from a 'real' world envisaged as a source of the energy or the troubles or the mobility that are absent from.

It is in the context of this other kind of story that domesticity is imagined as a first place of wholeness and rest, but a place from which – and in order for it to be retrospectivley seen as such – a separation has always taken place. Two books from the late 1950s, one English, one French, illustrate this in very different ways. Richard Hoggart's *The Uses of Literacy* gives a nostalgic portrait of a working-class culture described in terms of concreteness, locality and oral expression, and in the process of being subsumed by a materialistic American mass culture.[3] In numerous vignettes, the home is represented as the focus and epitome of this all-but-lost world, which is seen as at once authentic and claustrophobic: it is not so much that it should not give way or give place to some other mode, but that it is being taken over by the wrong kinds of force. In place of the false commercial culture, endlessly secondarised through images of superficiality – tinsel, glitter, tawdriness, show – Hoggart would substitute something else, the abstract and general thinking of which his own argument, by implication, is meant to serve as an example. So the sequence here is not unlike the anthropological schema deployed by Goody, from oral to intellectual and from local to generalised; but here the terms are reversed, so that the domestic figures as the first, and in this case limited, devalorised state, prior and vulnerable to a mutation which may be negatively or positively viewed – in the direction of commercial fake, or in the direction of intellectual generality.

In a different genre, Gaston Bachelard's *The Poetics of Space* lyrically evokes the peace and dreaminess of the home as a place of corners and nests, with its secret and private spaces. Houses are associated with primitiveness and childhood, and thence with a capacity for maintaining throughout life the qualities of stability, habit and restfulness in which it begins. There is a lovely section on chests of drawers, which Bachelard sees as full of imaginative possibilities of a kind which are lost when a philosopher like Henri Bergson uses them as no more than a polemical metaphor against the tidy separation or compartmentalisation of concepts, as though into drawers.

Bachelard, for his part, wants to bring out the full poetic suggestiveness of such seemingly insignificant domestic things: 'When Bergson speaks of a drawer, what disdain!'[4]

Nestlingly benign as Bachelard's enclosure is, it maintains itself nonetheless partly in its firm distance from two other, related schools or homes of thought. First, there are the twentieth-century philosophers with their hyphen-crazy abstractions: a being-in-the-world that is always already split up. And second, there is the psychoanalysis of negativity, refusing a primary sense of oneness and always finding evidence of a threatening sexuality.[5]

Bachelard's distinction from Freudian psychoanalysis appears most clearly in his tranquil hymn to homeliness as a source of poetic inspiration: 'In its freshness, in its specific activity, the imagination makes of the familiar something strange [*avec du familier fait de l'étrange*]. With a poetic detail, the imagination places us before a new world.'[6] This version of strange familiarity is a far cry from the covertly menacing reversibility of Freud's analysis of the uncanny, the homely *heimlich* which is also, within the same word, the unhomely, marking that unwelcome presence within what is most apparently reassuring in its familiarity and familiality. The house of Freudian psychoanalysis is irredeemably riven by the presence of ghosts, its comforting appearance of womblike unity doubled from the start by intruding forces, such that human life can never securely make a return to a place untroubled by the untimely and dislocating hauntings of other times and places, and other presences that interfere with the imagined separateness and identifiability of places and people who are known and loved.

I don't want to dwell – if that is the word – too long on Freud's uncanny.[7] But it is obvious that in psychoanalysis, the home is no place of harmony – and all the less for functioning so forcefully as the embodiment of a harmony that has always been lost. The home is where the muddle begins and continues; here domestication is not a smoothly operating process of adjustment or progress. And Freud in fact is rather specific about possible domestic disturbances, pointing out in *The Interpretation of Dreams* that 'The ugliest as well as the most intimate details of sexual life may be thought and dreamt of in seemingly innocent allusions to activities in the kitchen'.[8] This is, after all, the world of what Freud called 'kettle logic'; and along such murky paths of connection, we might reflect that if you hear, rather than write, the word 'domestication' – if you return to that famous pre-civilised primitiveness of an oral culture – what you get, out of sight but not out of earshot, and none too neatly tidied away into this capaciously polysyllabic word, is 'mess' and 'stickiness': an

Anglo-Saxon sprawl that screeches for attention out of the nicely abstracted Latinate term. As every housewife knows.[9]

Which is perhaps the point at which to turn to look at the ways in which domestication has been treated as a theme in feminist writing. At first sight, the situation would seem to be quite straight-forward, as with the deployment of the word in a figurative sense: just as feminists are sure that the 'domestication' of feminist theories is to be regretted, so the rejection of domesticity has seemed a principal tenet of feminist demands for freedom, if not the very first. The home figures as the place where the woman is confined, and from which she must be emancipated in order for her to gain access to a world outside that is masculine but only contingently so, and which offers possibilities of personal and social achievement that are not available within its limited sphere.

In various forms, this representation could be said to run right through the western tradition of feminist writing from the past two hundred years – including in different ways Mary Wollstonecraft, Simone de Beauvoir, Betty Friedan, and at many points Virginia Woolf (the infamous 'Angel in the House', derived from Coventry Patmore's bestselling nineteenth-century poem, whose Victorian insistence on domestic virtues must be violently abolished before the freer twentieth-century woman can emerge[10]). Before going into more detail about some of these versions, it's worth noticing some of the strong common denominators.

These representations literalise the imagery of inside and outside, in such a way that the home is figured as something close to a prison, walled off against a 'real' world of events which is elswehere. The condition of femininity, inseparable from women's domestication, is artificially imposed by social and/or masculine forces which women have been powerless or unwilling to resist, or have not recognised as limitations at all. True selfhood is attainable only by moving beyond the domestic, local, private boundaries. Though presently allowed chiefly or only to men, this status is not inherently gendered: it is rather a right, or a nature, of which the present organisation of things has unjustly deprived women.

In the second volume of *The Second Sex*, Beauvoir's chapter on marriage delivers a resounding critique of that state or estate's effect on the woman insofar as it 'confines her to immanence'.[11] As so often, the metaphor of confinement is given a naturalised foundation, a home base, in that it turns out to refer to a life contained within the domestic space. Beauvoir does begin by quoting some passages – from none other than Bachelard and Woolf's *The Waves* – on the positive symbolic associations of the *foyer*, of being indoors and sheltered. But the critique is for the most part relentless: the housewife with her 'days leading nowhere'[12] is deprived of the capacity to form and carry out projects; her work is mere repetition with no product at the end or in the future, and this automatically casts it into a secondary, devalorised mode:

> She simply perpetuates the present; she does not have the sense of conquering a positive Good but of struggling indefinitely against Evil. It is a struggle renewed every day. . . . Eating, sleeping, cleaning . . . the years no longer mount upwards to the sky, they stretch out identical and grey in a horizontal sheet; every day imitates the one that preceded it; it is an eternal present, pointless and without hope.[13]

There is a combination of, on the one hand, temporal and spatial stasis – no progression as no movement outwards, outdoors – and on the other no building up towards the accomplishment of a lasting work. But this stasis is sustained by the need for it to be constantly, daily, reproduced – by the routine that is deplored for being always identical, and by the endless cleaning and cooking for an immediate consumption which leaves neither record nor surplus.

A woman's work, proverbially, is never done, to the point that this never-doneness can come to define it: an interminable task with no lasting result or addition. Beauvoir's account in some ways resembles the Marxist theory of the home as the site of the reproduction of labour power. No additional or measurable value is produced there; instead, its 'reproductive' function is one of the essential conditions for the production of surplus value to take place elsewhere. 'Reproduction' operates here in a curiously devious way. On the one hand it is the day-to-day servicing of the workers as one of the elements of production. They need to be fed, cleaned and rested in order to be physically capable of going out again and doing the next day's work. On the other hand, it is the reproduction of lives, so that there will be more workers to man the factories. In this second implication, the term moves covertly from the biological to the economic, as the teleology of embryo development in the first of these discourses latches or hatches itself onto the parallel but quite different teleology of the needs of capitalism (workers as a supply to be kept up).

In Marxist theory, then, 'reproduction' evidently does a lot of work for all its apparently secondary status. As in Beauvoir's version, the domestic sphere figures as the place which both makes possible and reinforces a difference attributed to the sphere of real projects or production. This difference is represented both spatially – in the respective 'spheres' or sites – and temporally, in the demarcation of the linear, cumulative time of production and projects from the repet-itive, cyclical time of reproduction and housework.

In Friedrich Engels's *The Origin of the Family, Private Property, and the State* (1884), an anthropological narrative of the develop-ment of human societies to their modern capitalist forms of organisation draws out the interdependence of the terms of this divi-sion in an especially sharp form. Engels's story is derived from the latest anthropological researches of the time, in particular the hypothesis that the present patrilineal, patriarchal order of things is not universal, but was preceded by forms of matrilineal (though not matri*archal*) organisation called 'mother right' (*Mutterrecht*). The changeover from one to the other is glossed in unequivocally dramatic terms:

> The overthrow of mother right was the *world-historical defeat of the female sex*. The man seized the reins in the house also; the woman was degraded, enthralled, the slave of man's lust, a mere instrument for breeding children. This lowered position of women, especially manifest among the Greeks of the Heroic and still more of the Classical Age, has become gradually embellished and dissembled, and, in part, clothed in a milder form, but by no means abolished.[14]

But the precipitating circumstances of the change are nothing other than the process of domestication itself. Previously, according to Engels's anthropological sources, societies were more or less polyg-amous, and they were communal: there was no private property, and extended households were not based on the nucleus of a single set of parents. The transition to patriarchy accompanies a whole series of other changes: the beginnings of monogamy, the one-couple family, the private home, privately owned property, competitiveness between men, surplus value in production, and the strict demarca-tion of male from female labour as between the household and what now becomes a separate site of work accorded a superior value.

At one fell swoop, one irrevocable crash and fall, this mythical moment resumes all the standard separations of the domestic from its outside, or that mark off the domestic as an enclave or 'separate' sphere within the generalised norm of a world that excludes it but which depends absolutely upon it. Crucially, domestication indicates the definitive division of masculine and feminine as operating in and governed according to spaces and times that are irreducible to one another but mutually dependent. Engels, bless his nineteenth-century feminist heart, is unequivocal about the specific implications of all this:

The woman's housework lost its significance compared with the man's work in obtaining a livelihood; the latter was everything, the former an insignificant contribution. Here we see already that the emancipation of women and their equality with men are impossible and must remain so as long as women are excluded from socially productive work and restricted to housework, which is private. The emancipation of women becomes possible only when women are enabled to take part in production on a large, social scale, and when domestic duties require their attention only to a minor degree.[15]

(It's worth noting in passing that Engels's emancipatory vision doesn't include the possibility that it might not have to be only women's attention directed towards 'domestic duties'; and in a similar fashion, he consistently assumes in his discussions of marriage and sexuality that there is a natural desire for monogamy or 'individual sex-love' on the part of women, and an equally natural desire for promiscuity on the part of men.)

In Engels's myth of origins, the overthrow of mother right brings in its train not only the three estates designated by the book's title but also, implicitly, the beginnings of various temporal lines – of history, of accumulation, of production (it is a classic instance of domestication in the sense described by Goody). Not only is the time before patriarchy thenceforth a kind of pre-time or non-time in relation to the forward directions that are now installed, but the private household comes to represent something like residue or throwback in the midst of the modern world.

It is in this sense that home can figure too as a refuge from the batterings and struggles of what is variously described as the 'real' world or the 'outside' world. Not long before Engels's manifesto in a very different mode, John Ruskin's lecture, 'Of Queens' Gardens', from *Sesame and Lilies* (1865), set in place an extraordinary cele-bration-cum-damnation of the domestic sphere. Ruskin sees this as the site on which to fight out and lay claim to a proper division of the sexes in terms of their respective natures, which he takes to be at once different and complementary.

Ostensibly, the argument is asserting all the well-known virtues of a peaceful, innocent Victorian womanhood – unencumbered by work, and simply blossoming forth with a natural spontaneity that balances the rather more turbulent nature of the man. But the context for the assertion of what Ruskin calls the 'harmonious idea' – glossed somewhat insecurely as 'it must be harmonious if it is true'[16] – is the opposite, a situation of antagonism. Ruskin has opened his question as having to do with what he calls women's 'queenly power', their 'royal or gracious influence', which should be exercised 'not in their households merely, but over all within their sphere'; the domestic space moves out effortlessly to comprise a set of individual 'territories': to each woman her own private colony for domestication.[17] At the same time, there is a specific contemporary background of disorder, which Ruskin explains in this way:

> There never was a time when wilder worder were spoken, or more vain imagination permitted, repecting this question – quite vital to all social happiness. The relations of the womanly to the manly nature, their different capacities of intellect or of virtue, seem never to have been yet measured with entire consent. We hear of the mission and of the rights of Woman, as if these could ever be separate from the mission and the rights of Man; – as if she and her lord were creatures of independent kind and of irreconcileable claim.[18]

It is a verbal unruliness – wild words – which needs to be tamed, civilised and constituted into its prescribed place. Unlike his contemporary John Stuart Mill, Ruskin's starting point has to do with a difference, not a relative sameness, between the sexes. Ruskin both acknowledges that this difference is somehow a tense one, productive of dissent and disturbance, and at the same time asserts almost by fiat that to that very extent – because it is not harmonious – it must be deemed and made so. 'Vain imaginination' has been reprehensibly 'permitted': the issue is one of legislation, such that a disruptive or distracting element must be arbitrarily forbidden, and/or put out of the way.

Ruskin then sets up his ideal social arrangements on the basis of a clearly distinguished difference of sexual natures:

> Now their separate characters are briefly these. The man's power is active, progressive, defensive. He is eminently the doer, the creator, the discoverer, the defender. His intellect is for speculation and invention; his energy for adventure, for war, and for conquest, wherever war is just, wherever conquest is necessary. But the woman's power is for rule, not battle – and her intellect is not for invention or creation, but for sweet ordering, arrangement, and decision. She sees the qualities of things, their claims, and their places.[19]

Wars and strife are taken to be inevitable, though not valued in themselves: they are subject to considerations of justice and necessity. And it is worth noticing too that in attempting to harmonise – to sweetly reorder, arrange and adjudicate the dissensions between the sexes –

Ruskin himself is 'eminently' less 'a doer' than a woman. The full expansion of this social arrangment then takes us swiftly away from all the worldly strife to the place of feminine security:

> This is the true nature of home – it is the place of Peace; the shelter, not only from all injury, but from all terror, doubt, and division. In so far as it is not this, it is not home; so far as the anxieties of the outer life penetrate into it, and the inconsistently-minded, unknown, unloved, or hostile society of the outer world is allowed by either husband or wife to cross the threshold, it ceases to be home; it is then only a part of that outer world which you have roofed over, and lighted fire in. But so far as it is a sacred place, a vestal temple, a temple of the hearth watched over by Household Gods . . . so far it vindicates the name, and fulfils the praise, of Home.[20]

Home must thus be constructed against, not in continuity with, the 'outer life' of 'anxieties' which must at all odds be kept out; it is defined not so much by its capacity to provide the basic needs of shelter and warmth, but by its exclusion of the outer, its standing against what is always trying to force or 'penetrate' its way in. Consecrated against the secular troubles of the outside, home has become the haven in an aggressive world; it is where the heart is, but a heart constructed desperately as a defence against an intolerable and ineradicable pressure from what is thereby rejected to an indefinite external source of disturbance.

Here, domestication runs its complete course. Home is set up as a response to and bulwark against something perceived as a threat; it makes an interior separate from and set off against the dangers or anxieties that can then be safely thrown out onto an outside, an out there, whose differentiation has to be constantly re-established with the risk of every questionable foot across the threshold. But despite this order of things, home is also represented as the place which has always been there, the original temple of the Household Gods, something that pre-dates and will by implication outlive the incursions from the outside which in this light appear as no more than contingent and ephemeral.

Just a little excursion at this point – though we won't stray too far from the front door – on the history of home. Witold Rybczynski's charming book called *Home: A Short History of an Idea* documents this in loving detail, through developments in bourgeois forms of living accommodation and their accompanying notions of family intimacy and comfort. It is a reassuringly developmental history: the home and its pleasures were just waiting placidly to be found, at the end of a smooth historical path leading straight to the modern armchair and all the rest – all the rest you could ever want. So Rybczynski begins one of his central chapters like this:

> Privacy and domesticity, the two great discoveries of the Bourgeois Age, appeared, naturally enough, in the bougeois Netherlands. By the eighteenth century they had spread to the rest of northern Europe – England, France, and the German states. . . . The house was no longer only a shelter against the elements, a protection against the intruder – although these remained important functions – it had become the setting for a new, compact social unit: the family. With the family came isolation, but also family life and domesticity. The house was becoming a home, and following privacy and domesticity the stage was set for the third discovery: the idea of comfort.[21]

Slowly and surely, in Rybczynski's story, things have been getting cosier and cosier: domestication is certainly a lengthy process (it took a while for people to discover how nice it is) but it is one that does no more and no less than fulfil wishes that are natural: 'Domestic well-being is a fundamental human need that is deeply rooted in us, and that must be satisfied'.[22] There can be difficulties in the way of its attainment in particular periods, as with the mistaken austerity of modernist functionalism, or the contemporary postmodern bric-à-brac of decors vaguely alluding to heterogeneous styles from the past. Rybczynski is clear this is a mistake: 'It is not watered-down historical references that are missing from people's homes. What is needed is a sense of domesticity, not more dadoes; a feeling of privacy, not neo-Palladian windows; an atmosphere of coziness, not plaster capitals.'[23]

The book ends with an argument which simply sets the natural home in relation to, and usually against, the machine, in the form of either outside experts imposing their views of what it should be, or mistaken and artificial contrivances, whether decorative or labour-saving. Rybczynski is not straightforwardly opposed to the presence or use of machines in the home, but they must be kept in their subordinate place to a natural form of domestic life that is clearly separable as such: 'We must rediscover for ourselves the mystery of comfort, for without it, our dwellings will indeed be machines instead of homes'.[24] As with Ruskin, nature has mysteriously metamorphosed into an injunction – 'We must' – that needs to be constantly re-legislated.

Rybczynski has taken us calmly to a world where the incursions from outside are not as formidable in their home-breaking potential as Ruskin's, but are nonetheless there as a permanent threat which is also a permanent bolster to the setting up of home as an ideal. In Ruskin, the most sinister aspect of the territorial arrangements is the role ascribed to the woman. We have already come across her vaunted capacities for 'sweet ordering'; more dangerously, she can be held responsible for all that goes wrong:

> There is not a war in the world, no, nor an injustice, but you women are answerable for it; not in that you have provoked, but in that you have not hindered. Men, by their nature, are prone to fight.[25]

So the inside/outside opposition between home and world is now directly transposed onto the difference of male and female natures; and now the inside, previously secondary and reactive to the troubles of the world, is being allotted a dominant, controlling power whereby the healing sympathies of the feminine home are to spread their influence outwards, taking over the uncontrolled masculine spaces of strife. In this way Ruskin argues against the present situation, in which 'You shut yourselves within your park walls and garden gates; and you are content to know that there is beyond them a whole world in wilderness – a world of secrets which you dare not penetrate; and of suffering which you dare not conceive.'[26] The movement of domestication thus ultimately reverses itself again, with a feminine force called upon to penetrate outwards to overcome the wilderness: sweet ordering through the exertion of a counter-power that repeats in the other direction the invasion from the troubled outside.

Returning now briefly to Beauvoir, who has no doubt been resentfully and repetitively darning the Sartrean socks all this while, I would like to highlight one moment in her section on the domestic life of the married woman. For the most part, Beauvoir considers both oppression and emancipation from an individual perspective: it is an affliction of single and separate cosnciousnesses, not – as in Engels's analysis, for instance – an effect of a structure bearing upon women collectively as a sex.[27] But here in Beauvoir is a moment of break-out from the confinements of daily life – within the text, and for the woman it describes – and it is when the housewife goes shopping:

> While they are doing their shopping, women exchange remarks in the shops, on the street corners, through which they affirm 'housewifely values', where each one derives a sense of her importance: they feel they are members of a community which – for a moment – is opposed to the society of men as the essential to the inessential. But above all,

buying is a profound pleasure: it is a discovery, almost an invention.
... Between seller and buyer a relationship of tussling and ruses is set
up: the point of the game for her is to procure herself the best buys at
the lowest price; the great importance attached to the smallest of
economies could not be explained merely by the concern to balance a
difficult budget: the thing is to win a round. For the time she is suspiciously examining the stalls, the housewife is queen; the world is at
her feet with its riches and its traps, for her to grab herself some loot.
She tastes a fleeting triumph when she empties the bag of provisions
onto her table.[28]

The shopping interlude is the one moment when domestication
becomes something other than the stifling repetition of itself in solitude, as the housewives move outdoors to take a breath of collective
fresh air and to enjoy what is practically the only pleasure that
Beauvoir recognises for them. Where Ruskin's woman is enjoined to
be a perpetual moral 'queen', Beauvoir's is granted this – 'the housewife is queen' – as a momentary release and a 'fleeting triumph'.

It is interesting to note that this one interval of relative emancipation involves a collective experience founded in an affirmation of
domestic values and a reversal of the normal hierarchy between the
feminine-domestic and the masculine-worldly. A later French feminism would pause on this moment of reversal, and hold it out as a
possibility of serious philosophical mutation. So Luce Irigaray,
eminently Derridean in this strategy, would in effect pick up
Beauvoir's denigration of the feminine condition in its absence of
forward direction, its lack of an individual project, by classifying
such values not as the neutral destination of the human individual,
but as specifically masculine. The hitherto subordinated terms – repetition, non-unity, otherness – come forward in Irigaray's account to
disrupt and break into what is thereby both identified and challenged
as a monolithic, but potentially mutable, phallogocentric order.[29]

Though the argument and its implications are not the same, Julia
Kristeva's essay 'Women's Time' operates upon some comparable
reversals. It identifies a quasi-tyrannical linear temporality – the time
required for the teleologies of western history and capitalist accumulation – with masculinity in the psychical sense, and suggests that
other structures of time associated with femininity may now be
coming to take a less subordinate place, alongside if not instead of
the linearity which has dominated modern western thinking and
experience.[30] None of the contemporary feminists, however, takes
back the abstract temporal questions into the daily life of the kitchen
which is where Beauvoir's disgruntlements begin. In fact, insofar as

domestication gets a thematic mention in these more recent theories, it is to perpetuate the assumption that of course women would and should want to leave home and enter the workforce; or at least, not to be spending their days solely as housewives, a situation still implicitly marked by the imagery of confinement within a space that excludes participation in a real world elsewhere.

But in the age of postmodern technology, such straighforward separations are perhaps open to rethinking in a way that they never were before. All sorts of technical innovations – faxes, computer networks, and so on – have altered the terms on which one hypothetically private space is related to another. Telephones and radios can now be seen as historically first in this series of instruments which abolish the communicational boundaries of interior spaces from each other, or from the 'world outside' in general. They have made possible, for better or for worse, a sharing of space between home and work, the reproductive and the productive spheres, in a way that had been excluded since the industrial revolution definitively divided the two for all but a few eccentric professions. But this is to put it too simply. For the new potential for blurring and overlap could also be said to show up the way in which the division of the domestic from its outside was previously sustained only through a literalisation of the figure of the house within and separate from a surrounding world, with its four walls marking off a boundary which was supposed to keep clearly apart each of the two sides, the domestic and its other, whether defined as the real world or the outside world or the productive sphere.

One last trip to the shops before we finally bring it all back home. For almost as long as the middle-class ideology of domesticity has existed, consumerism has provided a bridge, or at least a very brisk walk, between the home and the outside world. From nineteenth-century department stores to twentieth-century supermarkets, via the development at the turn of the century of brand-name goods and the vast expansion of advertising in all the media which enter the home – newspapers and magazines and later radio and television – consumption has been intimately bound up with the changing forms of domestication. So much so, that it has at various times been identified as the key to a female oppression now associated with a false, commodified form of home life, implicitly differentiated from something more authentic that either preceded the present situation or might be available in the future, if women could rid themselves of their subjection to the lures of commodities.

Betty Friedan's *The Feminine Mystique* (1963), the book that was so influential for the 'second wave' of feminism on both sides of the

Atlantic, is probably the best, as well as the first, example of this type of argument. It is also one of the quirkiest. For Friedan in effect claims that women won their emancipation – votes, professional rights – and then let it go, foolishly seduced by the determined operations of the men of Madison Avenue and their avatars in other areas of life who wanted to ensure their return to that homely place which Friedan uncomfortably names 'the comfortable concentration camp'. Here, consumption figures not as momentary freedom, but as a forceful social pressure driving women, against what are nonetheless their potentially better judgments, back to the 'feminine' home.[31]

But the deeper accusation of Friedan's polemic is the fear that this creeping and artificial domestication is affecting men as well, who are sinking and sudsing into the ghastly 'togetherness' of conjugally shared household activities--and the pattern is in danger of becoming perpetuated through the lack of paternal discipline and excess of mother-love. The renunciation on women's part of real-world achievement values – 'human' values, in Friedan's terms – in favour of the circumscribed and secondary values of the home seems to be leading inexorably to a corresponding domestication of the men, who are going soft in the head. Domestication implies for both sexes an alienation from a true, whole self whose field of operation is out there, somewhere else.

It will be clear that there are common elements between this argument and Beauvoir's. In both cases, domestication represents a deprivation of full human potential, and domestication is associated with a false version of femininity. Women should be allowed access – out of the home, into the wide world – to the prospects and projects of an authentic subjectivity which is not in itself gendered: the feminine exclusion is contingent, not structural, and identity is in fact diminished to the extent that it is bound to sex (women's lot as feminine, kept in their secluded place, rather than fully human). Because of their individualistic frameworks, both Friedan and Beauvoir see women's liberation as their own responsibility: resistance is up to each one on her own.

We have come full circle several times, repetitively but also with some differences, looking at various constructions of domestication in relation to its outsides, seen diversely as either a wilderness waiting to be tamed, or a neutral space of social reality and opportunity. The home itself functions as either a residual sanctuary for and source of moral values seen to be absent from the outside world, or (and the two are not mutually exclusive) as a place of rest, its dailiness and removal from the progressive, linear time operating elsewhere seen as complementary to, rather than subversive of, the dominant external order. In feminist versions, this becomes a stagnantly artificial prison or cage for a woman whose fulfillment can only be 'outside'.

How then might we think of the domestication of deconstruction or the domestication of feminism? As for deconstruction – well, in one sense, of course, deconstruction is always already domesticated, or never not yet domesticated, to the extent that it does not pretend to set itself up as something outside, radically separable from, the structures and logics it comes to analyse. There is no such thing as a pure deconstruction; instead, it can only be seen insofar as it works in and through particular texts or structures. However, this is not much use in thinking about the more dismissive use of domestication that I began with: always-already structures tend all too easily to slip into 'it's-all-the-same' structures, as though there were then no distinctions to be made between uses or adaptations of deconstructive methods. But I would like to say something about one of the processes which get damned as domestication: the transmission or presentation of deconstructive ideas.

The metaphor of accessibility is regularly used in this context, with a connotation of diminishment and simplification: insofar as you make the theory accessible, you automatically simplify it, abolishing a complexity which is seen as the virtue of the original. This characterisation operates with particular force in conjunction with the idea of translation and importation, in a weakening that is assumed to occur in the movement from French to English. Associated with this is an implicit devaluation of English as the language of common sense, and behind this again lies the whole history of the development of theory in Britain and other English-speaking countries, where it has been valorised for qualities of Frenchness, complexity and difficulty seen to be absent from domestically English or Anglo-American traditions of thinking. In this context, inaccessibility and obscurity of presentation come to be linked as positive and indissociable terms.

Yet there is nothing inevitable about this state of affairs, no reason to assume that complexity has to go with obscurity, or accessibility with simplification. Deconstruction is assuredly finding some homes in English-speaking intellectual culture, but such domestications need not be considered as necessarily following a pattern of decline and distortion. There are doubtless more domestications, there and elsewhere, than are dreamt of in any common or kitchen philosophy of domestication as meaning the moment which marks the end of the interesting story.

A different, though related argument applies in the case of feminist domestication (though I don't mean to imply a necessary separation between feminism and deconstruction: there are many points of overlap between the two, in practice and in theory, and most of those who bring them together would claim that they are inseparable). The use of 'domestication' as a straightforwardly negative metaphor, in need of no further analysis, implies simple binary oppositions and two-stage stories, whereby something initially natural, spontaneous or subversive gets pushed into a conformity or homogeneity which deprives it of whatever made it different. This much would apply to any deployment of domestication; but in feminist contexts, there is an added irony because the would-be abstract term is rich in thematic ambiguities and histories which, from the point of view of feminist demands and aims, could hardly be closer to home. Feminism cannot just get away from domestication, whether by sweeping it under the carpet as a dusty old error, or by identifying it with an uncomplicated and inevitable process of asssimilation.

Domestication, as the examples should have demonstrated by now, is not such a firmly fixed, univocal concept in the first place. And feminism, with its inherently undomesticated place – neither at home nor away from home – is uniquely placed to engage in productive forms of domestic deconstruction.

*Written for a lecture series at Cambridge in the autumn of 1992, organised by Thomas Baldwin and Gillian Beer in the wake of the contested vote on Derrida's nomination for an honorary doctorate at that university*

1 Judith Butler, *Gender Trouble: Feminism and the Subversion of Identity* (New York: Routledge, 1990), pp. xiii, 139.
2 See Jack Goody, *The Domestication of the Savage Mind* (Cambridge: Cambridge University Press, 1977).
3 See Richard Hoggart, *The Uses of Literacy: Changing Patterns in English Mass Culture* (1957; Boston: Beacon Press, 1961).
4 Gaston Bachelard, *La poétique de l'espace* (1957; Paris: Presses Universitaires de France, Quadrige series), 79.
5 On hyphenating philosophy, see Bachelard, 128 and 192; for the critique of a negative version of psychoanalysis, see e.g. 112–13 and 155–7.
6 Bachelard, 129.
7 But I must add a domestic detail from the last half hour: as I was typing this, to the reassuring dim backing of the radio, the voice of Dave Lee Travis – a household name on British radio until he faded ignominiously from the airwaves in the summer of 1993 – filtered itself across, asking

some quiz question to some pub team somewhere in East Anglia, about – as I subsequently reconstructed it – the total weight in tonnes of the quantity of cargo shifted through Heathrow Airport every year. A few moments later the reply came back, as it turned out just one or two off the correct answer, somewhere in the hundred thousands. With what sounded to me like genuine disturbance, DLT returns: 'That's a little too close for comfort, that's a very uncanny guess.' To me, about to start a paragraph on the uncanny, this too was a little too close for comfort, as if the radio, habitually used in some nebulous way to be alternately soothing and enlivening, or just <u>there</u> in an unremarkable domestically familiar way, had suddenly jumped out to take on a quite different role, unsettling in its apparent reinforcement of the main direction of my attention.

8  Freud, *The Interpretation of Dreams* (1900), trans. James Strachey (Harmondsworth: Penguin, 1978), 463.

9  In which connection, there is the following searing passage from the end of Upton Sinclair's *The Jungle* (1906; Harmondswroth: Penguin, 1986), spoken by an advocate of cooperative communities:

> 'Surely it is moderate to say that the dish-washing for a family of five takes half an hour a day; with ten hours as a day's work, it takes, therefore, half a million able-bodied persons – mostly women – to do the dish-washing of the country. And note that this is most filthy and deadening and brutalizing work; that it is a cause of anaemia, nervousness, ugliness, and ill temper; of prostitution, suicide, and insanity; of drunken husbands and degenerate children'. (406)

He goes on to imagine the hygienic twentieth-century wonders of a collectivly owned 'machine that would wash and dry the dishes, and do it, not merely to the eye and the touch, but scientifically – sterilizing them' (406-7).

10  See Virginia Woolf, 'Professions for Women', *The Crowded Dance of Modern Life: Selected Essays*, Vol. 2, ed. Rachel Bowlby (Harmondsworth: Penguin, 1993).

11  Simone de Beauvoir, *Le Deuxième sexe* (1949; Paris: Gallimard, Folio essais series, 1986), vol. II, 259.

12  Beauvoir, 259.

13  Beauvoir, 267.

14  Friedrich Engels, *The Origin of the Family, Private Property, and the State* (1884; trans. New York: Pathfinder Press, 1972), 68.

15  Engels, 152.

16  John Ruskin, 'Of Queens' Gardens', in *Sesame and Lilies* (1865; London: J.M. Dent, Everyman Library, 1970), 50.

17  Ruskin, 49.

18  Ruskin, 49–50.

19  Ruskin, 59.

20  Ruskin, loc. cit.

21 Witold Rybczynski, *Home: A Short History of an Idea* (London: Heinemann, 1988), 77.
22 Rybczynski, 217.
23 Rybczynski, 220–1.
24 Rybczynski, 232.
25 Ruskin, 75.
26 Ruskin, 75.
27 This is a point eloquently made by Michèle Le Doeuff in *L'Etude et le rouet* (Paris: Seuil, 1989).
28 Beauvoir, 272.
29 See Luce Irigaray, *Speculum: de l'autre femme* (Paris: Seuil, 1974).
30 See Julia Kristeva, 'Women's Time' (1979), trans. Alice Jardine and Harry Blake, in Catherine Belsey and Jane Moore (eds), *The Feminist Reader* (London: Macmillan, 1989).
31 I discuss this in more detail in '"The Problem with No Name": Rereading Friedan's *The Feminine Mystique*', in *Still Crazy After All These Years/ Women, Writing and Psychoanalysis* (London: Routledge, 1992).

# 13
## The Joy of Footnotes

Dear Darian,

I've been reading yours and I just have to sit down and write to you. Don't know what I'll do with it when I've finished. I might give it to a toddler to draw aeroplanes on the back of. Or I might just bin it. But I won't post it, don't worry, I'm not about to spoil the fun.

But before I get on with what the rest of this, I just wanted to tell you about a letter I read the other day. A friend was describing the break-up of his marriage and he put it like this: 'I woke up one morning in love, opened the wrong file on Word Perfect and found a letter from her to her lover.' That was it. Now there's no way of knowing whether she – his wife – ever printed out, let alone sent that letter. But it was certainly received, at least by someone who was not its official addressee, and she may have intended that or she may not.[1] Posting, you see, not being the main issue here – what this seems to show is that there are many ways of sending a letter, though the sender may be the last one to know where the thing has ended up, or indeed where they meant to send it in the first place. Lacan, I seem to recall, once said something about a letter always arriving at its destination, and I think there was some kind of debate with that deconstruction philosopher, can't remember the name, but I'm sure it will come back to me and when it does I'll put it on a postcard. Anyway, my question to you, Darian – it's the question I think I'll be continuing to ask, in various ways – is, who do you think you are writing to?

Now in the book, you say something near the beginning about what you're going to do which set me thinking, it's at the end of the Introduction. It's this:

> I have avoided heavy footnoting and quotation of authorities, a prac-
> tice perhaps first made famous by Prynne, the seventeenth-century
> critic of the theatre teased by Milton as always having his wits beside
> him in the margin so as to be beside his wits in the text.

Okay, so you don't do footnotes. Well, not 'heavy' footnoting. In fact there aren't any – whether heavy, light or middleweight. But I wondered – what is the significance of announcing the lack of footnotes. What, indeed, is a footnote?

For footnotes seem to have two rather different roles. On the one hand, they are like signposts. They say where what you say has come from, and they say where readers can go if they want to investigate the source themselves. They point to something outside this particular text, they provide information in a conventional and quickly comprehensible form.

On the other hand, alongside this scholarly role, footnotes can do something rather different. They are the place to play, the place where you can digress or speculate about something outside the main frame of your argument. They are the space where what you say does not have to be substantiated in the same way as what is said in the main text. The footnote in this sense is what doesn't need to be footnoted in the first sense.[2]

Now it seems to me that what you have written, footnoteless and pedantry-free, is in fact a long footnote of this second type. As such it's very entertaining and suggestive, full of little stories and teasing details. But I kept asking myself––what is the main text? What's this based on? Is this just a little anecdote or is it a serious argument, and does the difference matter?

Let me give you an example or two of what I mean. I'll start on page 62 – I'll give proper references, you see – when you are talking about, more or less, the Freudian account of the development of femininity and the trouble for girls of having all that shifting about to do, from mother to father to some other man, if they're to end up as heterosexual women:

> Theorists and scholars have been commenting on this problem for many years, but what matters in this context are less the specific vicissitudes of Freud's theories than the very simple question: if the girl's first object is the mother, why does she have to have a relation with man at all? After all, her wish to receive a child from the father, one reason she turns to him, is thwarted. Freud argued that this wish to receive a child is first represented in oral form (the phantasy image of receiving the phallus through the mouth), but surely this does not square with empirical observation. Why is is that a woman may find it easier to perform fellatio on a man she does not know than to kiss him?

(Funny, I thought that was what gay men did, so I've heard, but never mind, it's all the same to me.) Now there are lots of things that could be said here about what's being given as the Freudian account. We're supposed to leave that to the 'theorists and scholars' and stick with the 'simple questions'. But just what is being presented here? what is the 'empirical observation' on which the challenge to Freud's argument is based? For one thing, you wouldn't expect to find any empirical observation necessarily operating as a refutation of a psychoanalytic argument about fantasy – quite the contrary. But even without this – we aren't told if the empirical observation is meant to mean something the author read in a book, or else a matter of generally accepted common knowledge – or is it just what you have observed for yourself – in which case the formal, not to say scholarly phrase 'empirical observation' still begs every question: in the street? in the laboratory? in analysis? – and if so, one case? or most cases? And then that last question: 'Why is it that a woman may find it easier to perform fellatio on a man she does not know than to kiss him?' May she? Who says? Again – is this meant as a statement about all women, most women, the odd woman, the woman who thinks she's a gay man (which might, who knows, be most women, but we aren't told that either)? The phrase 'a woman may' leaves it all open. And what is the evidence? 'Empirical observation' would cover a multitude of sins in this case.

My next example also raises the question of the nature of your observations, and it also made me think more about what sort of a reader your text is setting up. So now we turn to one of the places when you move from one sex to the other, here from women to men, with one of those quick bridging sentences: 'Masculinity, of course, is also beset with problems, albeit different ones' (this is page 17, by the way). Okay. Then you go on:

> Many recent books have tried to define the nature of these problems, yet they have had the unfortunate tendency to transform themselves into encomiums for either the 'new', weak man or the lost warrior type, something that can hardly fail to bring a smile to the reader's lips.

Let's just pause there for a moment. Are you smiling comfortably, dear reader? Who, indeed, is the reader here? Someone of no particular sex, it seems, and easily aloof both from the pathetic tendencies of these 'many recent books' and from the things they praise, those silly new men and those equally silly Iron Johns (see, we get the reference even without a footnote). We readers know a real man when we see one. Then the passage goes on:

It is a notable fact that many modest and homely gents purchase jungle warfare magazines just as furtively as the porn magazines of their adolescence. After work, in the privacy of their sitting rooms, they can learn how to survive on berries after the next nuclear holocaust and how to combat marauders with their bare hands. The popularity of these regrettable publications tells us more about the modern man than the academic volumes which treat directly of the subject.

Who is looking at who here? We are given a delightfully detailed sketch, somewhere between the voyeuristic, the affectionate and the patronising, of these 'modest and homely gents' in their continuing 'furtive' practices, sneaking back home 'after work' (I expect it's a crummy little job too, probably selling insurance) into 'the privacy of their sitting rooms' (shouldn't it be their lounges? and probably in somewhat downmarket flats, rather than the nice 'apartments' which are scattered around the rest of the book), where their habits have not gone unnoticed. 'It is a notable fact' that they do these things. But who, exactly, has been watching them? Is it 'us'? And have we been watching openly or furtively, and with what kind of interest? And then that last sentence – 'The popularity of these regrettable publications tells us more about the modern man than the academic volumes which treat directly of the subject'. Regrettable for whom? Who is the 'us' being bonded together in our snug or rather cool superiority at once to the homely gents poring over their war pornography, and to the 'academic volumes' on masculinity? The modern man' is a topic or a type that we're somehow interested in but apart from – we are not him, and nor is he one of our friends.

I think this passage raises some questions about the form of rhetorical address that the book deploys. Another element in what's going on, as part of the bonding of us, is the assumption that certain things go without saying, don't have to be argued at all – they are beliefs which we are bound to share (remember that 'surely' in 'Surely this does not square with empirical observation'). In this instance, it's the complicity of the reader's smile. *Of course* we already know what we think about these wimps and warriors, so that we're not then actually told why we should think this, or what is to be regretted in these unfortunate publications. This is particularly striking because the book does produce an implicit theory of masculinity that is universal, in the sense of being cross-cultural and transhistorical. There is a diagnosis of modern culture as not providing a proper frame for the symbolic initiation into manhood. This is a functional account which identifies a problem about contemporary society. You say (page 28):

'But today, what remains, in our culture, of the initiation ceremony, of the formalized passage to adulthood? . . . The less a civilization provides a symbolic framework for initiation, the more it will return in a crazy, real form'. This passage could very well be read as welcoming the warrior man home again, especially as no such claim is made in relation to rites of initiation into womanhood – on the contrary, that is given as always having been an impossibility. There seems to be some kind of anthropologically universal structure that differentiates between the sexes which is being both declared and advocated (we shouldn't have let it drop). Now I don't suppose that Darian does mean to be arguing for the return of – for instance – warrior men; but the problem is that he doesn't tell his readers how to understand this passage and these general claims about culture in relation to the one a few pages earlier when we were all sneering at men who fantasise about being fighters.

A last example of the sort of footnotelessness that bothers me. This is one of a number of places where you use shopping analogies to illustrate a point. In this case it's about supermarkets and children, used to explain the Lacanian idea of the limitless demand for love:

> When a child asks its mother for various products at the supermarket, the mother might indulge the youngster. But as all mothers know, what she gives will not be enough. The child will ask for still something else. This is no doubt the reason why there is always a little display of sweets just at the checkout and one sees so often the child's last demand at this moment. Supermarkets are alert to the unconditional nature of demand. They know that all the objects from the shelves which weigh down the mother's trolley are ultimately inadequate. The key is that in asking for something, the child's request becomes something more . . . Thus, in making the request, the specificity of the original object – the sweets – is lost; what was a demand for a particular product is transformed, via the act of speaking, into a demand for love. Which of course cannot be satisfied by sweets. (55)

There are two subjects supposed to know in this passage: first, mothers – 'as all mothers know . . . ' – and second, supermarkets: 'Supermarkets are alert to the unconditional nature of demand. They know that all the objects from the shelves which weigh down the mother's trolley are ultimately inadequate.' Now, I happen to know a thing or two about supermarkets – what they think they know, what they say they know, what they think or want mothers to think they know about mothers and small children. I could give you all sorts of footnotes to all kinds of documents on these points, if you were interested (and some of them are quite interesting, I assure you). Or I could take you into Safeway's and we could see what a bit of empirical observation might tell us here. Either way, I think you'd get a different story from the one suggested above.

Here's one version. When there are sweets at the checkout the kids hardly ever ask Mummy. (Or Daddy – remember, please that mother is no longer, either in reality or in the supermarket imaginary, its advertisements and other self-representations, the primary shopping caretaker, and that is itself an interesting development in the distribution of sexual differences which shouldn't be too easily dismissed as a simple matter of soft new men.) They don't ask, they take. The sweeties are at toddler level and they're at toddler level so that the toddler then has hands-on bypass-parental-intervention access. Little he or little she is not necessarily demanding love from the parent. There may be a reference to the parent – such as defying them, attracting their attention, provoking them: any of which could be understood in terms of the demand for love – but it takes the form of what's done with the sweets, not the form of speaking. And sometimes there is no reference to the parent–the toddler is just passing the time, pleasing itself and responding like a good little economic subject with a demand – in the economic sense – for what is offered to her. (Quite often, as well, they will pick the things up, play with them a bit, and put them back again.)

What supermarkets 'know' is that children will take these things without asking, and that if they get them open their parents will then have to pay for them. That is why they put them there, not because they think the child is going to use them as a test of parental love (though the two versions certainly aren't mutually exclusive). But recently, another more elaborate kind of reasoning has come into play: this is the look-how-ethical-we-are supermarket which wants to impress its customers with just how responsible it is in *not* putting such little displays of sweets in front of the checkout, thus leading to excess toddler demand, parental payment, parental annoyance, and toddler obesity and tooth decay. The psychology of this knowing supermarket is simply the inverse of that of the first one, the crude one that thinks it knows that toddlers will want what it offers. This supermarket knows that its restraint is itself a selling point – it will be appreciated by parents for not resorting to the visibly manipulative ruses of the older, hard-sell techniques.

Now that demand in the economic sense that I spoke of is not unrelated to what Lacanians mean by demand, far from it. There is much to be said about the sorts of psychology utilised implicitly and explicitly by economics and by supermarkets in their theories of and their forms of address to their customers. This isn't the moment to go into details, or footnotes, about the differences and the overlaps between the two. The point I want to make is a different one: that just as it would be a mistake to assume that the supermarkets' psychology of toddler economicus could be transferred smoothly to a situation where there are no checkouts and no sweets, so you might find, if you're a believer in toddler Lacanian, that checkouts and sweeties might show you a thing or two that Lacan's theory of demand didn't bargain for. The issue then is related to the one I mentioned before about universality. In the very ease with which you can move among examples from here, there and everywhere, from great thinkers to small toddlers or from car alarms to St Paul (that happens from one sentence to the next), I think you may also run the risk of missing what also make it difficult to compare them in the same paragraph. Call it history, call it difference, call it footnotes.

1   This paper was written for an ICA panel in March, 1996, centred on Darian Leader's book, *Why Do Women Write More Letters Than They Post?* (London: Faber, 1996); page references will be given within the main text. The event was organised by Helena Reckitt and chaired by Alison Hall. In addition to Darian Leader, the other participants were Chris Okely, Maya Okely and Natasha Walter

2   Note added 2018: The year after this event, the footnote rose to centre-page in Antony Grafton's *The Footnote: A Curious History* (London: Faber, 1997).

# 14

## Clichés in the Psychology of Advertising

'Nothing new under the sun.' What could be a more redundant way to begin? Unless, perhaps, the context of your utterance was a conference on the cliché – and they must exist, after all: the sun has seen it all.[1] In tht case, you could let yourself off the hook by saying that 'nothing new under the sun' was a mere example, a citation of an anonymous citation – whatever. There are many tricks of that kind to be used on such occasions, or so I understand. And you could go on, I suppose, to discuss what a very odd cliché this is, how in a sense it is the cliché of clichés, the one that says there was never anything new in the first place or the first time, that it has always been cliché and nothing but cliché. Surely, you would say, with just the right hint of distancing irony, this must be the oldest cliché in the world, the very *fons et origo* of cliché itself, if they had anything original about them. So yes, if you began with this phrase at a conference on clichés, you could doubtless find quite enough to keep things going.

Thankfully, however, my own usage of the expression has no such pretensions or potential embarrassments – it is simply a direct quotation. 'Rien de nouveau sous le soleil' begins the chapter on slogans in Pierre Herbins *Manuel pratique de publicité*, a guide to advertising for advertisers published just after the war. Herbin's deployment of the phrase might seem in some ways an unexpected one. This is how he proceeds:

> Nothing new under the sun, nothing, not even the use of *devises* in advertising, which the Americans think they invented because they have named them *slogans*. I am looking forward to the doctoral thesis some expert *chartiste* is bound to present to us one day on 'the advertising *devise* in the time of the Pharaohs'.[2]

You might have thought that slogans were something new, but in actual fact, no: and Herbin goes on half playfully to cite a few 'slogan ancestors', beginning – where else? – with Homeric epithets. Thus, '"swift-foot" Achilles and "white-armed" Andromache have gone down in history and in human memory' (15). Skipping on through heraldic inscriptions and the popular, childlike associations he ascribes to various forms of the pre-slogan, Herbin taks only a page or so before returning to complete his circle. 'In truth, nothing new under the sun ! After this kind of proof from usage and universal agreement, is there any need to make a more ample demonstration of the utility and necessity of slogans?' (16).

Herbin's suggestion that advertising's practices have a history as old as literature is meant, I take it, to strike the reader as something new. This is not the normal way of looking at things, whether for advertisers or for literary people. According to the usual view, whereby literature is old and advertising is not, the two of them appear in mutually defining complicities and antagonisms of various kinds. In the more negative representations, literature is the place of value and authenticity, but advertising has come on the scene as an imitative, superficial double to haunt and taunt it with its crude simulation of literary techniques. Advertising is cliché as anti-literature *par excellence*, quite simply the worst that has been thought and said in the world. Or, in another version, which posits literature as invention rather than tradition, post-Romatic literature seeks originality, but advertising mocks and disrupts that by its loud promotion of a manufactured novelty, a psuedo-newness inseparable from its second-rate quality and its deceptive aims.

This general perspective that defines the two together does not alter when the causal sequence is turned around by rotating the two positions and letting the sun shine first on the Antipodes of advertising. In this regard, it is the worls of technical reproductions, the world of the copy, including advertising 'copy', which pushes literature into its newfound modern quest for the originality of new words.

From the point of view of advertising, on the other hand, there is no such opposition; indeed novelty is often claimed as its own hallmark – novelty as modernity, progress, innovation But this does not imply a pejorative attitude to literature anything like the frequently pejorative attitude of literary culture to advertising. On the contrary – and this is where Herbin joins a tradition of thinking about advertising – literature tends to be regarded by advertising writers as a fund of usable primary material. What else do eadvertisihg writers call themselves, after all, but 'copywriters'? At the same time, advertising manuals of the first half of the twentieth century – the golden age of such texts – regularly liken the work of copywriters activity to that of literary writers, insisting that they are just as 'creative'. Book after book takes the student through all the intricacies and possibilities of rhetorical and poetic terms; book after book advises and advertises the pleasures and profits of immersion in great literature as the necessary foundation for the writing of advertising, and more often than not will claim that advertising is at least ewual in creativity to literary writing of the conventional or time-honoured sort.

In this connection, advertising seems to be indistinguishable in its aims from literature, each of them seeking at all costs, economic or otherwise, to make their marks by original expression. If literature got there first, it is often only because literature has managed to anticipate something that is also a perfect device for advertising. Such devices include, for both, the necessity of avoiding cliché in order to maintain the power of making an impact. Thus in an earlier book of 1938, Herbin describes the origins of the use of negative superlatives like *unfathomable, ineffable* or *undying* in the efforts of ltierary writers to avoid the repetition of overused, overblown rhetoric, in other words of clichés:

> In literature, however . . . all these decorations were already well used. It was then that writers renewed these negative adjectives, so as to give their style a new lease of life . . . to produce effect of unheard of verbal violence, of unsurpassed extremity.[3]

The last clauses, by the use of *inouïe* (unheard of) and *insurpassée*, exemplify the very effects they name. These are strong words for strong words; we shall return to the implications of this 'verbal violence'.

Slogans – or *devises*, as Herbin insists they be called, against the Anglo-Saxon locution – take on the flagship or campaign-cry role of representing the verbal wit and inventiveness that advertising is deemed to be just as capable of producing as literature. But slogans are subject to precarious conditions of existence. They are devised to be striking, fresh, origina: hitting hard to mark off this brand from all its competitors in the minds of potential buyers. In which minds – so the psychology goes – at the point of purchase, the slogan will magically and mechanically resurface, rise up into consciousness, as a stimulus to the making of the appropriate choice. But the very success of slogans, described in these terms, depends on their becoming the stuff of everyday language and thinking, dwindling inevitably from their first fine force of novelty to the banality of the commonplace and ultimately the rubbish-heap of the cliché, when the slogan is no longer regarded as effective at all and has to be replaced by a newer coinage. (And there may now be a further possible stage in this development, namely the retro-slogan: in the early 1990s Esso petrol was readvertised in Britain with the once renowned invitation to 'Put a tiger in your tank!' – the sloganly beast now rising again from its generation-long slumber invested with a new capacity to represent the very essence or *essence* of 1960s nostalgia.)

Slogans present to advertisers a whole complex of questions about the mutability of linguistic expressions from invention to cliché. The prohibition of cliché in advertising language, as in literary language, is itself a commonplace. In Herbin's pre-war book, for example, he is quite explicit:

> For let there be no mistake about it. It is not aged adjectives, stereotyped formulas, worn-out metaphors, or well-worn clichés that will keep us in touch with our public. . . .
>
> [Advertising] should not make do with this ready-made, fossilised thinking, hardened into stereotyped formulas. What it needs is a spurt of fresh inspiration and the novelty of a rejuvenated vocabulary. (219)

Such a statement, in its cliché-heavy repudiation of clichés in favour of an equally clichéd evocation of originality, might just as well be talking about literature as about advertising.

Advertising writers wax lyrical and wane prosaical on these issues of the life and death of slogans. In one manifestation slogans may be treated as the key to success, a kind of magic 'Open Sesame' to consumers' minds. This passage is from a French book of 1930 by Louis Angé:

> There must be nothing ordinary or over-used. It must be something as concentrated and as condensed as an elixir – an advertising elixir.
>
> The importance of the advertising slogan [*devise*] cannot be overestimated. Because a slogan of this kind is what is best engraved in the memory and as a result, when we are thinking of making a purchase, the memory will offer to our minds, at the opportune moment, the name of the product or company it applies to.[4]

'Nothing ordinary or over-used – in order for it to make its impression it must not be a cliché; but in making that impression, engraving itself in more and more minds, the slogan will in the end presumaby become both commonplace and over-used. In its turn it will set and settle as as the cliché from which it is freshly distinguished at first.

At the other extreme is the debunking of slogans as mistakenly thought to hold magical powers. Here, for instance, is the forthright American duo of Brewster and Palmer, cutting out the bullshit back in 1931:

> There has existed in the past a popular idea that if an advertising man cold think out the right combination of words, it would mean instant success for the product he was advertising. In order to disillusion those who still have that belief, we shall make two statements:
> 1. If it were possible to invent a better slogan than anyone has ever invented, the slogan would be of little value until many hundreds of thousands of dollars were spent in advertising it to the public to make it valuable.
> 2. A large percentage of the slogans in use today have no particular effect except as any selling phrase has an effect in an advertisement.[5]

For these two, the effectiveness that a slogan does have depends not on an intrinsic verbal brilliance that could assure 'instant succes', but on a slow, costly gravitation over a period of years until it 'sinks into the public consciousness' (137). Bqnqlisqtion is the condition of success, not the end of it.

So cliché does not always figure as the bogey of successful advertising. There is a quite opposite tendency which emphasises not the deadness and ineffectivenss of the recongised phrase, but its usefulness. For from this point of view, at its mildest, anything wholly new will scare potential customers away; familiarity has its functions, and they are not to be despised. Clichés are not often named as such in this regard, though I have come across one British text of the late 1920s by J.C. Toohill which has a short paragraph on the subject as part of a guide to rhetorical and litrary terms and their importance in advertising:

> Cliché is a stock phrase which has been used so often that it is a bit threadbare at the knees and elbows. Literary highbrows, who try to make every sentence an epigram, avoid it like a plague; but this is no reason why it should be shunned by the copy writer. An amiable cliché will pay a higher dividend than the most laboured gaucherie. Though useless for portraying the important qualities of a product, the cliché is a kind of literary shorthand; the reader, having seen it so often, unconsciously takes in the meaning with his eye. It can therefore be used to help the reader and thus keep his attention until the main point has ben reached.[6]

This personification of the cliché as a comfortable old suit of clothes plays friendliness and familiarity against the studies poses of literature. In reality, Toohill's scene is a chummy version of an idea common at the time that it is of no use to seize hold of readers' attention with something that disturbs the balance of their existing thoughts, usually conceptualised as a stock of separate articles 'stored' in the memory as in a tidy shop. What is taken in – understood and received into the mind – will be what seems to fit with what is already there, what appears to be nothing radically new.

American advertising psychology between the wars is much occupied by the question of what determines belief in what an advertisement is proposing. Put more forcefully, Toohill's position approaches the more exclusive theory that familiarity, and familiarity alone, breeds belief; no other mental operation comes into play than a form of unthinking recognition such that nothin new is ever taken in. In an influential article, A.T. Poffenberger puts it like this:

> If belief in an advertisement does not depend upon the truth of the statements made and does not depend upon the reasoning of the reader, on what does it depend? Tro state the matter simply, we may say that ideas which are present in the mind and are not interfered with by any opposing ideas will be believed.[7]

Nothing new is the psychological desideratum. If people seem to accept the most unlikely claims, that is not because they are perversely or stupidly amenable to the counter-factual, but because their belief has nothing to do with the validity in objective terms of the advertisement's claims, or with any attempt at evaluating those claims. Only grasp the 'ideas which are present in the mind' of the re'ader, and you will then be in a position to offer ideas designed not to oppose them:

> It is not enough to say that the American people like to be fooled and that there is no scheme too wild to arouse the confidence of a large proportion of them. The advertiser should know that action is dependent upon belief and that belief in advertising depends upon conditions, some of which at least are under his control. (1)

In place of the rejected hypothesis, that it is a question of wild appeals to wild minds, Poffenberger presents advertising techniques as a matter of calculated appeals to fit in with known mental conditions: reasoned approaches to unreasoning minds.

It was this kind of view of the psychological power of advertising which itself turned out to shock, by its own suggestion of advertising's potential to insert itself into the minds of buyers, against – or rather, in the absence of – their judgement. Claiùs of this kind on an advertisingùs own part go back a long way – as it happens; the earliest example I've found is from a book published in Tours in 1914, *Sa Majesté la publicité*, in which the author refers to an American definition of advertising:

> An American writer said that advertising is the force that makes it possible to get an idea into the crowd . . . If we consider it as a science, we can say that it teaches us the best means of making a collectivity think and act in a certain way.[8]

The unselfconsciousness of the declaration of manipulative intent is striking here, at a time when advertising does not usually represent itself as dealing with collective rather than individual minds. Later – from the 1930s – advertising in Britain and France started to adopt a defensive tone in an attempt to distinguish its own practices from the unacceptable forms of Nazi propaganda. And it was in the Cold War period above all that the powers of advertising came to be imagined as a dark, inexorable conspiracy to make all minds the same. In the popular denunciations of the 1950s and early 1960s – Vance Packard's *The Hidden Persuaders* was a bestseller – American advertising, far from promoting a freedom denied to those oppressed by Communist regimes, is seen as an inhuman application of mechanical techniques whose mindlessness matches te mindlessness thereby produced int he mentalities who are their target. In the ew language of the time, consumers are 'manipulated' and even 'brainwashed' into robot-like responses. The image that rises up spontaneously, if not naturally, as typical of this kind of critique is that of the housewife shopping in one of the garish new supermarkets, dumbly picking up just the packet of washing powder the experiments showed that she would.[9]

The remarkable feature of such critiques is the way that they adopt the very assimptions about collective psychology that they denounce in its applications to consumer behaviour. Mental responses are predictable and modifiable; it is simply that it is immoral to take advntage of the knowmedge of them. There are some unlikely examples of this. In his essay 'Rhetoric of the Image', first published in 1964, Barthes analysed a humble magazine advertisement for an Italian brand of dried pasta and tinned sauce, Panzani. The essay was not ostensibly about advertising or psychology, let alone about clichés, but about images. In order to say something about how images mean, Barthes chooses to analyse an advertising image because, he says, it makes the job more straightforward:

> We will start by making it considerably easier for ourselves: we will only study the advertising image. Why? Because in advertising the signification of the image is undoubtedly intentional; the signifieds of the advertising message are formed *a priori* by certain attributes of the product and these signifieds have to be transmitted as clearly as possible. If the image contains signs, we can be sure that in advertising these signs are full, formed with a view to the optimum reading: the advertising image is *frank*, or at least emphatic.[10]

Loud and clear – in the advertising image, we know they know what they are doing, the thing is easier to read because it is made to be easy to read. No advertiser could have put it more confidently. Barthes then proceeds to a *tour de force* application of *Mythologies* method to the unpretentious little photograph of the fishnet shopping bag with its mixture of Panzani products and fresh vegetables. Under the semiotic regard, it is miraculously made into a paradigmatic illustration of how the supposed innocence of the phtographic image, the image without a code, functions to naturalise the signs of culture. The bare identifiability of the objects in the photo, so that we know where we are and what thi is, makes way for the slipping in, 'surreptitiously' (45), of all the cultural connotations which, rather than the things themselves, are really what make the product attractive: in this case, its likeness to still life paintings, its touristic appeal to French consumers as an image of *italianité*, its suggestion; even while it is advertising convenience foods; of fresh products and home preparation. To understand this, Barthes says, 'requires only a knowledge which is in some sense implanted as part of the habits of a very widespread culture where "doing your shopping yourself" is opposed to the speedy provisioning (preserves, chilled goods) of a more "mechanical" culture' (34, tr. mod).

Readers' responses to advertisements are not all the same, for people vary in the number of these chunks of ideology that they have taken in. But it si assumed that if the appropriate bit is there – barthes calls them *lexiques* – then the siginifying of it in the iùage will have its effect, automatically:

> There is a plurality and a coexistenc of lexicons in one and the same person, the number and identity of these lexicons forming in some sort a person's *idiolect*. The image, in its connotation, is thus consti-

> tuted by an architecture of signs drawn from a variable depth of lexicons (of idiolects); each lexicon, no matter how 'deep', still being coded, if, as is thought today, the *psyche* itself is articulated like a language; indeed the further one 'descends' into the psychic depths of an individual, the more rarified and the more classifiable the signs become – what could be more systematic than the readings of Rorschach tests? (47)

Here, at the bottom of the mind, where all soundbites are equal, the sun never shines, and all parrots are grey, Lacan meets behaviourism with no unhappy consequences. Every one of Barthes's connoted meanings for the pasta advertisement – the tourist stereotype, the high-art reference, the evocation of a home-grown culture – boils down to ideology's disingenuous refusal of the 'more "mechanical" culture' of function and derivative copy that it actually is and promotes. Yet the underlying psychology here accords perfectly well with the mechanical mode of the culture whose surface values disavow it, as the mind consists of little cliché-deposits only awaiting their appropriate trigger from the outside.

In *Les Discours du cliché;* Ruth Amossy and Elisheva Rosen speak of what they call the '*hantise du psittacisme*', the obsession with parroting which gives the cliché its bad name in our post-Romantic culture of standardised, 'mass' communications.[11] This parroting preoccupation seizes on the cliché as the antithesis of a desired but impossible self-expression: in the worst scenario, the cliché-scenario, we are condemned to repeat, mechanically, the phrases and thoughts of a world that comes to us ready-made – ready-to-consume, ready-to-eat, ready-to-repeat. It is perhaps not surprising to find this cliché-world dawning bright in the fantasies of some of those who take it as their business to szeek to control the minds of their buyers, to understand those minds as minds whose reactions can be known in advance. But when this parrot-psychology appears in the critiques of such practices as well, then it does begin to seem as if there might be no escapt from the cqge or cave – no air or sun to be sought at all.

Barthes, of course, went on to reject the instant semiotic recipe – denotation underneath, connotation on top, flip the whole thing over and you have a perfect ideology-critique – which by the early 1970s had been tried and tested so thoroughly and frequently that it had itself become a kind of cliché. In laying more emphasis on the distinctions to be made between different kinds of writing, though, he did not cease to make use of advertising or consulption to stand for a mechanical, functioning foil to the complexities of literary and other texts. In this brief sampling I have tried to show that there may be more to the discourses of advertising than meets the eye – and by more, I do not necessarily mean the complexity of literature (though that is often to be found), but something else: a continual reflection on how minds respond to what they take in as old or new ideas, old and new forms of words. It is a question as old as the study of rhetoric, and I think it has been given a few new spins in the light of advertising.

1  This paper was written for a conference in September 1995, organised by Claudine Raynaud and Peter Vernon, on 'Fonctions du cliché: Du banal à la violence', at the Université François Rabelais, Tours.
2  Pierre Herbin, *Manuel pratique de publicité* (La Chapelle-Montligeon: Editions de Montligeon, 1949), p. 15. Further citations will be in parentheses in the main text.
3  Herbin, *Comment concevoir et rédiger votre publicité* (Paris: Editions de la revue *La Publicité*, 1938), p. 212. Further citations will be in parentheses in the main text.
4  Louis Angé, *Pour bien faire sa publicité* (Paris: Editions J. Oliver, 1930), p. 232.
5  Arthur Judson Brewster and Herbert Hall Palmer, *Introduction to Advertising*, 2nd edn. (New York: McGraw-Hill, 1931), p. 136. Further citations will be in parentheses in the main text.
6  J.C. Toohill, *The Art of Advertisement Copy Writing* (London: John Bale, Sons & Davidsson Ltd., n.d., p. 60. Further citations will be given in parentheses in the main text.
7  A.T. Poffenberger, 'The Conditions of Belief in Advertising', *Journal of Applied Psychology* 7:1 (1923), p. 4. Further citations will be given in parentheses in the main text.
8  J. Arren, *Sa Majesté la publicité* (Tours: Maison Alfred Mame et fils, 1914), p. 16.
9  Such a picture is found in chapter 10 of Vance Packard, *The Hidden Persuaders* (1957; Harmondsworth: Penguin, 1991), 'Babes in Consumerland'.
10 Roland s Barthes, 'Rhetoric of the image' (1964), trans. Stephen Heath, in *Image Music Text* (London: Fontana, 1977), p. 33. Further citations will be given in parentheses in the main text.a
11 Ruth Amossy and Elisheva Rosen, *Les Discours du cliché* (Paris: CDU-SEDES, 1982), p. 148 *et passim*.

# 15
# Who's Framing
# Virginia Woolf?

In *Between the Acts*, Virginia Woolf blurs the boundaries between embedded and framing forms until the reader wonders whether it is fruitful to distinguish between them at all. To show that the most complex interpretation is, in fact, as limited as the simplest story, an author may place the key to the necessary perspective in an obvious detail of the narrative, hidden by its conspicuousness, like the frames within Virginia Woolf's novels.[1]

Placed quite conspicuously at the end of the middle chapter of the book, these two sentences look as if they were intended as a characteristically modest elucidation of Ruth Miller's own project in *Virginia Woolf: The Frames of Art and Life*. No previous critic had systematically drawn out the details and the complexities of Woolf's many representations of the frame and its analogues. But there it was, obvious once it was noticed and meticulously brought into focus, and traced out through this admirably concise and suggestive book.

In three neatly delineated chapters, Miller explores first, the frame which separates but also merges 'art' and 'life' in Woolf's writing; second, the ways in which Woolf frames the novel in relation to other genres; and lastly, the various frames and enclosures – rooms, thresholds, mirrors and windows – which recur within her writing. These figure the edgy or smudged boundaries between different spaces, different perspectives, different orders of representation or understanding, that Miller spots as the key her author left lying around all over her writings. Nothing is out of place here: so convincing is Miller's account that it seems as though Woolf's work had only been waiting all this time for the appropriate reader to come along and pick up this explanatory implement, showing up the frames in all their significance.

Miller sees Woolf's art as being a more or less deliberate and always provisional circumscription of what she perceives as the structureless nature of that other category called 'life', a kind of catch-all term for the uncapturable, what does not fit into a frame. Woolf opts for the novel as that genre which, by its own lack of definition, of fixed boundaries, will best enable her to keep open, while still minimally controlling, a distinction between art and life, or between form and what it at once keeps out and puts in order. For her own part, Miller would seem to have chosen a firmer, less fluid outline. There is no messing here: with not a word wasted, each chapter and section is minutely distributed into satisfyingly measured points. Like the momentarily unifying, more poised effects of a mirror's reflection of the 'life' around or outside it, which Miller sees Woolf exploring, her own exposition is eminently clear-cut in its demarcation of her subject's hazier shifts and crossovers. Though the equivocal two-sidedness of thresholds and frames is the matter of its argument, the book itself never oversteps or blurs the boundaries of expository decorum.

Miller adroitly guides us through and among Woolf's writings viewed from the perspective of the observer interested in every aspect of her framing question. She expressly eschews what she calls 'the developmental fallacy – the often implicit assumption that each work in a writer's canon represents a refinement of its predecessor' (p. x). In parallel fashion, she refrains from making her own study into the developmental narrative she does not find in or project onto Woolf's work. Her sections are elaborated by accretion and expansion rather than by a sequential argument; in a preview at the beginning, she summarises the separate but overlapping approaches of each chapter; and the elaboration that follows, a model of unobtrusive organisation, makes use of no unannounced keys.

All this must be seen in the context of Miller's denial of any consistency to Woolf's pronouncements on art and life: 'Virginia Woolf never systematically outlined her aesthetic priorities: the terms of her argument changed continually and the attitudes she held towards the relationship between life and art are so various that it is quite easy to find support for contradictory conclusions' (3). Yet inconspicuously, a kind of coherence does seem to emerge.

The tripartite organisation of the text might give rise to the expectation of some kind of dialectical argument or narrative resolution. Looked at with this possibility in mind, Miller's book seems to offer something more recognisable in this line, or within this frame. At several points she stresses a function of reconciliation: 'By enhancing both the particularity and the universality of the figure it encloses, the threshold becomes a means of reconciling Virginia Woolf's respect for the thing in itself with her vision of assimilative unity in which 'everything was partly something else' (89). The theme of reconciliation is linked to that of redemption: 'Such deliberate failures are at least partially redeemed by the self-consciousness they represent' (72). And both these can be seen as related to a further notion she employs, that of compromise: 'It would seem that Virginia Woolf envisaged art and life as a series of compromises. The necessity of frames must be weighed against the distortion they entail' (40).

On one side, on the other side: different pairings – of inside and outside, art and life, the novel and other genres – are posited and then held in a tenuous equilibrium which is seen to have been Woolf's artistic aim as well. The negative suggestion of the compromise – both sides must lose something – is itself counterweighed by the more positive metaphor of the scales or balance, where one side supplies or adds what the other does not: 'The artist, then, must balance the distance and isolation provided by his room with the immediacy and diffusion of the outdoors. If he does not intermittently allow himself to be inspired by life outside, the withdrawal necessary to acquire a perspective becomes a confinement which distorts it (83)'. Woolf may have veered from one side to the other of her different dualities, and may have been identified as definitively situated here or there; but that in itself becomes the background for her location poised, just about, between.

The passage acknowledging the evidence for 'contradictory conclusions' about Woolf's writing continues with a reference to another balancing act, involving this time a significant general distinction not attributed to Woolf:

> While some maintain that her work is governed by an unprecedented commitment to the representation of life, others see it as the reflection of a belief, considered characteristic of Bloomsbury, in the autonomy of art and the primacy of formal concerns. Her vacillations, however, give a more detailed sense of the balance she hoped to achieve in her writing rather than any explicit statement of her aims. ... Quite reasonably, she allowed herself a writer's liberty with words and arguments rather than restricting herself to a philosopher's exactitude. (3–4)

As before, there is a 'balance' lurking after all in Woolf's work; and it is the philosopher's task to locate or specify what is there, to draw it out in its precise outlines. The two functions or modes are clearly separable: 'exactitude' on one side, 'liberty' on the other. The philosopher's job is at once more narrow and confined ('restricting herself') and a broader or superior definition of the space of liberty, framing and making explicit what the writer has left all over the place. Miller thus draws up a minimal balance or reconciliation between what she identifies as the two alternatives on eithr side for both Woolf herself, free and floating in the 'writer's liberty with words and arguments', and her readers, who have seen in her work either life or art, eithr commitment or aestheticism, but never both and never, by implication, the 'balance' which is nonetheless there in her own aim, and there in the works for the critic or philosopher for formulate exactly.

There are, however, two sides to the frame itself. Miller also stresses at other points that the frame suggests not so much balance as unsettlement. And when it is regarded from this point of view, rather than as a reconciler, the bearer of minimal order, it is associated for Miller not with Woolf's own intentions, explicit or not, but with more recent concerns in literary criticism and philosophy:

> Still, the frames in her writings and her exploration of the principles of framing reveal the extent to which she anticipated the contemporary interest in the threat that the marginal poses to the integrity of the centre. (ix)

> In pursuing what is bound to fail and renouncing complete beauty, Virginia Woolf reflects current critical attitudes rather than those of her time. . . . Deconstruction provides the appropriate metaphor: Virginia Woolf may be said to show 'the crumbling, abyssal, nontotalizable edges of the story's frame'. (72)

The second quotation is glossed in a footnote: 'As Barbara Johnson describes Derrida's intention in his essay "The Purveyor of Truth"' (118), and elsewhere Miller refers to the 'Parergon' chapter of Derrida's *The Truth in Painting*. Now, Woolf's writings are being promoted, brought forward, as sketches or previews of a critical frame, that of the insecure frame, whose outlines have only recently come to be visible.

These two frames, the secure and the insecure, the frame as precarious artistic unification and the frame as deconstructive undermining of frames, are suggestively juxtaposed in Miller's text such that neither is finally, definitively superimposed upon the other. The holding together and apart of the two could itself be described as deconstructive. But what might appear less so is the implied situation of the two modes in historical places associated respectively with Woolf's time and with ours, 'current critical attitudes rather than those of her time'. From this point of view, Woolf's interest in decentring, an aberration in relation to her own time, is refocused as belonging to another critical time, that of the present time of centre-lessness or threatened centres. This would indicate a straight, not blurred, division between two times which would each be consistent and unified in themselves. By the installation of a historical narrative which concludes with their disintegration, centres have been securely restored after all.

But if Miller sees Woolf's work in one respect, from one aspect, as an anticipation of present-day critical interests, this also draws attention to a quite different feature of her own framing of Woolf. This is its eccentricity – both an original peculiarity and an off-centre unrecognisability – in relation to much of the criticism that has recently been published on Woolf. A detail which may hae struck the reader of the qutoations I have cited so far becomes more conspic-uous at this point: Ruth Miller refers to her subject throughout not as 'Woolf' but as 'Virginia Woolf'. In this, she is in effet situating herself – though she does not say so – somewhere before or behind what has emerged as the convention for referring to Woolf, or indeed to any woman writer. The use of a feminine marker by the inclusion of the first name (male writers are generally referred to by surname alone in the book) paradoxically has the effect of setting Miller's text at a distance from the norm that feminist criticism has established.

Even more strikingly, and even less neutrally, Miller uses the generic masculine rathr than the 'he or she' which most contempo-rary readers and writers would now expect. This leads to some oddly anachronistic impressions, in sentences like these:

> In her diary, she maintains that it is her 'outsider's vision' which enables her to see things 'composed & in perspective'. An outsider's alienation is counterblanced by his increased self-awareness; he can see the frame as well as the scene it encloses. (75)

> Paradoxically, the moment at which a character appears memorably distinct in Virginia Woolf's writings – standing at a threshold – is also the moment at which he seems irresistibly enigmatic. Lily Briscoe, looking at Mr. and Mrs. Ramsay . . . (88–9)

Miller does not explain or justify this uncontemporary practice; and yet its oddity reveals the existence now of a feminist frame which she does not herself note as characteristic of the present picture.

In this connection, it may be interesting to look back briefly at what now show up as the main landmarks in the past half century of writings about the novelist who began critical life, not so long

ago, as someone generally referred to as 'Mrs Woolf'. For this per-
sonage has undergone more critical vicissitudes, more veerings up
and down and from one situation to another, than most; and they
reveal some sharply differentiated frames or contexts in the history
of her reception.

Until fifteen or twenty years ago, Woolf was usually regarded as
writer to be considered alongside Forster and Lawrence and sometimes (depending on the critical perspective) Joyce as well (or
instead), as one of the principal early twentieth-century British novelists. More commonly, she was placed as almost, but not quite, the
best: she was not in the second league, but nor was she right at the
top of the first. An outstanding exception to this is Erich
Auerbach's *Mimesis*, published just after the war, with the English
translation appearing in 1953. Auerbach's famous concluding chapter on *To the Lighthouse*, 'The Brown Stocking', compared Woolf
favourably to Proust and in effect represented her narrative technique as the culmination of what his book's subtitle dubbed
nothing less than 'The Representation of Reality in Western
Literature'. For Auerbach, the claim was grand indeed: the narrative technique used by Woolf could be regarded, hopefully, as a
foreshadowing of a global 'unification and simplification' in its
'unprejudiced, precise, interior and exterior representation of the
random moment in the lives of different people'.[2] Most of the time,
though, studies of Woolf did not attempt to promote her work to
anything approaching this level of significance.

Parallel to her evaluation in terms defined as primarily literary,
Woolf was also placed in an elusive and weakly defined, but endlessly fascinating frame called 'Bloomsbury'. Its hovering quotation
marks at once cast doubt on its identity and at the same time constituted part of its mystique. This framing made Virginia Woolf
part of a group of radical artists and intellectuals whose cult status
was already annoying people in the 1930s. The writers associated
with F.R. Leavis and the journal *Scrutiny* had shown either condemnation or, more often indifference to what was regarded as the
weakness, aesthetic and moral, of Woolf's writing; this was associated with a general effeteness and snobbery attributable to her
exclusive milieu.[3]

Before the 1970s, there were various full-length critical studies of
Woolf in existence and their number was growing; still, nothing
would have led anyone to predict the massive reorientation of interest
since then, which has brought about the fulfilment of Auerbach's case
for her significance from a direction he did not imagine. The situation since then has been so different in regard to both the volume and

the preoccupations of writng about Woolf that the time before appears now as a kind of prehistoric period, lost in the mists and myths of when she had yet to come into her critical own. Before considering the effects of this turn, it is worth pausing to glance at what may now appear as a minor mark of its momentous consequences. The interest of this little memorial is in the very fact of its obscurity in the context of what followed or overtook it: it appears today as belonging to a kind of pre-Woolfian period, all but hidden behind or before its more prominent successor.

In August 1974, the topic of one of the prestigious Cerisy conferences in France was 'Virginia Woolf et le groupe de Bloomsbury'. An opening statement by Jean Guiguet, the author of one of the early scholarly monographs on Woolf, notes with satisfaction the increasing number of works appearing about her in recent years. From 1968 to 1973 the total came to six books, about one a year (that figure could now itself be multiplied by six). Most of the contributions to the conference concern other Bloomsbury authors as well as Woolf, though the question of the usefulness of this context is something that bothers some of them. The most revealing paper (as well as the most suggestive and critically acute) comes from a British critic, Anthony Inglis. It is stated in one of the discussions prior to his paper that he had been invited as a kind of Leavis henchman, to make a *Scrutiny*-style attack on Woolf as a provocation for her defenders. This Inglis pointedly does not do, and you get the impression that the annoyance his paper nevertheless does produce in the discussion that follows it is partly a substitute for the anticipated response, all the more heated for having no real object. Inglish argues that *Scrutiny*'s dismissal of Woolf is mistaken; she could be read as a modernist as Benjamin reads Kafka, and appreciated even by *Scrutiny*'s own criteria, in the way that D.W. Harding was able to appreciate Shelley, normally not a *Scrutiny*-favoured poet. The paper runs through some of the existing books on Woolf and concludes that they do not do her justice because they have not moved outside their own intra-Woolfian interests to make a cogent case for her valuation against the more canonised modernists.

The proceedings of this conference have never been translated into English (though they were published in a cheap paperback in France[4]): it is as thought they were out of date before their time. What had happened? 'Bloomsbury' was already established as a staple of the literary-cultural market, even if the name of Virginia Woolf did not yet arouse all the critical and other forms of interest that were later to accompany it. A clue is provided by the titles of two of the books cited in Guiguet's introductory speech: *Feminism and Art* by Herbert

Marder, and *Virginia Woolf and the Androgynous Vision* by Nancy Topping Bazin. It was already beginning, and soon Woolf would be firmly established as that newly celebrated being, a 'woman writer' – if not the woman writer *par excellence*, in the age of feminist criticism. For the great majority of the output of articles and books on Woolf is now, and has been for some time, from points of view which declare themselves to be feminist. This is so to such an extent that anything now appearing which does not consider her in connection with that frame seems at first sight to be somehow out of place.

Since the early 1970s, Woolf has been first and foremost a woman and a fminist writer; she has been for many the first among women writers, seen to have made way for many of the developments in feminist criticism which have now taken place. This, I think, is why reading Ruth Miller's book today produces the effect of a time-warp or distorted perspective. Though she refers to deconstruction, Miller does not mention any of the feminist arguments in relation to Woolf which have been the principal focus of her criticism for a considerable period now. Most of her references, in fact, are to books that pre-date the feminist turn and which are rarely cited nowadays.

Only at one point does a feminist question appear, and interestingly enough in the form of a foregone conclusion. In the course of her first chapter, writing about the first appearance of the character of Richard Dalloway, in *The Voyage Out*, Miller states that 'The unity Richard Dalloway conceives justifies his sexism as well: the sexes, he argues, complement each other – men fight while women retain their illusions' (27). Miller's claim that Dalloway's belief in unity is related to a view of the complementarity of the sexes which implies sexism (a term that is taken for granted) prompts all sorts of further questions; first, about the conflicting feminist understandings of sexism and of the fundamental difference or sameness of the sexes (there is no feminist unity about what counts as sexism); and second, about the possibility or necessity of connections between an abstract idea, in this case that of unity, and an attitude to sexual difference. But Miller tantalisingly leaves it at this, an inconspicuous detail that cannot but point itself out, despite its minuteness, in the context of the contemporary frame in which her book on Woolf is situated.

This disturbance of what is now the normal standard of vision repeats the peculiarities already noted in some of Miller's linguistic choices. Miller might have her reasons for wanting to restore 'Virginia' to 'Woolf', or to return to the practice of using a masculine pnroun rather than 'he or she'; but she does not see a need to provide them. Even if Woolf had not herself been a feminist, these stylistic features would still jar in relation to conventions which feminism has nowadays succeeded in establishing, outside as well as within the domain of explicitly feminist contexts.

My surprise at this is augmented because it seems to throw out of the window, or down to a lower storey, everything that Miller is endeavouring to maintain as her highere, more visible argument about the significance of frames. By extension, the whole subject of the book has to do with the context in which we see or read a work of art. So it is as though the book's own focus on frames had ruled out, framed out of sight, the question of how it is itself to be read in relation to the contexts in which it appears.

If Miller's particular stylistic choices and thematic interests did not already show up as different from current norms, the issue of feminist context and writing conventions might not have emerged at all. This difference is all the more noticeable in that Miller's meticulously ordered book is clearly not intended as an undermining of the norms of the critical monograph. But there is also a second aspect in which her book highlights what then looks like its own omission or blind spot, which is the question – named in the subtitle – of 'life'. Here too, by what she does not address as much as by what she does, Miller brings to the fore some features of the recent history of writing about Woolf and and other non-living authors.

Miller's first chapter, 'Art and Life', discusses the relation of art to life as it is represented in Woolf's own writings (and in those of some of her Bloomsbury friends, relations and associates); it is a relationship that Woolf herself discusses with just those terms. It does not, however, look at the kinds of frame which mark off or merge the art and the life in critical considerations of artists and writers like Woolf. In Woolf's case, this issue is particularly striking because of all the material which has been made available in published form in the years since her death: there are copious volumes of letters and diaries, and there is also the collection of autobiographical texts written for friends which was published in 1977 as *Moments of Being*. Woolf's art – her novels – has thus come to be framed by reference to a whole corpus of 'autobiographical' or 'personal' writings, some of them written for publication and others not. There are also early drafts of published texts; and there are the numerous reviews and essays written by Woolf throughout her life. Of these three groups, arbitrarily separated according to divisions which already form part of the problematic frame of discussion, only the last would seem to be exempt from the charge of being doubtful as evidence of the same order as that of the published fictional work. Even here, though there might be questions: all Woolf's reviews for the *Times*

*Literary Supplement*, for instance, were anonymous (as were those of all its contributors at the time).

Ruth Miller makes use of material from all these kinds, as well as of writings by Woolf's Bloomsbury friends, especially Roger Fry and E.M. Forster. The intention in the latter case is to supply a context within which the significance and the connections of Woolf's own statements will appear: the book begins by juxtaposing a paragrph of Fry, on streets as opposed to pictures of streets, with one from Woolf's short story 'The Lady in the Looking-Glass', on rooms and their ref'lection in mirrors. But this then raises the question of where such comparative frames from Woolf's own 'life and times' might begin or end, or where they should or might be found or sought. Where is the frame that marks off the area of texts to be looked at for evidence of Woolf's view of the frame? And where does Woolf's life end or begin in relation to the art from which it is customarily curtained off?

These questions are further related to the discussion in Miller's second chapter about genre, which she treats as a variant of the question of frames. She shows how Woolf both distinguished the novel from other genres and, at the same time, was interested in the breakdown of generic boundaries and conventions, attempting to blur them in her own writing. While she remarks on Woolf's interest in the genre of biography – she herself wrote both a real one (of Fry) and a fictional one (*Orlando*) – and particularly in its new, looser form as practised by her Bloomsbury friend Lytton Strachey, she does not pursue this into the treatment of Woolf herself. Yet biography's own peculiar generic position would seem to provide a focal point for Miller's concerns. It hovers on the edge between the categories of art and life, neither pure fiction (it has to be true) nor pure fact (it is a story). Biography both puts a life into an artistic form and at the same time pulls the art of narrative away from fiction and towards the constraints, or the different conventions, of fact. It can be seen as either a point on what is only a continuum that joins and divides art and life, or else as an uncertain measure of a qualitative difference, involving elements of both.

Foucault's essay 'What is an Author?' (1969) includes a discussioin of the notable absence of what he calls a 'theory of the œuvre': there are no fixed rules to determine how far a critic should range in looking for valid additions to an author's writing.[5] The establishing of an œuvre implies that the aim is to define a body of texts for interpretation or commentary. Ruth Miller herself uses Woolf's diaries, letters and early drafts as sources for quotations in her discussion, without more ado; in this respect, there is no frame. But also, she does not discuss the relation between Woolf's life and her writing. The life she does discuss is its use as a concept in opposition to art, where it tends to figure as the unframed or orderless, which art seeks to capture or evoke without at the same time pushing it out of sight. But in Woolf's case, the question emerges from the other direction, since the woman's existence has been subject to so many kinds of framing and historicising apart from (though often in connection with) the reading of her literary works.

Miller's sharp focus on Woolf's blurred frames makes her writing, and the history of writing about it, appear in new perspectives. Paradoxically, it is perhaps her very indifference to contemporary feminist frames, whether of thematic interest or stylistic practice, which makes her book most provocative and open-ended for its readers now. For seeming to have stepped outside the current feminist conventions, Miller's book is all the better placed to make them visible. Her book implicitly suggests new questions, and ways of framing them, about the varius overlapping contexts – of childhood seduction, mother–daughter relations, psychoanalytic narrative, and female development, to name a few of them – in which Woolf's life and her art have lately been considered. By its anachronism, as much as by any reflection of some present-day critical preoccupations, Miller's is a timely book: ahead of its time and before it, inside and outside what it reveals as being the contemporary picture.

*A review in the journal* Diacritics *of C. Ruth Miller,* Virginia Woolf: The Frames of Art and Life *(1989)*

1   C. Ruth Miller, *Virginia Woolf: The Frames of Art and Life* (New York: St Martin's Press, 1989), 74. Further page references will be given within the main text.
2   Erich Auerbach, *Mimesis: The Representation of Reality in Western Literature* (1946), trans. Willard R. Trask (Princeton: Princeton University Press, 1953), 553, 552.
3   See for example *Scrutiny* reviews by W.H. Mellers of *The Years* and other novels, and of *Three Guineas* (1938) by Q.D. Leavis, reprinted in Robin Majumdar and Allan McLaurin (eds), *Virginia Woolf: The Critical Heritage* (London: Routledge, 1975), pp. 395–8, 409–16; see also Francis Mulhern, *The Moment of 'Scrutiny'* (1970; London: Verson, 1982).
4   *Virginia Woolf et le groupe de Bloomsbury*, Colloque de Cerisy, ed. Jean Guiguet (Paris: 10/18, 1977).
5   Michel Foucault, 'What is an Author?' (1969), trans. Donald F. Bouchard and Sherry Simon, *Language, Counter-Memory, Practice*, ed. Bouchard (Oxford: Basil Blackwell, 1977), 113–38.

# 16
# Woolf's Working Window

In London there are certain shop windows that always attract a crowd. The attraction is not in the finished article but in the worn-out garments that are having patches inserted in them. The crowd is watching the women at work. There they sit in the shop window putting invisible stitches into moth-eaten trousers. And this familiar sight may serve as illustration to the following paper.[1]

Here, in the opening to Woolf's piece on 'Reviewing', a shop window contains not new merchandise and mannequins but real women and old clothes; a crowd is attracted by the display of 'women at work', not by the fashion of the 'finished article'. The 'familiar sight' is at first sight what the crowd sees – but it could also be what we, as readers, are being shown, the crowd and the window together. And the passage continues by suggesting that this peculiar spectacle is itself being presented only as a window onto another one:

So our poets, playwrights, and novelists sit in the shop window, doing their work under the curious eyes of reviewers. But the reviewers are not content, like the crowd in the street, to gaze in silence; they comment aloud upon the size of the holes, upon the skill of the workers, and advise the public which of the goods in the shop window is the best worth buying. The purpose of this paper is to rouse discussion as to the value of the reviewer's office – to the writer, to the public, to the reviewer and to literature. (195)

First, let us note that the crowd in front of the window has become two groups: performers (the reviewers) and audience (the rest). So now we have no fewer than four removes or stages from work to ultimate reader: those behind the window, then the reviewers, then the public, then finally the viewers of the whole lot, the present readers. There is also the question of the fit between the window-world and the writing world which it is meant to show.

The women in the shop window differ from the feminine figures usually to be found in such a place because they are working; but they are also unexpected as author-equivalents. They are women and they are in a group, not men alone with their writing. And what they are doing is not new making, but repair work – Roland Barthes's metaphor of modern literature as a fabric or weave of citations finds its literal version here. Yet the aim is to produce not a fragmented modernist work in pieces, but its realist antithesis. The moth-eaten gaps are covered over by 'invisible stitches', so producing that object so despised of contemporary theoretical criticism, an apparently seamless whole.

After this characteristically multiform beginning, Woolf launches into a brief disquisition on the history and state of the art of reviewing. I can't, of course, cut it up and put it back together again without losing much of the texture and the material – but basically, her point is that reviewers nowadays have so little time and so little space that they don't fulfil a useful function, either in telling the public whether a book is worth buying, or in giving the author constructive advice. There might as well, she says, be a simple 'hit or miss' system, whereby the reviewer, having been issued with a *précis* of the book by a character called the Gutter, would indicate with an asterisk or a dagger whether the thing is worth the money.

Authors, Woolf thinks, dislike bad reviews not because of their effect on sales, but because they hurt; and they hurt not because they criticise, but because other people see them. The author is on display, shown up, put in the window as a target of criticism. Woolf therefore proposes, alongside her parodic proposal, a serious reform. The author wants real criticism – she assumes. In place of the present public arrangements, why not have private one-to-one consultations? The author would pay three guineas (three guineas always being what Woolfian people are willing to pay for a good cause) for an hour talking to the critic about his work; 'the fee', she says, 'would be enough to ensure that the interview did not degenerate into tea-table gossip'. Somewhere between a therapy session and a tutorial (assuming there's a difference), here is the scene:

> They would talk seriously and privately. . . . The consultant would speak honestly and openly, because the fear of affecting sales and of hurting feelings would be removed. Privacy would lessen the shop-window temptations – the temptation to cut a figure, to pay off scores. (202–3)

Not an unconscious in sight. There is a full and frank exchange of ideas, untroubled, it seems, by any difficulty of communication, now that the public context is out of the picture. Reading and writing, ideally, come down to a two-person conversation.

The shop window comes back once again, in answer to the question hypothetically put: 'what effect would the abolition of the reviewer have upon literature?' To which Woolf answers:

> Some reasons for thinking that the smashing of the shop window would make for the better health of that remote goddess have already been implied. The writer would withdraw into the darkness of the workshop; he would no longer carry on his difficult and delicate task like a trouser mender in Oxford Street, with a horde of reviewers pressing their noses to the glass and commenting to a curious crowd upon each stitch. Hence his self-consciousness would diminish and his reputation would shrivel. (204)

The violent smashing of the dividing glass paradoxically leads to what is now a much more clearly cut separation between the dark, private interior and the exposure of the outside. For the crowd in front of the shop window has degenerated since we last set eyes on it. It's now a 'horde', and the reviewers are repulsively sticking their noses against the window. We as readers are presumed to share in looking from a different vantage point, from which this distasteful and rather alarming vulgarity is apparent to us.

This opposition, between the safety and privacy of the interior and the unpleasant exposure of the outside is so much at the forefront of the passage that it is easy to miss something else which has occurred to the image. For the complaint against the reviewer here has shifted oddly, and against the grain of the main line of argument. Pressed up against the window, he is presented now as being not so much superficial as too nosey, too detailed, altogether over-interested in the process of production. He comments on every single stitch, and that is what the equally 'curious crowd' wants to hear.

The passage continues:

> No longer puffed this way and that, now elated, now depressed, [the author] could attend to his work. That might make for better writers. Again the reviewer, who must now earn his pence by cutting shop window capers to amuse the public and to advertise his skill, would have only the book to think of and the writer's needs. That might make for better criticism. (204)

The reviewer's performance-as-self-advertisement distracts attention from the real work of the writer, who neither performs nor advertises; the exaggerated contrast serves to enhance the sense of the writer's authenticity as a craftsman. In the new, improved version of things, neither writer nor critic would be in the public eye. But ironically, that means that readers – with the exception of the one privileged consultant – seem to get no look-in whatever.

This is the start of Woolf's concluding summary:

> The review, it is contended, increases self-consciousness and diminishes strength. The shop window and the looking-glass inhibit and confine. By putting in their place discussion – fearless and disinterested discussion – the writer would gain in range, in depth, in power. And this change would tell eventually on the public mind. Their favourite figure of fun, the author, that hybrid between the peacock and the ape, would be removed from their derision, and in his place would be an obscure workman doing his job in the darkness of the workshop and not unworthy of respect. (205)

The author of present times here joins the reviewer as a vaunting 'figure of fun'; and now the imagery is consciously turned inside out, as shop window and mirror 'inhibit and confine', while the closeted interior opens up a 'gain in range, in depth, in power'. Yet by the time the 'obscure workman . . . in the darkness of the workshop' has emerged, or rather disappeared, at the end, it is almost as if Woolf realises that she may have gone too far. Just in time, the last sentences save writing from a complete absence of publication or publicity by bringing back a now reconstructed 'public mind' as witness:

> A new interest in literature, a new respect for literature might follow. And, financial advantages apart, what a ray of light that would bring, what a ray of pure sunlight a critical and hungry public would bring into the darkness of the workshop! (205)

But then it was Woolf who had smashed the shop window and consigned the poor writer into that darkness in the first place.

In many ways, then, the shop windows of 'Reviewing' dramatically show up ambiguities implicit in Woolf's reflections about the connections between creative writing and the mass literary market. In the opening image, it is menders, not original designers or makers, who draw the crowd. Woolf seems to associate the women's reconditioning work with the bad publicity-culture of the present-day literary market; but the spectacle, one of skilled craft, actually comes close to her ideal of the writer as an artisan.

To pursue the sense of such ambiguities, let us look briefly at the shop window itself, in relation to other literary windows in Woolf that might be looked at or through. The vulgarity of the big show window with its gaping crowd is at one end of a spectrum which includes many types of window-gazing. For instance, Woolf often evokes a pleasure in looking at a private window open to view but not deliberately on view. An example of this would be a passage from the essay 'How should one read a book?':

> Shall we read [books] in the first place to satisfy that curiosity which possesses us sometimes when in the evening we linger in front of a house where the lights are lit and the blinds not yet drawn, and each floor of the house shows us a different section of human life in being?[2]

Here is the curiosity of the reader before the window, just as in 'Reviewing'. But in this instance, it is a single reader, and she is like 'us'. She is loitering, making the house into her own private theatre. She is seeing but unseen, gazing into a private space from the permitting neutrality of a public one, a virtual *voyeuse*. Even more directly, in an earlier version of the same essay: 'The windows of the house are open; the blinds are drawn up. One can see the whole household without their knowing that they are being seen.'[3]

The window can be even more private than this. In 'Reviewing', the show window scene is contrasted to the inner sanctum where the author and consultant ideally sit in conference:

> The author wants to be told why Mr. Nicolson [the reviewer] likes or dislikes his work. This is a genuine desire. It survives the test of privacy. Shut doors and windows; pull the curtains. (201)

Such a passage has something in common with the famous androgynous images for the creative process in *A Room of One's Own*, in which the mind goes about its eroticised creative business with 'the curtains . . . close drawn', well concealed from view – and from the light.[4] The writer's work is hidden, intimate, figured through an image of the privacy of the interior – and there is someone looking on, or rather imagining from outside what is going on, with a child's-eye curiosity. The secret and private atmosphere of these scenes of literary making seems to be meant to guarantee their authenticity in relation to the window scenes where the show is deliberate and the spectators are a crowd. Both the writer's practice and the reader's interest are shown as private, almost illicit pleasures, for their eyes alone. When writer and reader come together for the dialogue of a consulation, they are not overheard. And there is not a bookstore to be seen.


*Written in 1995 for a talk at the University of Michigan, Ann Arbor*

1   Virginia Woolf, 'Reviewing'(1939), in *The Essays of Virginia Woolf*, Vol. 6: 1933 to 1941, ed. Stuart N. Clarke (London: Hogarth Press, 2011), p. 195. Further references to this essay will be given in the main text.
2   Woolf, 'How should one read a book?', *Collected Essays*, ed. Leonard Woolf, vol. 2 (London: Hogarth Press, 1968), p. 3.
3   'How should one read a book?', *The Essays of Virginia Woolf*, vol. 4: 1925 to 1928, ed. Andrew McNeillie p. 394.
4   Woolf, *A Room of One's Own* (1929; London: Panther, 1984), p. 99.

# 17
# Woolf in Scholarly Form

Today's event has been given the title of 'Woolf in the twenty-first century', and I'm sure I'm not the only person here to have thought of that passage at the end of *A Room of One's Own* which returns to the hypothetical figure of Shakespeare's sister, whose thwarted sixteenth-century life had been imagined earlier on:

> She lies buried where the omnibuses now stop, opposite the Elephant and Castle. Now my belief is that this poet who never wrote a word and was buried at the cross-roads still lives. She lives in you and in me, and in many other women who are not here to-night, for they are washing up the dishes and putting the children to bed. But she lives; for great poets do not die; they are continuing presences; they need only the opportunity to walk among us in the flesh. This opportunity, as I think, it is now coming within your power to give her. For my belief is that if we live another century or so – I am talking of the common life which is the real life and not of the little separate lives which we live as individuals – and have five hundred a year and rooms of our own . . . then the opportunity will come and the dead poet who was Shakespeare's sister will put on the body which she has so often laid down.[1]

Well, we have lived another century, more or less, and so has Virginia Woolf, who did write a word, these words and many more words, and whose individual life has become a common life shared across thousands and millions of books and screens and classrooms and kitchens. Woolf has herself become Shakespeare's sister, as she imagined her coming into her own, into every woman's own, in the twenty-first century. She is queen of women writers, across all centuries, and without any sign of a possible successor. Her presence and visibility enable and inspire the writing and thinking of others. Where once she might have been sidelined or subordinated to some of the modernist men who were her contemporaries, today she is up there alongside and often above them. Her writing has come to occupy the place that Erich Auerbach prophetically gave her more than half a century ago, in *Mimesis*, as the culmination of the tradition of European literature that begins with Homer. (And is she on Facebook? Yes, of course. You can go to a page and personally connect with Adeline Virginia Stephen.)

Nowhere is the 'continuing presence' of Woolf more tangibly evident than in the many editions of her work that have appeared since she first came out of copyright in 1992. These editions have moved, in broad terms, from the general to the scholarly – and from the light weight of paperbacks to the more solid volumes that will make up the Cambridge list. Far from being kept off the Oxbridge turf, as she is at the beginning of the roamings of *Room*, Woolf is now a fixture in the library, her footnotability a continuing and never-ending work. (For there will always be new footnotes needed, old ones outdated, as times and questions change.) What would Virginia Woolf have made of this new Woolf, these many new Woolfs, that she has become?

That's an unanswerable question, of course, if only because a Woolf born in 1982, a century after Virginia Stephen, would or will have been seeing the world of books and universities and courses in a completely different way from the one who was born in 1882. But I want to go back for a moment to that decade a century after Woolf's birth, a somewhat earlier phase than our own in the growth of Woolf studies, Woolf seminars and Woolf notes. Back then in the mid-1980s, another country from now in economic terms, several British academic publishers were starting series of short monographs about individual authors. The idea – and some of you may even be able to access a distant memory of this – was to produce new readings in light of the new kinds of theory and criticism that were quickly gaining currency as teaching tools – with feminist criticism prominent among them. One day, I got a letter asking if I'd like to write a book on Virginia Woolf for one of these series. I was taken aback – in fact I was scared. I hadn't read any of Woolf's novels – ever. Some years before, I'd come across *A Room of One's Own* by chance in a library and read it then and there, one Saturday morning. A handsome old hardback, in fine condition and hardly ever taken out (you could tell in those days, from the return dates stamped in the front). For all I know it may have been a first edition. I loved it, but it didn't occur to me – why didn't it? – to then go and seek out the novels. When subsequently I was studying for an English degree, there were no books by Woolf on the course. If I *had* got around to reading her – and this was still true when I finally did – the likely medium for doing that would have been those unappealing little black books with cheap paper and no margins for notes.[2] (They did have the merit, though, of being highly portable.) Those were the Woolf paperbacks in print in the 1980s, before she came out of copyright.

So, when I got the letter about the book, I felt, and I was, completely unqualified, and my instinct was to retreat. At the time I'd been writing something on *Dorian Gray*, and maybe it seemed that one W might sound much like another – at any rate, I wrote back to the series editor and said could I do Wilde instead? There was a pause – in those far-off days, remember, communications of this kind passed on paper and via the post; there was no rush. Eventually the response came back. 'Wilde? But isn't that just drawing room comedy?' And so, eventually, I decided to get down and read my Woolf, and of course in a very short time I was hooked.

The story I think captures something about the vicissitudes of authorial canonisation. Five years later, a book on Wilde would have been an obvious candidate for such a series. A few years before, I don't think that Woolf would have been on the initial list herself. ('Virginia Woolf? But surely that's just Bloomsbury introspection?') Yet both Woolf and Wilde have stayed the new canonical course since the 1980s. Woolf above all has been repeatedly reborn or relaunched in the form, among many other forms, of new editions. Her words, her continuing presence, are kept alive and in motion through constant new interpretations and incarnations. At the same time, she is drawn on and called on for the wisdom and critical power of her words in relation to the cultural conflicts that face us today, as they faced Woolf then. That also is and will be the role of Woolf in the twenty-first century.

1   The occasion was an event at Senate House, University of London, in February 2011, to launch the Cambridge University Press edition of the works of Virginia Woolf. It was organised by Ray Ryan, and the other speakers were Gillian Beer, Susan Sellers and Ali Smith.

2   Virginia Woolf, *A Room of One's Own* (1929; London: Panther, 1984), 107–8.

3   The inside covers of these refers to them as 'Triad/Panther' books; the copyright page says 'Panther Books' and 'Granada Publishing'.

# 18
## Ginny Whizz

'No additional book about her is strictly necessary, but then neither is chocolate.'[1] Deliciously combining the tart and the indulgent, Victoria Glendinning's remark a few years ago about lives of Virginia Woolf has stayed in my mind – long after the book that prompted it will have disappeared into the deeper recesses of Amazon's warehouse. In a few aphoristic words Glendinning suggests a great deal about the relatively harmless and mainly feminine addiction to Bloomsbury biographies, which is the counterpart to publishers and writers regularly producing the things in their many hundreds of pages – and reviewers reviewing them.

Now along comes Alexandra Harris's book with the latest version of Virginia.[2] But this one is different. It carries no promise of radically new discoveries or lines of thinking about its subject. Instead, its selling point is a simple one: it's short. At well under 200 (and many of them photographs), this particular *Virginia Woolf* checks in at less than a quarter of the normal page expectancy. Gone are the days when you might have spent months on end minutely following the young Virginia Stephen as she and her many siblings meandered back and forth between Cornwall and London in the final decades of the nineteenth century; as Julia, the mother, tragically died when Virginia was just thirteen; as a half-sister, Stella, also died, not long afterwards; as Leslie Stephen, the father, raved through the years rehearsing his future destiny as *To the Lighthouse*'s Mr Ramsay, before finally dying himself in the early years of the twentieth century. Only then, after page upon page, would you be down to the second layer of the chocolate box, with Virginia now setting off on a semi-independent, post-Victorian life of her own; and Leonard waiting faithfully in the wings, for better or for worse.

Imagine then the shock of sitting down after breakfast one morning with Harris's slim volume and finding, after what felt like a very short while, that we were already heading towards the major breakdown of 1913. I got up to make a quick cup of coffee, but by the time I came back not only was the crisis long over, but the woman was apparently passing forty. Oh no! Have I gone and missed Vita? But it's okay, we're actually just pausing for a moment of reflection. 'She wanted her life to have form in the way that her novels had form. Now, at the end of 1922, she could feel herself being tugged in different directions and making the choices that would determine who she was in middle age.' Good to take a moment to sort that out. But now there's no time to lose for Ginny Whizz: 'She wrote very quickly, one after the next, four major novels, each completely different from the last, each taking a huge gamble by adopting untried methods'. Amazingly, she also found time for the 'growing mid-life relationship' with the glamorous Sackville-West.

And so onwards into another decade, with more great books and another passionate female attachment, this time with Ethel Smyth, always good for a spiky array of cartoon epithets: 'this large, deaf, outspoken septuagenarian warhorse of the feminist cause'. By way of some serious preoccupation with 'politics' (this is the 1930s, after all), it is now almost time for the end we all know to be on the way. But this is followed, in properly twenty-first-century style, by a further short chapter, called 'Afterwards', which has capsule accounts of various kinds of published and performed Woolfian lives after Woolf – her own letters and diaries as well as biographies, and also novels and plays.

Don't get me wrong. The book is a very good read, assured and infectious in its wish to impart an enthusiasm for all that Woolf made and was. Harris writes compellingly about Woolf's love of the rural places that she knew – and this, as the author of *Romantic Moderns*, is something she is very concerned to convey as a neglected feature of Woolf's writerly affections. But when she expresses regret that 'East Sussex is not signposted "Woolf Country"' (170), I think she is going a stile too far along this particular path. Apart from the fact that Woolf only lived part of the time, for part of her life, in one part of what's now East Sussex, and that quite a few other writers, women included, are known to have lived in the county too, this would surely be a form of authorial celebrity that she would have deplored. In the first paragraph of *A Room of One's Own*, she mocks the expectation that a lecture on 'women and fiction' should include, amongst other predictable names, 'a tribute to the Brontës and a sketch of Haworth parsonage under snow'.[3]

More of a guidebook for first-time visitors to a famous site, Harris's brief life is not presented as offering an original version of Woolf – or as doing away with an existing one. It is avowedly indebted to Hermione Lee's 1996 biography, much the most important and influential of recent times; and it follows Lee in the stance

that it takes on crucial biographical debating points like the qualities
of the marriage with Leonard or the understanding of the recurrent
episodes of depression and mental breakdown – for Harris as for Lee,
an intermittent 'illness' that Woolf partly learned to live with. Harris
is perhaps less directly interested than Lee in Woolf's status, in her
lifetime and later, as a woman writer; or in whether her creative
achievements should be seen as specifically that of a woman. You
wouldn't, from reading this account, pick up any sense of the critical
battles that were fought to claim Woolf's place as what Harris calls
'one of the greatest writers of all time': or the way that those battles
were very much bound up with a contested sense of what might count
as great writing – for women or men, let alone for all time.

As this big picture implies, Harris takes her distance from what
she presents as hyper-detailed studies of Woolf s work: 'the telescope
as well as the microscope has its uses'. Focussing on its established
star, this *Virginia Woolf* is lucidly readable. It doesn't change what
has been seen in Woolf, but it should serve, as Harris hopes, as a pleasurable and informative 'enticement to read more'. To read Woolf's
own writing – and, of course, to read more Woolf biographies.

1   Victoria Glendinning, review of Julia Briggs, *Virginia Woolf: The Inner
    Life*, *Guardian*, 9 April 2005.
2   Alexandra Harris, *Virginia Woolf* (London: Thames and Hudson, 2011);
    page references will be given within the main text. This review was written
    for the *New Statesman*.
3   Virginia Woolf, *A Room of One's Own* (1929; London: Granada, 1977),
    5.

# 19
# The Pinker Thinker

Steven Pinker says he loves reading style manuals, and I had high hopes of his.[1] A linguistics professor who's known for writing accessibly, Pinker is also the chair of the Usage Panel of the American Heritage Dictionary, a role that he evidently relishes. Prescription ever-so-lite is his mode. He wants us to know how different he is from the characters he mocks for their 'graybeard sensibilities' – those who hold that language is 'the' language, established with rules and meanings for all time. But he also has plenty of specific directions for how to get on with writing that language effectively and attractively.

That's all fine by me – I'm an anti-prescriptive prescriber too when it comes to correcting my own or my students' prose. So why did I find it so hard to get through this book? Part of the problem was figuring out who it was meant to be for. The book's subtitle ('The Thinking Person's Guide...') refers to one of those characters rarely sighted outside such contexts; but it sometimes feels as if the Pinker thinker addressed in these pages is someone learning English as a second language, or perhaps a brightish Year 6 child, happy to take a mix of real technical terms and jolly stories. For instance: 'Pronouns such as *he, she, they,* and *it* do more than save keystrokes. They tell the reader, "You've already met this guy; no need to stop and think about a new kid in town".'

At the beginning there's much talk of 'graceful' writing and 'classic' style. Long commentaries follow long quotations from writers whom Pinker admires (including one 'to whom I am married'). These passages are offered as taster experiences of 'savoring good prose', something the would-be good writer is encouraged to do. The bulk of the book is given to lengthy expositions of how to do sentences, drawing on various kinds of terminology from grammar and linguistics. It can be confusing. Pinker will give you a barrage of made-up examples of badly formed sentences, and then, as it were, put them right. Or else an invented sentence that's first paraded as maybe wrong, one that the 'style mavens' wouldn't like, is after all *not* wrong because 'great writers in English' have been sticking their adverbs in this forbidden position 'for centuries'. A mild and distracting irritation surfaces each time you can't stop yourself from coming up with more realistic or more convincing examples, whether to make the same point or to argue against it. And a feeble resignation when you're presented with yet another nudge-nudge joke or hilarious real-life linguistic blunder.

Pinker is much more interested in grammar and syntax than in semantic change. When it comes to talking about new words and meanings he just offers – for fun, more or less – the list of first-time entries in a recent edition of the dictionary he's involved with. Disappointed, I went back to a long-age book that Pinker mentions, Sir Ernest Gowers' *Plain Words*. Here is Gowers, in 1954, on the subject of new American words in British English:

> Nor do I see why anyone should turn up his nose at *teenager*, for it fills a gap usefully. We have no word that covers both sexes in what it is fashionable to call that 'age-bracket', except *adolescents*, which vaguely suggests what I believe the psychologists call 'imbalance', *juveniles*, which has been tainted by association with delinquency, and *young persons*, which, though adopted by the law, retains a flavour of primness.[2]

In just two sentences Gowers evokes a complex contemporary picture, in which the invention of a new generation is inseparable from a cultural debate about how to name it. In the *teenager* case, thinking about words is far more than a matter of fussing and anti-fussing about the validity of this or that form (though Gowers, like Pinker, has pragmatic advice for clear writing). Instead, the contestation of words and their uses is itself vitally part of the changing social world.

Beyond all the pedagogical paraphernalia, Pinker – I think – thinks that too: he's concerned, for instance, to do the right gender things with his pronouns. But Gower's *Plain Words* involves you in an ongoing discussion about the implications of particular linguistic choices; *The Sense of Style*, for the most part, just gives you more guidelines.

1   Steven Pinker, *The Sense of Style: The Thinking Person's Guide to Writing in the 21st Century* (2014). This review was written for *Times Higher Education*.
2   Sir Ernest Gowers, *The Complete Plain Words* (1954; London: HMSO, 1960), 34.

# 20
## Cultural Studies and the Literary

In their editors' introduction to *Cultural Studies* (New York: Routledge, 1992), the monumental volume from the 1990 Champaign-Urbana conference, Cary Nelson, Paula A. Treichler and Lawrence Grossberg state in passing that 'although there is no prohibition against close textual readings in cultural studies, they are also not required'.[1] A slightly grudging Venn diagram is being sketched out here: close readers may overlap with cultural studies if they must. 'No prohibition' – whence a possible new formula for acknowledgements pages: 'We thank cultural studies for generously giving permission for this book's occasional dependence on a close reading.' To judge by the desk-sagging weight of the cultural studies anthologies that have appeared over the last few years, there won't be much time, never mind inclination, for close reading anyway. This damning with faint inclusion occurs after a high-sounding reference to 'the heritage of disciplinary investments and exclusions and a history of social effects that cultural studies would often be inclined to repudiate.' Close textual readings are the chosen illustration of this unfortunate heritage and history, singled out as more guilty than most of the exclusions and exclusiveness that cultural studies seeks to avoid. But after the sentence not prohibiting them, there comes a further charge: 'Moreover, textual analysis in literary studies carries a history of convictions that texts are properly understood as wholly self-determined and independent objeccts as well as a bias about which kinds of texts are worthy of analysis. That burden of associations cannot be ignored. The problem now is not the way that literary analysis operates – through close reading – but the objects it operates on and the assumptions it makes about their conditions of existence and their value. And this time there will be no turning of blind eyes: this hangover 'cannot be ignored'.

So the authors of the introduction draw a nervous distinction between cultural and literary studies, ignoring the fact that the history of literary criticism is as diverse and contested as the practices of the rather younger discipline of cultural studies. It is as though cultural studies were afraid of being sucked into a celebration of Great Works at the very mention of the word *literature*. Analogously, literary studies seems to fear being swallowed up by an all-devouring, all-levelling new disciplinary force that refuses it the right to ask other than self-evidently social or political questions of its texts.

If cultural studies can represent itself as the locus of social critique, as opposed to a quiescent literary criticism forever closely reading its canon, then disaffected literary people can identify with cultural studies as the cutting edge of what they see as their complacent discipline. But this is not a new formation for literary studies. Literary criticism has often been accused of being indifferent to cultural concerns, and there have always been tendencies within literary studies that seek to open close reading: to make reading politically relevant or to place texts in frames wider than or different from those encompassing whatever are identified at the time as literary concerns. Semiotics was a field that situated literature as exemplary for examining how cultural meanings are made. Before that, sociology, especially Marxist sociology, promised to make literary studies political. With the advent of theory and then the 'turn to history' in literary studies, sociology more or less dropped out of discursive sight, to be mentioned only as a distant domain of benighted number-crunchers. Then along came cultural studies to assert the pertinence of contemporary social analysis, incorporating into its anthologies the work of authors historically associated with various forms of radical sociology.

In the work of such writers as Benjamin or de Certeau, close reading of cultural texts becomes creative sociology: the reading changes the objects, shows it up in a new perspective. Here is a place where cultural studies can and does meet literary studies on common, critical ground. By prompting unfamiliar questions and juxtapositions, close reading can discover and make connections between as well as within diverse texts. The objects of study may be imaginative writings, with a history of interpretations and with established cultural value, or non-canonical writings, or writings from any cultural field where close reading may yeild new perspectives not available through other methodologies. To use the same method in readng a poem, a newspaper editorial and a piece of philosophy is not necessarily to treat literature of different kinds as the same sort of matter. Closely reading non-literary writing doesn't imply an aesthetic valuation of that writing any more than asking a cultural question of an established literary text implies that the text is no different in its history or its provenance from, say, an extract from a marketing textbook. Not all literary work is cultural studies, and not all cultural studies involves modes or objects of reading that are literary. But the area in which the circles cross can unsettle both fields in potentially challenging ways – as the awkwardness of 'no prohibition' suggests.

1   Lawrence Grossberg, Cary Nelson and Paula A. Treichler, 'Cultural Studies: An Introduction', *Cultural Studies* (New York: Routledge, 1992), 2. Further quotations are taken from the same page. The present piece was written as a contribution to a forum in 1997 on 'Cultural Studies and the Literary' in the journal *PMLA*.

# 21

# Derrida's 'Once and for All'

'I recently fell in love with the French expression *"une fois pour toutes"*', said Derrida. The words were part of of an interview given in 2000 which I was translating into English a few weeks before he died.[1] Often enough, translating Derrida or trying to, you come across something for which you have to resort to a laboured expansion or parenthesis that takes away all the force and panache of the French. But here, for once, despite the pointing up of the Frenchness of the idiom, it seemed to me that English and French were in perfect harmony – that *une fois pour toutes* – literally, 'one time for all (times)' – was pretty much identical to 'one time and for all (times)' – in other words, 'once and for all'. How confusing, then, to read what came next, when Derrida added: 'I think it is untranslatable, but never mind.' Now, it is too late to ask him about this. And now 'once and for all', most final of phrases, resonates with a changed sense of ending.

A once which is not one – not a fixed finality, not one final meaning only: this is just what Derrida loved about the phrase, as an everyday encapsulation of a deconstructive idea. He goes on to explain – in much less translatable phrases – what he saw in *une fois pour toutes*: 'In a very economical way it states the singular and irreversible event of what or who only comes about or comes along once, and so is a one-off [literally, 'is never repeated']. But at the same time it opens up onto all the metonymical substitutions that will take it somewhere else. The new arises, whether we like it or not, in the multiplicity of repetitions. This is what suspends the naive opposition between tradition and renewal, memory and the future, reform and revolution. The logic of iterability ruins in advance the logic of countless discourses, philosophies, ideologies . . . ' (136–7).[2]

'What or who only comes about or comes along once': here I have clumsily translated a phrase that is much smoother in French – that I would like, defensively, to call untranslatable, but never mind. It involves the verb *arriver*; in French both events and people commonly do this, whereas English separates things that 'happen' or 'occur' from people who 'arrive'. Derrida's sentence is thus able to merge the unique event and the unique person, or rather to leave open the question of how or if they can be told apart. But English has to distinguish them from the outset, just as it differentiates verbally between the ways that they make their appearance – and Derrida's point is lost.

It is this kind of difficulty, or impossibility, of translation – *arriver*, in particular, turns up all the time – that frequently makes Derrida's writing seem obscure. Translators do their best, but it is very hard to retain both the complexity and the readability of sentences which depend on or write about French words or idioms that cannot easily be naturalised into the 'destination' language. The peculiar discourse in which Derrida's words have had to make their way into English is often laden with glosses and neologisms. Derrida comes over in English as a semi-foreign language, an alien arrival. As such, his thinking has repeatedly been dismissed. But it has also taken root and become established in the form of deconstructive writing in English with an idiom of its own.

In this sense, unquestionably, Derrida was a 'French' philosopher, in practice and in principle. He rejected the view that an idea could be separated off from the language of its formulation (why else would he happen to mention, in the course of a conversation in French, that *une fois pour toutes* may well be untranslatable?). In another late interview, Derrida spoke of the 'singular idiomaticity' – the translation is cumbersomely unidiomatic, but never mind – 'of what I write.' He continues: 'That is why some people (starting with those who have a slightly simplistic idea of the universal and think that philosophy has to be written in a sort of all-purpose Esperanto) consider my writings too 'literary', and philosophically impure. It is true that idiom is resistant to translation. But it doesn't necessarily discourage it; on the contrary it often provokes it.'[3]

Other twentieth-century French thinkers of the past few decades have met and meet with comparably divided linguistic and intellectual destinies, as Derrida points out himself in the same interview. 'The "success" abroad of some philosophers of my generation has to do, among other things, with the fact that each in their own way they remain extremely "French". In the 1960s there was a "French" configuration of philosophy (and of lots of other disciplines – psychoanalysis, the social sciences, literary studies) that was absolutely unique; we are its actors or these days its heirs. We have not yet weighed up what happened there, which has yet to be analysed, beyond the phenomena of rejection and fashion that it continues to provoke.'[4] Derrida marks out the collective 'Frenchness' as being bound up with its export but he returns, at the end of the interview, to the point of departure: 'Without being chauvinistic, anyone can see that the philosophers who are the most present, certainly the most influential, at any rate the most taught and the most translated in the world today are French thinkers of the generation of Levinas or Lacan, and afterwards that of Althusser, Foucault, Deleuze, Lyotard, and so on.'[4] (And most of all Derrida.) 'In philosophy', he goes on, 'or on the border between philosophy and a large number of other "domains", something singular and new occurred in France, only in France, in the course of the past forty years. Why only in France? That would be worth a lengthy analysis which I won't try to improvise here.'[5]

These reflections on the movements of cultural history, equally focussed on the identification of what is singular or radically new, may seem to take place on a quite different plane of analysis from the thinking that moves out from the meanings enfolded in an everyday idiom of the French language. This apparently effortless versatility of approach and emphasis is, I think, part of what made Derrida so extraordinary a thinker. In 1979, as a new graduate student, I started attending Derrida's seminars at Yale. Apart from a seminar when he was a visitor at my undergraduate university, this was the first time I had experienced the patient, step-by-step exposition of his utterly engaging speaking style. And I was taken aback by the material. He spent the first sessions giving a detailed exposition of the context in which an author in seventeenth-century France would have made a choice as to whether to write in Latin or the vernacular. It was a prelude to, and an integral part of a reading of Descartes' *Discourse on Method*. Up till then I had come across only the 'high theory' Derrida, as he had so far mostly appeared in English translations here and there. To British fans of 'French theory' at the time, proud in the repudiation of English common sense, the prospect of an account of legal and linguistic history would have sounded like something to be dismissed with the withering label of 'empiricism'. What I realised in those first weeks of listening to Derrida was that for him there was no division or contradiction between thinking historically and analysing texts: and that there was no once and for all to either kind of interpretation, or the two together.

This was long before Derrida came to be congratulated on a belated 'turn to history' or 'turn to ethics', as if he had eventually got the message that that there ought to be something outside the word-play. In fact – and as he steadfastly maintained each time the predictable question came up – there was no change of heart or direction. His thinking had been political and historical all along, though not always in the same ways or in all his writing all the time (if it had been he would have been a duller writer). But in his last years, the politics became more explicit or more recognisable as such. *Paper Machine*, for instance, the book I have been translating, is a mixture of articles, interviews and short journalistic pieces. Some of it is easy to read and some of it very demanding. Its subjects include immigration policy, the politics of language, the history of the book, the Frenchness of French philosophy. Derrida analyses what is new and not new in electronic, as opposed to manual technologies of writing and signature. Or he responds at length, and late, to articles written for and about him with a discussion of excuses. Or, in the way that only he could do and declare, he falls in love with a phrase, once and for all – for the last time.

1    Jacques Derrida, '"Others are Secret Because They Are Other"', interview with Antoine Spire, *Paper Machine* (2001), trans. Rachel Bowlby (Stanford: Stanford University Press, 2005), 136. This piece was written for a forum on Derrida in *Times Higher Education*, 12 November 2004, following his death. The other contributors were Derek Attridge, Simon Blackburn, Simon Critchley, Nick Hewitt and Richard Rorty.
2    Derrida, 'Others', 136–7.
3    Derrida, 'What does it mean to be a French philosopher today?', interview with Franz-Olivier Giesbert, 1999, *Paper Machine*, 113.
4    Derrida, 'What does it mean . . . ?', 112–13.
5    Derrida, 'What does it mean . . . ?', 120.

# 22
# Derrida One Day

One morning at the end of last month, I was listening to the beginning of *Woman's Hour*.[1] It was the lead-in to the opening item. There
were a few teasing sentences about long-gone pop stars, teenage
mooning and bedroom walls. 'Who was yours?' asked Jenni Murray
– adding enticingly, 'Mine was Elvis.' We can all relate to this, she
seemed to be saying, and there were more suggestions for faces that
might have been stuck above the bed next to sometime girls of a post-
Elvis generation – the Beatles, David Cassidy, possibly Donny
Osmond. Then finally out it came: 'Let's *deconstruct* the pin-up!' The
word was articulated with such bravura and such relish that you
couldn't but want to follow. Any deconstructing that sultry voice was
about to speak would be good enough for me. Ears pinned, I forgot
the usual academic twitchiness about the term being used as a simple
alternative to 'analyse' or 'think' about'. Here was a happy show-
casing of a bold, strong, glamorous word: *deconstruct* as pure phonic
pleasure, all voice, all signifier, without any special historical or technical meaning.

Did Jenni Murray's *deconstruct* have anything to do with
Derrida? Not by name. But it should be remembered that Derrida
was not averse to some of the more spectacular and seemngly outra-
geous appropriations of deconstruction in popuar culture.
Deconstruction was itself a pin-up and a label – a real record label
and a cutting-edge item in the contemporary vocabulary of fashion.[2]
Derrida's own head and shoulders photographed pretty well, too,
and he even starred in an arthouse documentary about himself. He
might well have been flattered as well as amused by the *Woman's
Hour* allusion. Deconstruct the pin-up – why not? Pin it down, take
it apart, put it back up, and move on.

I thought no more about deconstructing the pin-up. Frustratingly,
I couldn't even stay to listen to the feature and find out what, if
anything, lay behind or underpinned the mid-morning deconstructive exercise. But later the same day I was in a bookshop, one big
enough to have a philosophy section, and there my eye was caught

by a row of identical books on an upper shelf, their thick spines prominently displaying the words *From Plato to Derrida*. It was a big American textbook, the Prentice-Hall *Philosophic Classics*, fourth edition, 2003.[3] A million miles it seemed – in fact fifty miles and a few hours – from the deconstructive moment on Radio 4 with its manifest ephemerality, its lively sound, its flaunted superficiality: the poster all image and surface. Here, at the opposite extreme, at the end of the day, was the solidity and endurance of a permanent object. Derrida was granted the ultimate endorsement of a consecrated fraternity with the greatest philosophers of all time. The book appeared to embody a kind of immortality. What could be more of a vindication of deconstruction and of Derrida?

And yet the sight of the object depressed me. Was it because it was such a heavy tome, and a pedagogical text, in contrast to the light tone and the playfulness of the radio voice? That was part of it, perhaps. The text of Derrida's included in the book – no prizes for guessing – is 'Signature, Event, Context'. Like 'Structure, Sign, and Play', this piece has been much anthologised, in a way that has come to seem predictable, and to offer an easy-read, 'already read' Derrida. Yet this is ironic, in that the text itself argues for nothing other than the unpredictability and necessary variability each time any work is read, including itself, and including (though not anticipating) itself being read, over and over again, in pedagogical contexts. 'Signature, Event, Context' may have become locked for the time being into a certain explicatory function, but in the longer term it will inevitably – like any work – keep changing for its readers, as well as providing matter for thought about the fixings and movements that occur as a text is differently presented and consumed. Despite its static position within the covers of the classical volume, nothing ensures or predetermines its future uses.

So the problem was not the choice of text. I think the real reason for my reaction was because the book's very permanence and air of finality – here is the canon, from beginning to end – seemed to highlight and point to Derrida's own death.[4] It was a concrete instance of that structure that he had analysed in relation to writers and their words, whereby the 'survival' of the work and name necessarily occurs through a life apart from the author's own, and one outside their control; it is a life that goes on, if it does, independently of and indifferent to the biological continuation or end of theirs. The work's survival therefore marks the author's own mortality, as much as it grants a perpetuation or extension of their name.

Last of all, perhaps, Derrida described this structure in the interview he gave in 2004 to *Le Monde*:

At the point at which I leave my book, or leave or let go of it for publication (no one makes me do this), I become, appearing-vanishing, like that ineducable ghost that never did learn how to live. The trace I leave signifies to me both my death, whether it is yet to come or has already taken place, and also the hope that it may survive me.[5]

Later in the interview, Derrida spoke directly and personally about his thoughts on the survival of his own work:

At my age, I'm open to the most contradictory ideas on this subject. At one and the same time – please do believe me – I have the *twofold feeling* that, on the one hand – and I say this with a smile and not modestly – I have not yet begun to be read, and while there are certainly plenty of very good readers (a few dozen in the world, perhaps), basically it's later on that there's a chance of all that emerging; but also, just as much, that, on the other hand, a fortnight or a month after my death, *there will be nothing left any more.* Except what is kept for library copyright purposes. I swear to you, I believe sincerely and at one and the same time in these two ideas.[6]

Derrida situates these extreme reflections in the context of a new kind of unpredictability about survival, owing to both the rapid expansion of technologies of storage or archiving and the accelerating deterioration, destruction or obsolescence of media (which would include, for instance, the paper on which the interview is printed). But in this passage it's hard to believe he believes what he twices asks us to believe he believes: that his name and his writing might be dead as soon as he was. Hard to believe because the idea (his word is *hypothèse*) is realistically implausible and practically unthinkable (and by now, definitively disproved). Twenty or thirty years, however, would have indicated the time it might actually take for a writer to fade away from the visibility of publications, citations or coursework reading lists. There is no reason to think that this will be what happens to Derrida; but it is possible.

Yet in just a few dozen years, forty or fifty, say, Derrida will have more or less disappeared from what we call living memory. He will, probably, presumably, still be being read, perhaps read more and read as he would have liked, in the first of his two hypotheses about his survival. Deconstruction, the name, may long have ceased to have the edge and cut of a sharp new word; the time may have come and gone for a minor feature on a minor channel of some future verbal network in which punters are invited to remember the intellectual passions or fashions of their youth. Or else, or also, with or without its name, Derrida's thinking may have helped to bring about as yet undreamt-of or impossible things. But for the time being, the time of mourning, we are still left with the present memory of Derrida: of the living Derrida, who always had more to say and write. Whence, I think, the sadness, at the moment, at seeing Derrida's work put in its place: put there, as writing must be, in his place.

1  For anyone unacquainted with the fixtures of British national radio, *Woman's Hour* is broadcast every weekday morning on BBC Radio 4; Jenni Murray is one of its long-standing presenters. This paper was written for a panel that was part of a series entitled 'For Derrida' at the Tate Modern, London, organised by Simon Glendinning, February 2005.

2  Derrida's comment on Scritti Politti's track 'Jacques Derrida': 'Je ne m'y connais pas, mais il me semble que c'est de la bonne musique' ('I'm no expert, but is seems like good music to me').

3  *From Plato to Derrida* is the subtitle of the book, compiled by Forrest E. Baird; it has 1217 pages. Fifth and sixth editions, still with the same subtitle (no superseding of Derrida – or Plato – yet) have appeared since 2005, the most recent in 2017.

4  Derrida died in October, 2004.

5  Jacques Derrida, 'Je suis en guerre contre moi-même' ('I am at war with myself'), interview with Jean Birnbaum, March 2004, *Le Monde*, 19 August 2004, rpt. 12 October 2004, special supplement, 'Jacques Derrida', p. vi. Derrida', p. vi. The interview is translated into English by Pascale-Anne Brault and Michael Naas as *Learning to Live Finally* (Basingstoke: Palgrave, 2007).

6  Derrida, Je suis en guerre . . . , p. vii.

# 23
## Yale Theory

Once upon a time, there was something called theory. It had migrated across the Channel from France into Britain, but it also seemed to have a second point of origin in New Haven, Connecticut. Seen from the American side of the Atlantic, the 'Yale school' of deconstruction is the subject of Marc Redfield's gripping and intricately woven study: part cultural and institutional history, part exegesis and critique of key writers' work – and part reflection on the impossibility of smoothly bringing together those two frames of analysis.[1]

Redfield is fascinated by the way in which a particular kind of literary criticism somehow became what he calls a minor media myth. Mass-market magazines ran occasional features about a phenomenon that they presented as threatening the integrity of the (perennially threatened) academic humanities. When the Nazi-sympathising wartime journalism of prime Yale critic Paul de Man came to light in the late 1980s, theory – or deconstruction – could appear as a natural development of, or else a covert apology for, an ineffaceable and original tendency.

But Redfield is less interested in this stand-out sensation, much documented already, than in the peculiar history whereby a specialist form of academic writing acquired a certain public prominence in the 1970s and 1980s. He highlights the complex connection between on the one hand the media fascination with human (or inhuman) person-alities – the 'larger than life' Harold Bloom and the coldly 'cerebral' de Man – and on the other, de Man's sustained analysis of the error, but also the inevitability, of authorial personification.

The book has separate chapters on the writings of four of the major figures who were part of that nebulous (and stellar) Yale school: Bloom, de Man, Geoffrey Hartman and J. Hillis Miller. This list repeats a common sidelining of women theorists, notably Shoshana Felman and Barbara Johnson, who were also significant. Redfield awkwardly, if not unreasonably, explains this mainly in relation to his tracking of a public legend in which the men's names were the ones that figured. For despite its title, this isn't a book about theory 'at' Yale in the sense of what happened in that place or that institution day to day or year by year; instead it's about 'Yale theory' as seen from academic and media vantage points. This is the rationale for dissecting both the (media) picture and the (scholarly) texts – but not trying to reconstruct a picture of Yale 'itself' in the heyday of this intellectual movement.

Jacques Derrida, who symbolised the Paris-Yale connection because of his visiting appointment at Yale, is not given a separate chapter, but he features strongly in Redfield's fascinating readings of 1990s paintings by Mark Tansley that take theory as their subject. One of these, 'Derrida Queries de Man', actually portrays an ambiguous duel between these two colleagues, both of them identified with deconstruction. Of the four œuvres that Redfield describes, you have the impression that his own critic's heart is with Hartman; but it is the bromantic tussle between Derrida and de Man that draws his most forceful response.

And not only in viewing the allegorical adventures of this particular couple. The de Man chapter is primarily an engagement with John Guillory's critique in *Cultural Capital*, as Redfield weighs in, point by point, to take out Guillory taking out de Man. In a proto-Bloomian way, something strenuously agonistic seems to take precedence, apart from the academy and the occasional theory match reports in the media. But like the rest of the book, this is an accomplished and riveting exhibition of critical skill and insight.

1  Marc Redfield, *Theory at Yale: The Strange Case of Deconstruction in America* (New York: Fordham University Press, 2016). This review was written for *Times Higher Education*.

# 24

# The Future of Literary Thinking

Here is Terence Hawkes, writing in 1987, towards the end of his short Editorial for the very first issue of *Textual Practice*. He has been describing the many disciplinary and cultural fields in which the new journal may hope to engage in its special new form of analysis, and he concludes: 'For if we live in a world in which texts of all kinds surround, penetrate and determine our lives, we need at the very least to know how they operate, to what end, and on behalf of whom.'[1]

*TP* task in hand: 'to know how they operate', these piercingly all-pervasive textual things. In 1987, it's fair to say, the present was terrifying and textual. And the future, meanwhile, was implicitly litless and thinkless. Implicitly, because nothing remotely identifiable as 'literary thinking' appeared on the radar or the agenda. *Textual Practice*: not a trace of the literary or the thinking in that name. In the *Practice* an echo, still, of Marxism – or a distant claim to connection. *Thinking*, meanwhile, if worth doing or acknowledging, would be something that only really happened in (French) philosophy. It wasn't what literature did or the way that literature worked. Looking at literature could still just about pass muster as a sort of antecedent activity to the current project. It is recognised in Hawkes's piece as the source of the newfound focus on texts – what he doesn't call (because turns had yet to be invented) the textual turn. But literature has no primary place for *TP*. As part of a very long sentence, Hawkes says:

the effect of new theory, and the pondering of major social, historical and political issues it evokes, has been to establish and foster a funda-mental and greatly extended notion of 'textuality': the perception, deriving from the study of literature, that a culture's significant activ-ities involve a process which may fruitfully be conceived in terms of the production and consumption, the reading and writing of 'texts'.[2]

'Deriving from the study of literature': did you spot it before it was gone? To have referred, in this subordinate context, to 'literary thinking' (*what?*), as if such a thing might have a future, or for that matter a past or a present, or as if it might be something worth invoking or inventing or otherwise alluding to, would have been – to say the least – a little embarrassing.

But that was a long time ago. At some point since the 1980s *TP* must have tipped over, backwards or forwards, to come to a time now in which, so it seems, we can take it as read and written that a future of literary thinking exists, out there for the imagining or making, and perhaps in the pages of *Textual Practice* itself. Times have changed! Turns have turned! And texts are something else!

Let's look forward to many more years of literary thinking in the pages of *TP*. Thirty more – or, in an old language and a new text: XXX. Many happy returns!

*In 2016, for a feature called '30@30: The Future of Literary Thinking', thirty contributors were invited by Peter Boxall, its editor, to write 500 words on this topic to mark the thirtieth anniversary of the journal* Textual Practice

1   Terence Hawkes, 'Editorial', *Textual Practice* 1:1 (1987), 2.
2   Hawkes, 1.

# 25

## *Passionate* about Literature

Let me begin with an anecdote. A little while ago I was on the inter-view panel for a university job in English – not at my own institution, as it happens. There were four candidates, and every one of them at some point in the course of the interview, came out with the same four words: 'I'm *passionate* about literature!' – it was as if you could hear the italics and the exclamation mark. The final candidate even used the sentence all by itself, in self-sufficient isolation. Standard opening question after the introductions: 'Why do you want this job?' Reply (no less, no more, no hesitation): 'I'm *passionate* about literature!'

There would be a number of ways to think about this utterance or these utterances – these public and individual declarations of something that sometimes came out sounding like faith. One would be to do a bit of simple structural swivelling with the words. For instance, try replacing the word 'literature' with the word 'criticism'. This was, after all, a job to, in some sense, 'do' literary criticism, 'be' a critic – to write the stuff, teach the stuff. But imagine if all these people had come out with 'I'm *passionate* about criticism!' It doesn't quite work.

Because let's face it, criticism does have a bit of an image problem. Calling yourself a 'critic' in an academic setting is not recommended; the word conjures up something semi-defunct, the caricature of a dozing don slumped into a college armchair with a small sherry and a tattered but genuine bound volume of *Scrutiny*. If – and it's an open 'if' to me – the 'critic' once had some cultural clout, the role now seems well out of date. There's the use of the term 'authority' in the blurb for this event.[1] 'Authority' suggests the sort of stern and, yes, masculine moral sureness from which, I think, the passionate candi-dates (they were all women, in fact) were implicitly seeking to distance themselves.

A second reason for criticism not being the chosen word is that it's seen as secondary. As second-choice, like being a dentist when you didn't achieve the grades to study medicine (a common fall-back pathway at one time). The critic is the also-ran, the also-wrote, the one who didn't get to do the real thing.

Somewhere not far from 'passionate about literature' there may be the echo of a not very captivating TV ad for Marks & Spencer which ends with a gutturally uttered '*passionate* about food'. It seems not unlikely that this is the most direct contemporary source – or intertext, to be up-to-date in the critical language – for the equivalent literary passion, even if there's no conscious allusion. 'Passionate about . . . ' is a form of expression that has seeped into professional language in all sorts of cultural and not so cultural fields. It fits with the development of what is now sometimes called a 'cultural economy', one of whose features is the increasing blur between what used to be separated as the professional and the personal. There is a new kind of professionalism which doesn't just not exclude but positively demands the performance of emotional involvement in the organisation you work for and its ethos. Employees are *expected* to be 'passionate about' what they do – and to talk about that enthusiasm.

Another way to think about the 'passionate about literature' phrase would be to historicise it. Twenty years ago – or thirty, and probably forty – passion would not have been an obviously allowable, let alone an advertised feeling or attitude in relation to literature and criticism. I don't think you'd have heard any candidate for a job in a department of English admitting to, still less boasting of a *passion* for anything, least of all – and this might come as a surprise – for something called literature. Passion could certainly be found in plays or poems, and possibly in authors' lives, where it would be called 'experience'; but it was not for criticism or critics. Yes, you were teaching the passion-ridden substance and writing about it. But no one was meant to get all emotional about it. It might have been okay for a girl to gush a bit in the personal statement part of a UCAS form – or an UCCA form, to be historically precise – but by the time you were a job-seeking academic grown-up you would far more probably be a man not a woman, and in any case you wouldn't want to be presenting yourself in the sort of way that had always made English literature seem slightly dubious as a subject for serious academic study.[2]

A soft option, in fact.

In his new memoir John Sutherland uses that phrase to describe his own choice to do English at school.[3] As it happens, the link between the soft option and the study of literature goes all the way back not just to the beginning of English as a common degree subject, but to the origins of the phrase itself. For its first use in Britain the

OED cites a defensively assertive statement of 1923 about the then quite new English degree in Cambridge: 'It follows that our Tripos must be difficult; that we have little use for "duds", for Tutors who misconceive it as being a soft option'. This is from the Cambridge magazine *Granta*.[4]

I've come across earlier published mentions of the phrase, and they are on the very same topic. First from the Newbolt Report of 1921, the result of a Government-sponsored inquiry into the teaching of English in England. (There may also be a more than tangential connection, since Sir Arthur Quiller-Couch, Cambridge English don and author of the Granta piece, was a member of the Newbolt committee.) Like the *Granta* piece, the Report refers to the phrase in scare-quotes, as if it's well known as a taunt commonly thrown at university-level study of English; there is actually a separate section (paragraph 194) with the title 'English not a "soft option"'. Thus: 'It is suggested that it is a "soft option." This is an accusation which affects the whole of our inquiry.' And in conclusion: 'It is clear, then, that the alarm of the "soft option" may be dismissed as a bogey.'[5]

Going back even further, to 1917, a 'soft option' appears in an essay on the study of English in a general book on education. The essay's author, Nowell Smith, was the headmaster of Sherborne School at the time; his essay makes a strong case for the study of literature as essential for all-round citizenship, but also for the pleasure it can give pupils both at the time of teaching and as a resource for the rest of their lives. He insists that the teacher must be enthusiastic because no one is going to be persuaded that reading literature has a use-value – and also because 'there clings to literature, and particularly to poetry, which is the quintessence of literature, an air of pleasure-seeking, of holiday, of irresponsibility and detachment from the work-a-day world, which must captivate the student'.[6] Nowell Smith then brings on a pedantic interlocutor:

> 'Ah! It is just as I expected,' says my friend Orbilius at this point: 'this literature-lesson of yours is to be mere play, a "soft-option" for our modern youth, who is not to be made to stand up to the tussle with Latin prose or riders in geometry."'[7]

There it is again – or already – complete with its regulation inverted commas, as if it is always being cited with embarrassment from somewhere else. And it starts with a hyphen, the soft and the option marked as inseparable from the outset. (And it's true: there is seemingly no such thing as a not-soft option; without a soft option, what you make is a hard choice.)

So it is not just that the academic study of English might have been considered a soft option very early on in its history; it is that the very idea of a soft option appears to have been invented in relation to nothng other than the study of English. This soft option appeared decades and decades before the question of the putative consumerisation of academic choices had been broached; you could almost say it was before the serious beginning of twentieth-century consumer culture at all. Who would have thought it? It all begins with English!

How does the Newbolt report set about its dismissal of the 'soft option' jibe? Well, mainly by saying that the study of English is hard after all. The objection is made, says the report, because it's assumed that anyone who can speak the language can read the books. 'But it is a pure delusion to suppose that the fact that a boy or man knows enough English to talk to his brother, to take a railway ticket, or even to conduct a business, leaves him nothing hard and difficult to learn when he comes to study English Literature.' On the contrary, you can get on to the real work much sooner if you don't have to spend time initially on the practical basics. And in any case, 'we do not think it can be contended that it is a "soft option" to be called on to understand the art, thought, imagination of such writers as Shakespeare, Milton, Wordsworth, Shelley'.[8] The argument is careful, though, not to omit the 'delight' of reading literature, along with the hard work, and also to stress that it is not to be thought of as a pleasure confined to a trained university set. 'The literature of England belongs to all England, not to the Universities or to any *coterie* of the literary or the learned: and all may enjoy it who will.'[9]

I've said that 'passionate about literature' wouldn't have made sense as an article of professional faith twenty years ago, and as for 'passionate about criticism', it's probably beyond the pale of imaginable declaration, then or now. But there *was* something, I think, that it was acceptable and quite common for academics, or some of them, to be mad about, if not fully passionate about, in the 1980s, and that was the thing called *theory* – or even *critical* theory. In those heady days – and they were heady, cerebral, not meant to be bodily-passionate in any way – in those days theorists, even the qualified 'literary' theorists, saw themselves as serious, intellectual, engaged, and very far from the belletristic meanderings or scholarly moralism of what was always disdainfully dismissed as 'traditional' English criticism. And theory really did raise the intellectual stakes of literature departments in very much needed ways.

As opposed to the soft touches of 'reading literature', or the seeming redundancy of the old-fashioned moral 'critic', theory came over as appealing and adventurous and above all as intellectually alive and challenging. For one moment, perhaps, the burial of the critic was the birth of the theorist – or so it could appear. Since that time, theory itself has branched off along many different specialised pathways, and it has often stagnated into predictable techniques of writing and reasoning that may have no more vitality than the duller practices of 'literary criticism' that at first it exuberantly sought to supplant.

So are theorists, as well as critics, past it? Ronan McDonald, in his new book, ends up by proposing a return to or revival of the notion of 'evaluation'.[10] The job of the critic is, ultimately, to say what's good and what's not good, and why, and to say this with an authority that the proliferation of media and outlets for opinion of all sorts has progressively diminished.

I can't agree with this, or maybe what I mean is I just can't get passionate enough about it. As a cast-iron product of the golden age of theory, I've never thought that the job of literary academics is to rate what they read. Or perhaps the problem is more with the present associations of the word itself: to me, 'evaluation' suggests all the negative tick-box counting and accounting that's come to be so familiar and oppressive in universities through the dominance of the RAE – Research Assessment Exercise, to anyone fortunate enough not to know what that is.[11] Making a case for how and why a particular work is or was interesting or important or powerful does seem to me something worth doing, and worth doing for people who may or may not call themselves critics; and yes, for shorthand, we could call that a form of 'evaluation'. But I'd still rather avoid the word because it suggests an attempt at a final verdict whose own criteria and forms of argument go unquestioned.

It also seems to me crucial to resist the sure separation of criticism and its objects – or of critical and creative writing. First, because in a significant sense what we call literature is itself critical writing as well, engaging directly or indirectly, consciously or unconsciously, with existing works. Literature too, like criticism, is writing about other writing. This was the point made most forcibly by Harold Bloom's argument about the Oedipal struggle for mastery between poets and the 'precursors' their own works are intended to supplant; but the point doesn't have to be about an authorial struggle for power. Beyond intra-literary or interpersonal issues, what we call literature – and that classification, of course, is historically a fairly recent one – may also be critical in a philosophical sense, engaging with arguments about ethics, aesthetics, society, or identity, as do other modes of writing. It may do it in different ways, and to different effects, from non-literary genres, but there is nothing settled about the differences.

The second reason for rejecting the separation of the critic and the author is that if critical writing is itself worth reading, then it had better be good writing, interesting writing, not just some mechanical superstructure or substructure that stands to one side, authoritatively or not, of the 'primary' texts. Otherwise, to my mind, it's just not worth reading and also, not worth writing. It has to be said that theory, in its heyday, didn't always make for good writing: there was a wish, perhaps, to flaunt the difference of a language that was meant to be a radical departure from the untechnical, common-sense styles of English criticism, whether heavyweight Leavisite moralism or gentler aesthetic appreciations.

So instead of talking about the death, or not, of the phantom body called the critic, and worrying about who is going to do our evaluation for us, perhaps instead we should be thinking about a much more inclusive sense of criticism – in which, for sure, some critics are more thought-provoking or more challenging or more pleasurable to read than others – just as some literary writers are. No less than 'creative' writing, criticism calls for critical response: calls for more writing. That there are so many more critics (and creative critics, and critical creatives) around, in so many more media than there were before, is not a reason for despair – for Arnoldian 'bewilderment' – at the lack of a source of sure authority. Nor is it necessarily a reason for celebration. But it might be a reason, for a change, to get a tiny bit passionate about criticism.

1  In a shorter version, this paper was written for an ICA panel on 'The Death of the Critic', October 2007, prompted by Ronan McDonald's book of that title. The paragraph publicising the event was this:

In an age of book clubs, celebrity endorsements and a blogosphere staffed with thousands of amateur critics, what role is there for the professional critic as an arbiter of artistic value? Is cultural value just a matter of personal taste, with one opinion as good as any other? What function does professional criticism fulfil now, and should we lament the passing of the authority which previous generations of critics enjoyed?

As well as Ronan McDonald, the other panel members were Michael Coveney, Adrian Searle and John Sutherland.

2  For those who don't know: these two acronyms have each in turn denoted the general application forms for candidates applying to undergraduate university courses in the UK.

3  John Sutherland, *The Boy Who Loved Books* (London: John Murray, 2007), xx.

4 Sir Arthur Quiller-Couch, 'A First Purpose of the English Tripos', *The Granta*, March 2, 1923, 315.

5 Board of Education, *The Teaching of English in England* (London: HMSO, 1921) ('Newbolt Report'), ch. VII, 'The Universities', 202, 204.

6 Nowell Smith, 'The Place of Literature in Education', in A.C. Benson (ed.), *Cambridge Essays on Education* (1917; Cambridge: Cambridge University Press, 1918), 114.

7 Nowell Smith, 115.

8 Newbolt Report, 203.

9 Newbolt Report, 204.

10 See Ronan McDonald, *The Death of the Critic* (London: Continuum, 2007).

11 And in the years since the occasion of this talk, the RAE has long sunk into oblivion, superseded by the equally compelling REF (Research Excellence Framework).

# Interview

# 26

# Interview with
# David Jonathan Bayot and
# Jeremy De Chavez

**DAVID JONATHAN Y. BAYOT:** It's perhaps a good idea to begin this conversational journey with you via a subject that has been close to you in your diverse studies of literature, culture, women, consumer culture, and psychology (among the foregrounded themes in your work). I'm referring to Freud and psychoanalysis. Would you like to give us a narrative of your critical romance with Freud as well as with the diverse field of Freudian studies? Could you tell us about the starting point(s) as well as the tours and detours in the course of what the title of one of your books calls 'shopping with Freud'?

**RACHEL BOWLBY:** Thank you for the question. And as you imply, I could answer it with several different kinds of narrative. The first, perhaps, would be the more or less academic rationale. I became interested in psychoanalysis because I was interested in feminism. In the 1980s, those two things often went together, especially for students in departments of literature. You were either a psychoanalytic feminist – if you were a feminist – or you weren't, with the 'not' version implying at least some familiarity with the issues. Those who were for it took psychoanalysis as essential for a serious analysis of the (patriarchal) situation of women; those against it argued that Freud's view of women was simply misogynist. On the pro-psychoanalytic side, there were many subdivisions, and there was a growing interest in the work of Jacques Lacan, the French psychoanalyst whose writings on sexual difference were provocative – more so, perhaps – in the same way as Freud's.

A less academic (though still bookish!) version of this story. I had come across Juliet Mitchell's book *Psychoanalysis and Feminism* in a bookshop in Croydon in the mid-1970s (before I went to university). It had been reissued as a Pelican paperback, which is a sign of the serious – and increasing – interest in both of the topics of the title at that time. Mitchell's book spurred debate and paved the way for the academic interest in psychoanalysis and feminism that took root over the next decade. She argued for the centrality of the woman question to a full Marxist analysis (this being the arena of much feminist debate at the time), and along with that, for the indispensability of Freud's thinking for an account of the position of women.

This was also the period when the Penguin Freud, many volumes and many colours, was beginning to come out, and that's probably where the academic and less academic stories flow into one another. When I began teaching at the University of Sussex in the mid-1980s, Freud was very much part of the arts curriculum, across a number of disciplines. The texts were easily purchasable for students, thanks to those Penguins. There was a course called Studies in Feminism, which was taught by feminists in history and literature, including Cora Kaplan and Jacqueline Rose. Lots of Freud got read and argued over in the seminars for this course. (Last week, on a second-hand book-stall in a town market in Shropshire, I found an old copy of the red *Introductory Lectures*, with a gold 'Sussex University Bookshop' sticker on the back. Inside was the name of a student, with 'Eng/Am' – the School of English and American Studies – and the year, 1982. Those were the Freudian days!)

As far as my own work involving Freud goes, at that point I was interested not only in the ongoing debates about feminism, but also about whether a psychoanalytic approach could be brought to bear on feminist historical questions. I had gone to Yale as a graduate student (in Comparative Literature) because I was fascinated by theory – by Barthes and Derrida and Foucault, in particular, who were all lumped together under that one word. Yale Comp. Lit. gave you a wonderful education in different kinds of reading that drew on French theory; the faculty included Paul de Man, Hillis Miller, Shoshana Felman, Peter Brooks and Geoffrey Hartman, and Derrida visited to give three seminars a week for a month each year. I was also able to take courses with Fredric Jameson (in French) – one on Flaubert and one on the 1960s! – and with Harold Bloom (in English). Shoshana Felman's course on the Oedipus myth as a narrative figure, which I took in my first semester at Yale, was a revelation. She pulled out elements of the Oedipus story and got you to see and think about their recurrence in all sorts of other texts across western literary history. And the seminars were also a brilliant demonstration of an inductively Socratic teaching method – which like many of her students I've always wished I could emulate.

During this period I became interested in 'French feminism' (not that it had that name in France, or that all its practitioners were all French): primarily Hélène Cixous, Luce Irigaray and Julia Kristeva; there were also, for instance, Annie Leclerc and Michèle Montrelay. These writers were all imbued with psychoanalytic argument, and in particular were writing against – or at least in relation to – the course of seminars that Jacques Lacan had given on femininity in the early 1970s, and which had been published as a book, *Encore*. (That word 'femininity', not exactly common in English and frequently mis-spelt at the time as 'feminity', took on a whole new strange life in English in the context of these debates. It came to connote an exotic and abstracted Frenchness, as opposed to down-to-earth Anglo-Saxon 'woman' and 'women' – or the clunky 'womanliness' and 'woman-hood'.) With many individual variations of emphasis, the French feminists all said that 'the feminine', as that which escaped the dominant phallogocentric mode, was inherently subversive or transgressive, and lent itself to avant-garde art and literature. It was a powerful argument that brought together literature, feminism and (French) psychoanalysis, and for a few years there was a vibrant academic debate in English-speaking countries about this phenomenon labelled French feminism, which was often set against another hypothetical entity called Anglo-American feminism. For Jameson's course on 'The Sixties' I wrote an essay about this new French feminist writing (actually from the mid-1970s), which was published in the journal *Social Text*. And then a few years afterwards, when French feminism had become a dominant term of arguments within (English-speaking) feminist criticism, I wrote another one, 'Flight Reservations', about the Franco/Anglo polarisation of feminist theory.

Going back to Yale – when it came to choosing a dissertation topic, after two years of coursework, I found that I wanted to do something outside the unofficial Comp. Lit. canon of the time, and something that would be historical as well as theoretical. I had come across a review of a newly published history book about the beginnings of the French department store on which Zola had based his novel of 1883, *Au Bonheur des Dames*. The book was Michael B. Miller's *The Bon Marché: Bourgeois Culture and the Department Store, 1869–1920*, published in 1981. It inspired me both because of the specific history – in effect, the beginning of what we think of as shopping – and because, at the time, there was really no such thing as the academic study of consumer culture – and so it was all to play for!

In a nutshell, department stores were one-stop shops, in today's vocabulary, in that you could buy anything and everything there: all the formerly separated categories of merchandise under one roof. But that one stop was not so much about speed and convenience as about giving middle-class women the opportunity of spending extended periods of time in this city place, the big store, engaging in an enjoyable activity called shopping. The history of consumer culture has become a major interdisciplinary field in the past few decades, but in the early 1980s it was non-existent, with Michael Miller's book one of the very first. I was riveted because here was a topic – the history of shopping – which had to be seen as both cultural and psychological at the same time, and was quintessentially to do with women (since women, far more than men, engaged in shopping both of the practical, provisioning kind and the more open-ended, leisurely kind promoted by the new stores). Freud's notorious question, 'What does a woman want?' could be replayed as the question that the (almost all male) proprietors of the new mega-shops at the end of the nineteenth century were asking themselves, to very different ends (their aim being to get women to purchase more – and more – of whatever it was that they could be persuaded they wanted).

The insatiability or indeterminacy of feminine desire is a starting point for salesmanship as well as for psychoanalysis, and there you have a first crossover question between these two very different practices. In terms of the Marxist-feminist debates of the time, there was also the issue of how to theorise – or historicise – department stores. Were they primarily capitalist or patriarchal institutions? In what sense were they new, or was shopping new – as a social or a psychological form? And how could we think about the boundary (or relationship) between the social and the psychological? (I'm saying 'psychological' here where I'd probably have said 'psychic' then. I don't mean psychological in any specific disciplinary sense. In theory circles at the time I'm talking about, psychology was more or less a forbidden word; to use it implied a foolish ignorance of the intellectual limitations of the discipline, in contrast to the scope and openness of psychoanalysis. Psychology, meanwhile, has always returned the compliment by relegating Freud to a couple of dismissive paragraphs in the A-level textbook.)

There was a great freedom in doing a dissertation in what was not yet an established field of scholarship. There wasn't that anxiety about whether you'd managed to 'read everything', because there wasn't yet a recognisable field. Also, the subject was inherently cross-disciplinary, and methodologically mobile. I found myself looking at department store archives as well as reading all of George Gissing's novels (I think there are twenty-three of them!) – and plenty of Barthes besides.

BAYOT: What would you consider to be the most significant contributions of Freud to the understanding of what literature is or could be: literature as a production in the terrain of culture and civilization, as well as its being a *differentia specifica* (as Roman Jakobson would term it)?

BOWLBY: For Freud, literature often figures as something that has anticipated the subsequent, scientific thinking whose role is then simply to formulate in its own terms what has been said already in a literary mode. Sophocles' *Oedipus the King* is the primary and obvious example here. Primary in the sense that it's the cornerstone of psychoanalytic theory: it gives Freud his 'complex' of incestuous and murderous infantile desires, and it also gives him the unconscious, because Oedipus – unlike any other hero of a Greek tragedy – does not know what he is doing when he marries his mother and murders his father (they are not the two people he knows as his parents). And obvious in that Freud states quite clearly the literary source of his theory.

There are many ways that Freud draws on literary thinking as he develops his own ideas. He will produce a hyperbolically grand and vague allusion, as when he throws up his rhetorical hands in mock exasperation in his lecture on 'Femininity' and says if you want to know more about this ever enigmatic, impossible subject, then turn to 'the poets'! And his literary talk does not always have the specificity or deference of the Sophoclean reference. In the essay 'Creative Writers and Daydreaming', for instance, he takes the narratives of popular fiction to be akin to dreams in the way that they show the fulfilment of everyone's fantasies. Literature in this view has no special or distinctive insight; it is just a continuation of the grandiose, happy life of wish fulfilment that happens to everyone in their sleep – which is why we enjoy these daytime equivalents. And in the *Studies on Hysteria*, Freud worries that his case histories might read more like short stories than scientific accounts: it is not a tendency that he is proud to contemplate.

One difference between these various examples is between poetry and prose: it's less easy, it seems, for a prose narrative to pass serious literary muster than it is for something written in metrical form. Another difference is between the modern and the ancient; one reason, we can speculate, as to why Sophocles' play might have presented itself as a proof-text for Freud's new theory is that Greek tragedy – and particularly Sophocles, at the time of Freud's writing – carried a great deal of cultural prestige. It's a fairly consistent dichotomy in Freud's thinking about literature: that modern texts –

novels and short stories – tend to be associated with surface fantasies, conscious daydreams; whereas the long-term and more weighty matter of repression is found in older, classical literature.

That doesn't mean that contemporary literature is always dismissed or always taken as simply generic. The long essay of 1907 on *Gradiva*, a novella by the Danish author Wilhelm Jensen which had been published just a few years before, is painstakingly detailed in its close reading of the hero's dreams (as if they were actual dreams), and the relation between fantasy and reality in his life. It's also no accident, though, that this particular story is itself about the contrast between the ancient and the modern. Its leading character is an archaeologist so absorbed in his passion for the Pompeian sculpture of an attractive young woman that he fails to notice her real-life equivalent in the present until he is 'cured' by the pro-active girl herself: thus repression is lifted and love is born!

So literature plays a number of different roles in Freud's writing: sometimes hugely important, sometimes fairly trivial, and not really treated *en bloc* as encompassing all the different genres and periods that we tend now to include under that one general word. In this respect – the absence of a generalised 'literature' – it is interesting to compare Freud's treatment of philosophy, another discourse or practice that he sees as being close enough to psychoanalysis to be worth (in this case) distinguishing from it. Repeatedly, in passing, Freud uses 'philosophy' as a sort of collective straw man, stupid and stubborn in its refusal to acknowledge that there is thinking beyond the conscious. Here's a fairly typical – and typically funny – passage, from *An Autobiographical Study* (1925):

> This of course provoked a denial from the philosophers, for whom 'conscious' and 'mental' were identical, and who protested that they could not conceive of such an absurdity as the 'unconscious mental'. There was no help for it, however, and this idiosyncrasy of the philosophers could only be disregarded with a shrug.

It's interesting that Freud was markedly different in his attitude to philosophy – or 'the philosophers' – from Lacan, who was almost at the other rhetorical extreme in this regard. Lacan's writings are full of both swift and extended references to (specific) philosphers, not as contrary to psychoanalysis but rather (as with Freud's use of Sophocles) as confirmation or anticipation.

BAYOT: In a way, this question is a continuation of the previous one. While the earlier question is interested in Freud's contribution to our knowledge of this thing called 'literature', this question, focused on the aspect of 'reception management' (as I call it), is more concerned with *how* Freud, directly or indirectly, contributed to the paradigm (which necessarily involves the methodology) of literary studies. Would you say that Freud is a critical figure in, for example, 'interdisciplinising' the field of literary studies? In relation to the previous question and to this one, would you say that your book, *Freudian Mythologies: Greek Tragedy and Modern Identities* (2007) is in a way a foregrounding of Freud's contribution to the study of literature, both as a 'close' reader of literature and as an 'open' one as well?

BOWLBY: In relation to receiption: I think you're right to home in on the idea of what literature does to its readers as being crucial to Freud's thinking, and crucial to a perspective which rejects the idea that art can be siphoned off into some separate sphere of aesthetic appreciation, set apart from ordinary experience. To take the stand-out example of Oedipus: Freud's premise (in *The Interpretation of Dreams*) is that Sophocles' play affects everyone, and it does so because it stirs up longings and hatreds from early childhood which have been suppressed because they are incompatible with the maturely reasonable identities of adulthood. The story of someone committing now unthinkable acts that everyone, as a small child, would once have wished to do is both shocking and appealing – shocking because, in the later consciousness in which these acts are utterly ruled out, beyond the cultural pale, it is disturbing to evoke them; appealing because once upon a long-forgotten time, to get rid of a father and be everything a mother wants is what we all supposedly wanted to do.

So Freud is drawing on a work of literature, and the myth it is based on, to create (he says rather, 'discover': it was there all the time) a new theory of human development. For one of the many twists in his own interpretation or remaking of the story is to move it from singularity to universality. It is no longer about a uniquely ill-fated hero; it is about everyone. (Or about every boy, at any rate: the revisions that became necessary to try to fit girls, or women, into the paradigm form a different story of their own in Freud's later writings.)

There are two things to draw out here in relation to your question. First, that Freud is connecting the powerful impact he claims that Sophocles' tragedy has for each and every spectator to (what he equally claims as) a universal feature of human psychological development. To spell out the interdisciplinary aspect of this: the literary work is explained in terms of a general psychology; you can't understand the first without the other, and you need to think about psychology if you are thinking about literature. And second, this process is very much a matter of reception. It is the effect on the reader/spectator that is the aspect of the play that needs to be thought about and analysed; and you reason from the effect back to what you then postulate as common features of human (or reader) psychology.

Despite the presumption of universality, though, Freud does introduce some nuances into his view of that very long Oedipal reception period (a couple of millennia and more). In the same way that he implicitly makes an analogy between the ancient (classical) times of western civilisation and the ancient (childhood) times of a human life, so he also suggests a kind of middle period in cultural development, whose literary emblem is *Hamlet*. Hamlet, Freud says, can't bring himself to do the deed that Oedipus does do: can't bring himself to get on and kill the man who has married his mother (the father-equivalent). And the reason for the difference is that by the time of Shakespeare the culture is that much more repressed than it was in fifth-century Greece. The criterion Freud is using here is not individual development but cultural development; and the presumption is that both Sophocles and Shakespeare are telling versions of the same story – the paradigm human myth.

So Freud historicises his psychology in a way – but the historicisation is actually also a further claim for the pre-eminence of this one basis for thinking – throughout cultural history – about the processes of human psychology, and (by extension) their manifestations in literary form. There is also a significant difference between the two tragedies in terms of Freud's own conception of human psychology which may also have much to do with why he came to light upon *Oedipus* in the first place – or why *Oedipus* struck him and moved him in the ways that it did. That difference is the unconscious. Hamlet knows what it is that he wants to do in murdering Laertes – he just can't bring himself to do it. Oedipus, on the other hand, married his wife and murdered the man on the road without any knowledge that these people were in fact his own parents; as far as Oedipus knows – as far as consciousness goes – he loves his parents (that is, the parents he doesn't realise are not his birth parents) with absolute filial devotion. At this level, *Oedipus* ought to be the later play according to Freud's model of progressive cultural repression, because the deeds have gone underground, not compassed within the possibility of the hero's thoughts or actions – whereas in *Hamlet*, there is a conscious design to murder a father figure.

The comparison Freud makes between the two plays brings out the double notion of repression and the unconscious, the core of psychoanlytic theory, alongside the particular intra-familial story concerned. For Freud, the unconscious is inseparable from sexuality and the paradigm story of Oedipus. You cannot become a more or less functioning social adult without having gone through the early period of multiple sexuality ('polymorphous perversity' in his enchanting phrase) and Oedipal emotions – all of which must subsequently be as if they had never been: repressed, unconscious, but nevertheless vulnerable to exposure or reactivation if the always precarious edifice of mature, post-Oedipal selfhood should come apart.

I've talked about the peculiar fittedness of the Oedipus 'nuclear family' model – continuity of the same two parents, small number of children – to a dominant twentieth-century actuality that was historically without precedent or succession (family set-ups have generally been much more diffuse than that, for changing historical reasons). So it intrigued me that Freud, on the brink of that particular moment in western cultural history, should have come out with a theory that made the nuclear family a symbolic universal. Or, to go back again to the beginning of this in your question, perhaps the immense take-up or reception of Freud as a cultural phenomenon – to the point that Oedipal is now a Freudian not a Sophoclean adjective, and that everyone has some idea of what that word is supposed to mean – has something to do with the emergence of his ideas at the point when they could speak to the real conditions of most people's development. In the twentieth century the minimalist family of two parents plus a child did not look like a theoretical abstraction.

But if we stick with this one feature of the correspondence or not of the Oedipal story to the historical reality of families, then it might seem, on the face of it, that far from making a perfect match, the Sophoclean story of Oedipus doesn't have much to do with that particular twentieth-century 'nuclear' phenomenon at all. Just keeping with Sophocles' version in *Oedipus the King*, we have a plot that includes three highly untypical nuclear families. There is the family of four children that Oedipus has with Jocasta; it is a second marriage for her, after a first marriage in which there was one dead child (baby Oedipus). There is Oedipus' adoptive family: in fact this is effectively a transnational adoption, across the borders from Thebes to Corinth by way of foster-care from the rescuing shepherds. Behind the adoption – the reason why those parents so gladly received him – is a problem of infertility (a common theme in Greek tragedy). Finally, there is the family into which Oedipus was born.

In theory this is the exemplary nuclear family, a firstborn son for married parents, yet it is this family that is destroyed by the parents (or at least, the father) from the outset, when the baby is exposed to die.

If we tell it like this – rather than the way that Freud goes over the story – we notice two things. First, these odd families, if they resemble any historical moment, appear to resemble our own: when second families and step-parents are extremely common; when infertility is a major issue, and adoption, including transnational adoption, one possible remedy for that; when married couples (as Oedipus' birth parents were) may well seek *not* to become parents (the opposite issue from the problem of infertility), with contraception being a socially sanctioned means and abortion, not unlike exposure in the Oedipus myth, an extreme resort for the same purpose. Different cultures and historical periods have known all sorts of non-standard family groupings (adoption, for instance, was the common counterpart of illegitimacy in the mid-twentieth-century decades).

The second thing to notice in these alternative tellings of the Oedipus story is that the focus is on parents (including Oedipus as a parent) rather than on one individual from birth to downfall or on childhood experience. It's the opposite – or the flipside – of Freud's preoccuption with childhood and sexuality. Actually, there is no mention of erotic feelings anywhere in *Oedipus*, on the part of either adults or children (the children who figure are baby Oedipus – in the reconstruction of witnesses' evidence – and the present-day children of Jocasta and Oedipus). (The one exception to this is the moment when Jocasta, desperately seeking to reassure her husband about his anxieties, comes up with a fully Freudian theory – which Freud glee-fully cites: all men sleep with their mothers in their dreams. In other words, it's normal – and universal! – and it's not real, it's only fantasy – unlike what has happened in fact in the tragic reality of Jocasta's own world.) But the fear and the longing of two sets of prospective parents – fear in the case of Oedipus' birth parents, longing in the case of his adoptive ones – do feature in the play. So you could argue – and this is what I do in *Freudian Mythologies* – that *Oedipus* is a dramatisation of parental feelings much more than it's a dramatisation of childhood feelings. And that seems to speak now – more 'reception' – to a twenty-first-century preoccupation with parent-hood (new family forms, new biological and social ways of becoming a parent), which is itself something culturally new, in the way that the twentieth-century (overt) cultural preoccupation with sex and sexualities was new in its time.

In saying all this I'm making a recognisably Freudian move – in the sense that Freud went back to *Oedipus* for insights that would bolster his thinking about contemporary issues of identity. It's arguably one sign of a classic work (of literature *or* philosophy) that it has this capacity for yielding new interpretations in the light of culturally changing questions.

BAYOT: Having discussed Freud's contribution to the understanding of literature in relation to other cultural texts, I'd like us to focus at this point on the topic of a 'Freudian style of writing'. There is a tendency among literature students to label a specific body of writings with a 'Freudian tag' (as Lionel Trilling would call it). And usually, these are works attributed to writers who are associated with modernism – Virginia Woolf's *To the Lighthouse*, James Joyce's *Ulysses* or Marcel Proust's *In Search of Lost Time* (*A la recherche du temps perdu*). To what extent do you think this is a tenable and productive academic disposition? Is the Freudian label a fair representation of modernist writers like Woolf, to whom you've devoted much attention?

Another reason for my raising this question has to do with a personal anxiety: is there no way to talk about the mode of realism and naturalism alongside Freud on a level and in a manner that is philosophical (in contrast to perfunctory and reductionist readings of those texts, say, as instances of the condensation and displacement of desire)? Don't these modalities stand a chance of being recognised alongside Freud?

BOWLBY: I share your anxiety – or scepticism – about the way that certain writers, certain styles of writing, get co-opted as 'Freudian', while others are never considered in that light. And it would be interesting to do a comparative study of the kinship that develops between particular schools of criticism and their preferred authors or periods – their own special canons, if unacknowledged as such. I'm thinking for instance about the predilection of new historicism for Shakespeare, of American deconstruction for the Romantic poets (plus Hegel!), of Marxist criticism for realist novels. While it's easy to see the attractions in all these cases, the effect is often to reinforce certain patterns of talking about the given text, and to close them off from other critical possibilities. So it's as if you wouldn't *not* talk about a relation of Woolf or Joyce to psychoanalysis (something would seem to have been left out if you didn't); whereas it might seem odd – you'd have to make the case – to bring it in with regard to a realist novel by Elizabeth Gaskell or George Eliot. (Not nearly so true, though, for French realism: Balzac and Flaubert seem to lend themselves to psyschoanalytic readings as naturally as Proust or Marguerite Duras.)

In the examples you give of 'Freudian' novelists a crucial factor, of course, is that they are Freud's contemporaries. So the argument is often made, if not for direct influence, then for some kind of 'in the air' Zeitgeist community of literary-psychological spirit. Stream of consciousness *à la* Molly Bloom, at the end of *Ulysses*, looks or sounds a lot like the free association of the psychoanalytic patient; Oedipal patterns turn up everywhere, from the prohibiting father in the family triangle at the beginning of *To the Lighthouse* to the father-son dynamics of *Ulysses*. Or we could add the *unheimlich* haunted domesticity that figures in Theodor Fontane's (realist!) novel of 1895, *Effi Briest* – almost as though the author had himself – uncannily – written a novelistic version of the theory of the uncanny two decades before Freud's (which itself drew on an earlier German story, E.T.A. Hoffmann's *The Sandman*). And just keeping with your own classic examples: *A la recherche du temps perdu* and *To the Lighthouse* both involve quasi-Freudian concepts of a past whose meaning continues to change and to matter in the present.

But of course, Freud himself was the original practitioner of 'Freudian' literary criticism, and the foundational psychoanalytic literary text was not a contemporary novel but an ancient tragedy. Freudian motifs, if not Freudian styles, have been identified in the literatures of almost every period and culture. As far as the habitual separation of certain genres like realism or naturalism from psycho-analytic criticism goes – except, as you suggest, for the sort of reading which assumes they are following very simple psychological para-digms – I think that this may well be for the same reason that (English-language) realism and naturalism don't tend to be closely read. I don't mean they're not studied, but that they aren't usually studied phrase by phrase. Readers of realism tend to go for the large symptomatic historical interpretation (how this novel does or doesn't 'reflect' the world it's describing), whereas psychoanalytic readers tend to be the sort who want to take each text on its own – as a text – and to attend to its idiosyncrasies, much as Freud does in his ever more detailed interpretations of the text of a dream.

I'm making very schematic and broad-brush distinctions here, and of course the critical world doesn't straightforwardly divide into these two sorts of reader, any more than literary works divide into those that are close-read and those that aren't. And it's important to bear in mind, all the time, that the preliminary separations – between, say, realism and modernism, or between psychoanalytic and histor-ical criticism – often tend to blind us to some features of a given text, even though they may also be initially useful for pointing out some important differences of aim and method. In particular: modernist writers were often explicitly engaged in the project of representing reality; they took their distance from the card-carrying realists in that they thought that the realists had got reality wrong, not that they thought that literature was meant to do something else. Or: it's presumed that because psychoanalysis makes a claim for some universal feature of human psychology, it must be incompatible with an investigation of historical differences. Or in a milder form: it's presumed that psychoanalysis is only interested in what's constant and unchanging, whereas history is about the details and the differences – so the two would have little in common. But historical criticism can have everything to do with grand overarching themes, and continuities of storyline. And psychoanalytic criticism can be as much involved with minutiae as with large explanatory frames – which is what makes for the interest of Freud's case histories, testing a unique and locally anchored story against the general hypotheses it may suggest or confirm.

That again might bring us back to the question of psychoanalytically minded literature that is contemporary with Freud, this time in a very different mode from the modernism of Joyce or Proust. Arthur Conan Doyle's stories of Sherlock Holmes cases, published in the 1890s, have exactly the combination of detail, storytelling and interpretation that are found in Freudian case histories – those case histories that Freud was afraid might sound too much like short stories. (As does Holmes! In a cross mood he says to Watson, who writes up his cases: 'You have degraded what should have been a course of lectures into a series of tales.') As in Freud, a Holmes story will typically give you a scenario in which character suffering from a problem of some kind comes to the home of the analyst/detective for a consultation. He or she then tells their story to a sympathetic Holmes. Just as with the analytic injunction to say whatever comes into your head, Holmes's clients are given instructions not to leave anything out on the grounds that it's not important. Then when the story has been told, and supplementary questions asked, it turns out that Holmes, the experienced investigator, is able – from experience, he says – to make connections and inferences that ordinary beings – especially those in the thick of it, the ones who have come for help – are incapable of making on their own. As with Freud, it's a process that is at once logical (all the connections are shown to make sense), and at the same time verging on magical (only the maestro can pull it off; yet once it's done, it is seen as something that must have been true all the time).

BAYOT: This question is a corollary to the previous one. I think we have good reason to say that Freud was one of the most powerful influences on the 'death of the author' event in contemporary criticism. His concept of overdetermination, for instance, unshackled the signification of the text as well as the readers from the authority of the historical author. And my question is: in view of the decentring of Authority, is it possible to speak of a 'correct' reading of Freud?

BOWLBY: The last part of your question makes me think of the time (beginning in the 1970s) when Harold Bloom's take on Freud was central to poetry criticism. Bloom would have said that there are no correct readings, only strong readings; and strong readings get us to see the text that they 'read' in a different way: they change it retroactively, which is to say that they make it subordinate now to the new version which is the reading. Bloom was talking about poems rather than criticism (a new poem as a strong reading of an existing one), and about an unconscoius process – an unconscious Oedipal battle between male poets, in fact, whereby the new poet is necessarily seeking to supersede the previous one, who thereby becomes just his precursor.

But the point about powerful readings – readings that appear to change the object of interpretation, to show it in a new light – holds good, I think, for a thinker like Freud whose work has prompted all kinds of divergent emphases over the past century. Along with Marx, he is one of those named by Foucault as a 'founder of discursivity', meaning that his œuvre has given rise to a continuing body of scholarship that is dedicated to interpreting and reinterpreting it – with no end in sight, no horizon of arrival at a final 'true' reading. At the same time, there *is* a more or less stable œuvre, so that each new reading can claim to have found what is really there in the source.

When I say more or less stable, I'm thinking about Foucault's famous example of the problem of Nietzsche's laundry lists: would something like that form part of an œuvre? They are unpublished (and not written for publication), and they have nothing to do, ostensibly, with the concerns of his philosophy. But they are words written by Nietzsche! Foucault is making the point that even if ostensibly we throw out the figure of 'the author', replacing him (or her) with the work, there will still be criteria operating, implicitly or explicitly, to determine what is and is not to count as part of an œuvre – and thus there is still, in effect, a model of individual authorship.

Leaving aside the establishment of an authorial œuvre, I don't think there can ever be correct readings in the sense of readings once and for all, which will remain fixed forever; in any case, no reading is itself fixed in its meaning: there are readings of readings too . . . (That's not to say, though, that there can't be mistaken readings involving factual mistakes or straightforward misunderstandings.) It is always in principle open to a new reader to come along and claim significance for some hitherto disregarded fragment of an author's work, just as it's also possible – as Freud did with Sophocles' *Oedipus* – to say no, this is not about X (about an inexorable destiny and a particular mythical hero), but instead it's about Y (about everyone's forbidden infantile longings). Freud's own turning, or overturning, of the prevailing ideas about Greek tragedy, and about human psychology, was momentous. But not all new readings, of course, are like that, and there's another way that I find Foucault's thoughts about founders of discursivity (clunky phrase though it is) to be very suggestive. There are certain writers – not just philosophers, as in Foucault's model, but also literary writers – whose cultural stature is such that they become available for citation to anyone (not just to specialists) in relation to any subject at issue. Their position is so well established that they can be taken as an authority on anything, with passages found to support the present writer's point. I became interested in this phenomenon in relation to Virginia Woolf, when I was first writing about her in the 1980s. At that point, she was just in the process of acquiring this kind of position. I was struck by how, like the Bible, her writings were taken to have something to say about all kinds of diverse contemporary questions, and how – also like the Bible – she was often cited in support of quite contradictory views, depending on the chocie of quotation.

I don't mean to suggest that this is straightforwardly a bad thing. The richness of some writers is that they do offer infinitely malleable matter for thinking with; a new question we bring when we read them may indeed be illuminated by what we find there, or by what we are then able to see differently – because the question is new – in what we have read many times before. Freud is now undoubtedly a writer of this order – as perhaps Sophocles was for him, both personally and culturally. If you cite as a precursor of your new theory a play by Sophocles, who comes with a whole tradition of respectful reading behind him, then you will gain a different sort of serious attention than if you cite, let's say, Sir Arthur Conan Doyle. (Freud worried, as I've said, that his case histories might sound like short stories, but he didn't worry that they might sound like Greek tragedies!)

I think too – and this is pertinent to your question about authority – that it's not necessarily a negative quality if contradictory views can be found in the works of one writer – which is true of both Woolf

and Freud. Why should we imagine that an author should have
known what it was that they thought from the beginning, and never
swerved from that view from the beginning of their writing life to the
end? For a 'creative' writer, at least in the modern period, it is taken
for granted that continuing experimentation and development
should be one aim, and Woolf, for instance, certainly saw that as
essential to what she was doing in her literary works: each of her
novels was to be a different kind of thing from the last one. But in
non-fictional writing, the opposite assumption is regularly made –
and Woolf is not necessarily admired for the marked differences of
her thinking within and between her essays about culture and literature. (Here I have in mind especially the many different and often
incompatible views put forward in *A Room of One's Own*, and also
the many kinds of contrast in the thinking and style of Woolf's two
extended feminist texts, written ten years apart, *A Room of One's
Own* and *Three Guineas*.)

With Freud, these issues are acute in a different way, for many
reasons. To begin with, he was developing what turned out to be a
whole new field of thought and practice. He wasn't only writing what
would end up (in English) as the twenty-four volumes of the Standard
Edition (counting the index!), but his work gave rise to a new kind
of patient–doctor interaction, the therapeutic session, and to professional organisations on a national and international scale. And he
was writing and thinking across a period of half a century,
responding all the time to new challenges both from within the
emerging field of practice and thought, and from the political and
cultural events of the times he was living through. There was also an
astonishing diversity in the kinds of topic he addressed, and in the
styles of writing he adopted: from informal but didactic 'introductory lecture', to detailed individual case history, to general cultural
critique, to quasi-philosophical speculation. For all these reasons, it
would be difficult to imagine how there could be anything like a
single 'reading' of Freud, any more than there is one Freud with one
consistent or correctly identitiable line of thought.

As far as the death of the author goes, and Freud's part in the
phenomenon – well, I think that that's very much bound up with your
question about correct readings of Freud, because you could equally
well argue the opposite. I mean that you could say that Freud gave a
new lease of life, as it were, to biographical criticism, by proposing
new ways of thinking about the relationship of a work to its author:
about how and why, in terms of their own experiences, someone
might have come to produce a work like this, or about what perhaps
unconscious purposes the producing of art might be seeking to fulfil

for the person, by making something out of otherwise hidden or unacknowledged wishes and disturbances. (I'm thinking here partly of Freud's strange study of the life and work of Leonardo.) But from the other direction, the one you are starting from, it can be argued that Freud takes away the sense of individual artistic intentionality. A work of art become symptomatic not of a personal pathology – because that cannot be known from the evidence, and because an artwork is something other than a confession – but of broader psychological tendencies that may satisfy or intrigue or disturb readers or spectators in ways that are presumably comparable to the feelings in the artist that sparked it. This essentially authorless model would apply to what Freud says (in *The Interpretation of Dreams*) about *Oedipus the King*. He does not mention the likelihood of anything distinctive in Sophocles' personality, but implicitly puts him in the same position as the audience, extended to 'all of us': if we all react the same way to this play, it must be that we all felt in child-hood the feelings that Oedipus acts out. In relation to a very different kind of literature, narratives that show the fulfilment of happy fantasies of omnipotence, Freud makes the same assumption about the generality of both the writer's and the audience's likely desires.

When it comes to the literary-critical take-up of Barthes's idea of the death of the author, there are different things to say. Barthes's primary target is the idea that a piece of writing can be explained by the life of its author, or some aspect of that. In Britain, where biography is a very successful publishing genre, and biographies of authors are widely reviewed and read, this is if anything more obvious as an issue than in France – only think of the number of biographical books about Virginia Woolf and other members of the Bloomsbury group (to the point that it is not uncommon to be addicted to Bloomsbury lives without ever having felt an urge to read a word of Woolf or any of the rest of them). Second, the 'death of the author' phenomenon came at a point when theory was in the air, and when it provided a rallying cry for doing away with the kind of staid old studies which looked at the 'life and times' of an author, his (usually his) 'background', both individual and social, as if it could offer a full account of the work. If this or that work could be entirely explained by its historical context or its author's life or genius, or a combination of both, so that each – the work and its source – rein-forced and reflected the other, then there was nothing distinctive about the work as such: you might as well just stick with the biography or the history. Related to this was a democratic point about works in general: that their importance was not so much in who had authored them, as in what could be made of them; also, each person might find in them something distinctive of their own. The other much-cited essay of Barthes' in this context was 'From Work to Text' ('La mythologie aujourd'hui') which, like 'The Death of the Author', stressed a new role for readers in actively producing the meaning they took from the text – rather than that meaning being something that was already there in it, once and for all. And third, that 'life and times' model was generally inseparable from a notion of conscious plan: writers knew what it was that they wanted to do, and went ahead and did it. This ruled out any thought of intentions or results that might be other than conscious, or not in the artist's complete control.

I was very much a product of the then relatively new critical climate in which authors were out, and only the text was permitted as an object of study or curiosity. I remember feeling slightly nervous when I wrote in my book on Woolf that her mother had died when she was only thirteen: this probably shouldn't be included, I thought, because, after all, wasn't it too sentimental (we were callous in those days!), and wasn't it coming close to the circularities of biographical explanation that my book was also meant to be criticising? And anyway, even if it might be relevant on semi-psychoanalytic grounds that a woman who had lost her mother in adolescence might feel compelled to write about mothers (compelled not to, you could just as well argue!) – still, there was that logical refutation of explanations by social background, which could equally well be applied to life events. So, just as – in Marxist criticism – it was clear that while Sartre might have been a petit bourgeois, not all those of petit bourgeois origin turned into a Sartre, so too – in terms of psychobiography – not all girls who lost their mothers at an early age became a Virginia Woolf. (There were also, in Woolf's time still, many more early deaths of mothers in Britain than there were by the end of the twenieth century.)

Looking back, it now seems odd that there should have been such a wholesale rejection of biographical thinking – to the point that it was almost an article of faith, something you'd never have questioned – among people who were also taking psychoanalysis seriously. After all, psychoanalysis is all about the distinctiveness of individual life-paths and their outcomes, and it has its own theories about how one should and should not understand the relationship between a personal past and its present manifestations. Freud often says that you can explain in a given case how it is that this particular state of things came about. You can track back through all the different strands that turn out to have led to it. But you cannot do this the other way round and read off, from any particular point in the back-story, that what did in fact happen was bound to. No destiny there! but instead, a strong theory of the importance and value of a certain kind of biographical explanation. Related to this is the concept of overdetermination, which Freud elaborates in connection with dreams. There is not just one single cause which then gives rise to a result; rather, a number of disparate elements have all combined in the production of the particular dream or particular action which now calls for interpretation.

For whatever reason, I now find that authors' lives are the first not the last thing I'm consciously interested in. This is probably to do with my own time of life – but I also think that the critical tide has turned back now from the prohibition on the life as a legitimate topic of curiosity. For one thing, there has been a surge in the theoretical and historical study of life-writing of all kinds, both biographical and autobiographical. Speaking personally – if not autobiographically – I've always been fascinated by diaries, both the kind that record or reflect on what's going on, and the more practical kind in which future events or appointments are 'pencilled in'. Both sorts are interesting for the way they involve, at close quarters, an intersection between personal and social histories, and for what they reveal about daily lives. What counts, for any given diarist, as worth noting as a prospective or completed event? What thoughts (in the first sort of diary) are put into written words, and why? The journal is essentially a modern mode, encompassing many variations of implied address, all the way from the public and documentary at one end to the private and confessional at the other. In its more personal forms in particular, the diary has been much studied – and has also given rise to fictional variations, from the philosophical (Kierkegaard's *Diary of a Seducer*) to the parodic (George and Weedon Grossmith's *Diary of a Nobody*).

The appointments diary, on the other hand, has had little attention. It's not an obvious place to look if what you're seeking is intimate revelations about a person, and its lack of detail means that it doesn't seem to offer much in the way of historical evidence either: at best, it might confirm the likelihood of a person's presence at some event. But what this kind of diary does show is the interaction of one user with a given template, itself historically interesting as conventions change for what counts as the normal way to display the days in view. Here an ongoing life is framed within a surrounding time-culture presented as weeks, with a double page of separate days for pre-notation. The marks of individual difference appear by the choice of what prospective events to put down, and by the many possible ways of noting them – from a pencilled diagonal scrawl of a friend's first name across the diary day's ruled lines, to a neat horizontal record in violet ink, confirming and covering a pencilled version after the event. (These two practices, oh so beautifully gendered, are those of Virginia and Leonard Woolf – respectively; I've been looking at their diaries recently in the archives at Sussex University, which has all of Leonard's and has just acquired some of Virginia's.)

BAYOT: As a scholar known for your Freudian affiliation, there's definitely a lot of history in your work and this was already evident in your first book, *Just Looking: Consumer Culture in Dreiser, Gissing and Zola* (1985; 2009). Can we say that your interest in history has something to do with seeking to demythologise the perception of Freud's ideas as ahistorical? Were you in any way reacting to trends and strands of Freudian criticism that claim to be ahistorical?

BOWLBY: This question follows on nicely from where we ended up with the previous one, in that it was while I was working on the history of nineteenth-century department stores – which is part of what lay behind *Just Looking* – that I came across large-format diaries, the size of what would today be called desk diaries, that had been specially created for customers of the Paris Bon Marché store. Complete with full-page cartoons and articles of would-be general interest, and with all the expected factual components of a French ladies' diary, from sunsets to saints' days, these *agendas* also incorporated information about shopping events – special sales and promotions, attached to particular months of the year. The effect was not only to draw the customer's attention to these, but also to naturalise an annual pattern of consumptiom designed to take its place alongside the established cycle of the Church's festivals. Not the least interest of these diaries is their role as a brilliantly inventive marketing device. We can also look at them in terms of the presentation of a new way for women to imagine their daily and longer-term lives, as shopping is incorporated as a regular outing: more like a leisure activity than a daily task, but still something you would plan to do.

When I was working towards *Just Looking* I became fascinated by the minutiae of the nineteenth-century shopping revolution, which was one beginning of the consumer culture that is still with us. It was about a new way for women to spend their days (by doing this thing called going shopping), and it was also about the creation of a particular kind of subjective orientation, whereby the shopper was someone who was presumed to be perpetually in search of something new – which was what was then offered to her at the store, and within its advertisements. There was a very deliberate appeal made to what were taken to be underlying feminine desires or vulnerabilities. So I was interested in this commercial process of imagining an endlessly wishful female subjectivity, and enlisting a feminine subject who would be adapted to the new stores, while at the same time I was interested in the psychoanalytic understanding of subjectivity, including female subjectivity, which was beginning not long after this (at the end of the nineteenth century), but without any overt reference to contemporary historical conditions. There seemed to be some sort of parallel between on the one hand the Freudian model of fundamentally insatiable human desires, and on the other the development of a shopping institution designed to pandere to and exploit exactly those tendencies.

It is easy – too easy – to set up Freud as equivalent to the department store entrepreneur in their shared understanding, if not creation, of a certain image of womanhood; or to look at shopping and psychoanalysis as comparable services: retail therapy! They aren't the same thing and they weren't the same thing; but that doesn't mean that there is no relationship between psychoanalytic thinking and the culture within which it grew (and reciprocally). There is a tendency, which perhaps you're referring to when you speak of a would-be ahistorical version of psychoanalytic criticism, to dismiss as reductive any attempt to connect psychoanalytic thought with its times. This is particularly true, I think, in relation to women. The whole Freudian mythology of sexual difference appears, in the way that Freud elaborates it, to depend on something that goes beyond culture – on a primordial differentiation of the sexes, and a subordination of one to the other. I feel it ought to be possible to think about this problematic in other than either-or terms. It does seem to me that it's still true – experientially as well as in other ways – that sexual difference matters in human identity more than any other (and is still posited and experienced in essentially binary terms, though that is being challenged more and more). At the same time, the changes (in some western societies) in the normal subjective possibilities for women have been remarkable: the differences in the available life-choices and the typical daily lives of men and women are far less than they were in Freud's time.

I can't really claim, though, as your question invites me to, that my interest in history stemmed first from a rejection of non-historical criticism in psychoanalysi. It was more that I've always been interested in history – above all in social history and the history of everyday life. This kind of history has a natural affinity with feminism – because most women, throughout history, have lived the kinds of lives that did not involve them in the public events of political history. It's also related to the realist literature of the nineteenth century, which took ordinary life, in particular the domestic life of women, as one of its themes: for the first time bringing it into the field of literary representation. The feminist history that began in the late twentieth century has explored the previously unknown or neglected history of women, but novels had been doing this too for some time. And the whole enterprise – whether as history or as fiction – brings in questions of relative value. Women's histories and daily, domestic life have suffered, as though by definition, from the association of triviality, with the implication that this is not what really matters, not where the history that counts is happening.

And to bring this back to Freud again, it can also be said that from this point of view, the invention of psychoanalysis was all about paying attention to the small things of women's lives: their longings, their sufferings, their complaints. The method of psychotherapy was discovered through Freud and Josef Breuer listening (for hours) to what their women patients said, and finding that changes occurred through the process itself of speaking and response – what one patient, 'Anna O.', famously called her 'talking cure'.

Also, remember that questions of history – on many different scales – are present throughout Freud's oeuvre. There are the large cultural histories, part myth, part anthropology, that appear in works like *Totem and Taboo*, *Civilisation and its Discontents*, or *The Future of an Illusion*. Sometimes these all-encompassing collective stories are said to repeat themselves – to be recapitulated – at the individual level, in accordance with one of the post-Darwinian models of development in Freud's time. An unusually detailed example of this is the suggestion (in Freud's later papers on femininity) that the recent discovery (in psychoanalytic research) of girls' early attachment to their mothers can be likened to another discovery in a very different field: of the Minoan-Mycenæan culture preceding and underlying that of classical Greece. There's a teleology as well as an archaeology to such analogies: this first female bond, it's being suggested, is prior to the culture recognised by all; it is destined to be superseded and forgotten.

There is also the presumption that a patient's personal 'history' is vital to an understanding of their present situation; and that it is a history which is largely forgotten and unconscious, and therefore in need of unearthing or reconstruction (the archaeological analogy is a regular one for Freud). That a knowledge or recognition of this past can be liberating for the person is one of the tenets of Freudian theory. Much of the controversy over psychoanalysis in recent decades has centred on aspects of this, with the accusation not so much that psychoanalysis is ahistorical as that it finds a history where there is none – finds a spurious history of childhood fantasy or abuse, for instance. The difficulty (as well as the innovation) is that Freudian history, at this individual level, is not sequential; instead it is based on a model of deferred effect. Initially, an event or experience might have had little or no conscious signficance: because it was too much to take, and was fended off, or because the person was not at a stage of development to understand it. The postulation of a primary precipitating event may then become partly a matter of speculation or reconstitution. The clearest and most famous example of such tracking back and retroactive hypothesis is in the 'Wolf Man' case history, in which Freud also lays out some of the hazards and challenges of this very peculiar new method of historical research and exposition.

BAYOT: After your discussion of the dimension of history in the theory and praxis of Freud and psychoanalytic criticism, I'd like to ask what's your view on the relation of psychoanalysis and ethics? Is it acceptable to speak of an ethical dimension of psychoanalytic criticism? To complicate the matter: how would you characterise the relation of psychoanalytic criticism to ethics, literature and politics?

BOWLBY: Yes, that's complicated all right! I find it difficult to know how to respond, because it's my sense that the categories of the question – starting with ethics, but also the other two – have moved around a lot in the debates of the past few decades, with many fluctuations in and arguments over both their individual importance and their relationship to one another. Ethics has come to be a prominent term in the interdisciplinary humanities, and to some extent – I would hazard – it has taken over the role that previously belonged to politics. In the British context, at least, it used to feel obligatory when you were doing literary or psychoanalytical criticism, or some combination of them, to make a connection with politics – with a politics that had to do with the possibilities of social change or the conditions of social oppression. Now, the connection would tend to be more to ethics and individuals. In one obvious way, that's a framework much better suited to psychoanalysis, whose model for change was primarily at the level of the individual: person by person, perhaps you could change the world. But it's also the case that increasingly, politics in the public sense has become preoccupied with issues that previously (if considered at all) would have come under a more private remit of personal behaviours and attitudes: issues like racism or sexual harrassment or sexism.

JEREMY DE CHAVEZ: It is very apparent from your work that you pay close attention to the vicissitudes in ideas as they traverse temporal, spatial and cultural borders. So, my questions will take advantage of your sensitivity for translations and transformations. First, I would like to ask if in your estimation there is a meaningful difference between window shopping in a mall and browsing on eBay? Between lining up at the checkout counter in IKEA and simply clicking on the checkout button on amazon.com? How does the consumer who not only goes shopping with Freud, but also goes internet shopping with him, revise your initial pronouncements about modern subjectivities?

RACHEL BOWLBY: Well, the first thing to say may be that many of Freud's bourgeois contemporaries in Europe (and its colonies) and America were already doing what now look like early versions of internet shopping. A lot of the things they bought – both daily food provisions and more occasional purchases – were delivered by the store, rather than carried home by the customer. Also, there was a lot of mail order buying. In the United States, catalogues such as Sears, Roebuck and Montgomery Ward were browsed in the home, in the same way that online shopping happens now. Other countries had their own types of home shopping; in the UK, in some places, there is still a 'book' (an illustrated catalogue) that you browse and choose from, and then put out on your doorstep for collection by the local agent with your order. So then, as now, the home might take over the functions of the shop – might become, in effect, a place of shopping: the display of goods to choose from, the moment of making the selection.

The middle and later decades of the twentieth century were perhaps the aberration, from this point of view – even though what happened then, because it's what we grew up with, probably feels to us like a long-term nature that internet shopping has changed. In the period before the internet most shopping, as opposed to just some shopping, was done by customers in person, in the store. You went to the shop, whether local or at a distance; you picked up what you wanted; you took the stuff home yourself. So in some ways, shopping has come full circle. Online browsing and ordering from the comfort (or tedium) of your own space is much like what often used to happen, before the attractions of city shopping, or the practicalities of supermarket shopping, drew the shoppers out.

But of course it is also true that in many ways, everything has changed for the person sat in front of their laptop or tablet, compared to any of the previous shopper incarnations: the weekly customer at a local market, say; or the one who first set foot in a department store in the 1880s; or more recently the one who would have been driving to the supermarket two or three times a week by the 1950s (definitely an American, that one: supermarkets didn't arrive in Europe until later). Not the least change is that the shopping person setting finger online is now of indeterminate gender, whereas previously – whether in the enjoying mode of 'going shopping', or in the 'job done' mode of 'doing the shopping' – shoppers were almost always women. The duties and pleasures and boredoms of shopping have become men's as well.

And for this indeterminate new kind of shopper, the place of shopping is less clearly defined as well. It's not so much that present-day clicking is like, or not like, standing in front of a window or standing in line, as that those other experiences aren't themselves so clearly differentiated in time or space. You can be shopping while on your computer; but you can also be on your computer, or more likely, your phone or your iPad, while you are in the store (I mean the actual one not the virtual one).

DE CHAVEZ: Marx is curiously absent in your reflections on consumerism. Is this a strategic repression or an unconscious omission? If the former, why strategically leave Marx out? Or if the latter, what could his absence be a symptom of?

BOWLBY: Well, I think that Marx is present in my first book, *Just Looking*. But you're right, his absence thereafter is odd. The first explanation – or rationalisation – that occurs to me is simply a matter of the intellectual Zeitgeist. Critical thinking about social history or literary history is no longer necessarily or predominantly Marxist. But when I was first working on consumer culture, Marx, and arguments within Marxist cultural theory, were still a baseline point of reference for anyone looking at marginal or different aspects of social history. And since I was thinking specifically about the history of consumer culture, then it seemed self-evident that there was a connection between Marx's theorisation of commodity capitalism in the middle of the nineteenth century, and the rise of shopping as a mainstream activity shortly after the same period. But this is a social and economic phenomenon that Marx doesn't actually mention – and when I came to look at the history of shopping in more technical detail, on its own terms, it didn't occur to me to make overt connections with Marxist readings of history (which also ignored it). For one thing, it was so obvious that what you were looking at was straightforwardly a form of capitalist expansion, big stores taking over little ones, creative innovation in the interests of profit, and so on.

A second issue was that shopping history is very much bound up with women, both as consumers and as workers (and rarely, but sometimes, as shop owners or entrepreneurs). But the feminist history that developed in the 1970s found it difficult or impossible to reconcile the specific questions and findings relating to women's lives with a Marxist approach in which class – and class struggle – took structural precedence over gender as a mode of analysis. Also, in straight Marxist terms shops and shopping were just part of the cultural superstructure (the froth and tinsel!) as compared with the underlying economic base of production. And this duality and hierarchisation was of course bound up with the difficulty of bringing gender into the analytical picture, since these theoretically secondary places were very much women's domain.

There's perhaps a particular reason, beyond the cultural Zeitgeist, why the Marxist reference dropped out in my writing about the history of shopping. I became interested in the field known as consumer psychology that had developed in the first half of the twentieth century. Although often backed by funding from manufacturers and advertising agencies, consumer psychology was a serious research enterprise in American universities, and there were versions of it going on in advertising agencies, and in other parts of the world as well. The point of the work was generally to find out how minds work, how people think, so as to be able to make informed guesses about what would make them want to buy this or that product – and to that extent the enterprise can be understood in cynically and straightforwardly capitalist terms. But at the same time, a lot of the writing is nuanced and complex and what's interesting in another way – if you look at this material as a branch of psychology rather than as marketing history – is that human psychology comes to be seen as the psychology of a potential consumer, of someone who might be persuaded to buy. What do people want? What will give them a sense of satisfaction? These are old philosophical and political questions, now given a distinctive new spin in a modern context in which consumption can appear as the exemplary human situation. As it is, in fact, in an influential book from a very different disciplinary domain, Claude Lévi-Strauss's *Elementary Structures of Kinship* (*Structures élémentaires de la parenté*, 1949), in which the paradigm situation for the mak-

ing of a human bond – informally, for the time being, not for life –
is two strangers across a tavern table, who rather than keep to their
own allocations, offer each other the wine they have each bought as
part of their set meal.

These pre-war consumer psychologists put forward all sorts of
ways of imagining likely and unlikely consumerly desires and practices. But in a great deal of later cultural criticism, far from being a
figure of complexity and historical variability, the consumer is
deployed instead to stand for the simple and simplistic fool. This
dumb consumer is a foil for the more thinking individual who is the
serious reader of serious literature or philosophy. The consumer
passively consumes, and that's that. If the category is given any identifying characteristics, they will usually be feminine: no image better
encapsulates the picture of idiotic susceptibility than that of the mid-
twentieth-century housewife wheeling her trolley along the aisles of
the supermarket, occasionally reaching out a hand for the packet of
washing powder whose primary colours she can't resist. By that time
the advertising philosophy was itself much more crude than the
interwar versions, and the (supposed) mindlessness of the shopper
was the logical counterpart of the psychological 'techniques' that
were meant to manipulate (persuade) her with perfect precision. The
prolific criticism of 'mass' marketing and 'mass' consumption, often
broadly Marxist or literary in origin, itself echoed and thereby
endorsed this simplifying would-be scientific psychology, because it
took it for granted that the techniques of persuasion succeeded: that
they had got the psychology right. These arguments did not say that
people were not, in reality, a bundle of reflexes or repressions
(according to whether the theory applied was basic Pavlov or basic
Freud) – but that it was morally wrong to exploit the fact that they
were by manipulating their desires.

My interest in these turns of the early and middle twentieth
century were very much influenced by what was going on in the
1980s in the UK. One of the effects of Prime Minister Margaret
Thatcher's form of conservatism was to create a newly positive image
of the consumer, who now became the exemplary, not the vilified
figure of political argument. As all sorts of previously public services
came to be privatised, or partially privatised, so the consumer, ration-
ally making his choices and acting in his own best interests, became
the new paradigm of the modern citizen. This new consumer-citizen
was the antithesis of the old one. Exit the dumb, unthinking woman,
at the mercy of every buying suggestion blowing her way – and enter,
instead, the rounded rationality of the new man (or woman) who
rightly seeks out the best deal in electricity or university education or

hospital treatment, just as he or she would when purchasing a vacuum cleaner or a car.

A word about that 'university education' and the rest. At that point – the 1980s – university education was still free in the UK, and there was even a 'maintenance' grant for every student. But already the prospective student – or the student's parent – was being ideologically groomed, as it were, for the role that would soon be theirs, by the fostering of a new attitude of consumerly choice and rights in relation to what was not yet called 'the student experience'. The same sort of persona was being cultivated in relation to (free) health services, not to mention the many services (like electricity or gas or the telephone) that really were moving away from state-run provision to be placed, officially, in the category of private profit-making enterprises. This development had two results in particular. On the one hand, it had the effect of naturalising the consumerly model in relation to practices and services that had previously had nothing to do with it – so that when, in fact, new fields did become marketised, that seemed like an obvious or even a necessary move. It was as if the students (and parents) had already been trained up as consumers of education ready for their taking on that role in the new situation in which they really were paying for what they got. On the other hand, it had the effect of making all the different services (or 'products') that were now opened up to competition and consumption appear to be directly comparable to one another because they were all placed within the same (commodity) framework.

And I say vacuum cleaner or car for the hypothetical purchases of the rational consumer, because those kinds of items – the serious investment in an effective machine – had always lent themselves to association with the level-headedly sensible consumer who could appear as the counterpart of the flighty female. Such a character had his (and her) official beginnings in the various consumer rights organisations that gained influence – counter-influence – over the course of the century. They pressed for trading standards and clear labelling, and in the case of the American organisation, founded in the 1920s, they also pressed for better working conditions and pay for the producers of consumer goods.

DE CHAVEZ: Psychoanalysis at a particular historical moment seemed to me to live a double life, simultaneously claiming (perhaps opportunistically) the credibility of science and the grandeur of myth. However, now that there appears to be a consensus that psychoanalysis is not a genuinely scientific theory, and many of Freud's radical ideas have been rendered impotent by its comfortable integration into the banality of everyday life, psychoanalysis seems to have neither scientific credibility nor mythical grandeur. But what strikes me as fascinating in your work is that you seem to suggest that psychoanalysis may establish its credibility precisely through myth, which may enable it to more fruitfully map out the coordinates of new subjectivities, respond to the changing structure of families, and (perhaps consequently) properly diagnose new psychic afflictions. What are the ways in which Freudian mythologies may revitalise Freudian theory?

BOWLBY: I'm taken with your image of psychoanalysis leading a double life – it fits beautifully with the theory (or is it the mythology?) of the unconscious as (from this perspective) the terrible timeless twin to the ordinary everyday person. But a twin whose co-existence could perhaps only have been divined or detected at the historical moment, at the end of the nineteenth century, when doubles and double lives of every kind were all the rage in popular fiction, from Stevenson's Jekyll and Hyde to the Sherlock Holmes stories.

I think though that there's a tension in Freud's own writing about the relative interest or significance to be granted to everyday life. Reading *The Interpretation of Dreams*, you get the impression that daily life really is seen as banal, to use your word, in comparison with the deep dark truths that lurk unconsciously, and for which the minor events of the previous day – what Freud calls the 'day's residues' – provide a kind of cover story to make the dream present-able to the sleeping self. These day's residues are quite simply a load of rubbish, in the role that Freud ascribes to them: they are waste material (there's a whole pile-up of dismissive trash synonyms for them). They have no value in themselves; they are of merely passing interest and temporary dream-use on their way to oblivion.

On the other hand, there's the Freud who took everyday life more seriously than anyone had before: what else is *The Psychopathology of Everyday Life* than an argument for the potential significance of every seemingly tiny gesture or incident or utterance? And also for the existence of minor forms of madness that are part of everyone's life, so that madness cannot be hived off into a world of its own? The Freudian slip is probably the best example of both these features. And what's more, everyone gets it. Like so much in psychoanalytic theory, the slip is counter-intuitive, or at least contrary to common assump-tions of agency and intention: it's a theory of saying precisely what you meant not to say. But its very acceptance – its popularity, even ('Freudian slip!' as a standard tease – an everyday tease – ) is an acknowledgement that in some things, no question, Freud picked up on and analysed a psychological phenomenon that no one had spelled out so clearly before, and that appeared irrefutably right once described in this way.

I don't think I'd want to make the separation between theory and mythology that your question suggests. These are words that Freud sometimes uses more or less synonymously, especially when he is thinking about children's search for sexual knowledge – or sexual 'enlightenment', as he half-jokingly calls it, making the deliberate link with grown-up and grander projects. Also, with his intensive secondary school education in Latin and Greek, Freud was a keen follower of contemporary arguments in a then new field (it still has a contemporary ring to it) called comparative mythology. Basically the question there was about whether all cultures develop in the same way, with virtually the same fundamental myths and their later modifications appearing at different stages of development; or whether it is rather that different cultures have different stories, different explanatory myths, so that you can't read off their developmental moment by knowing what kind of tales they tell – and conversely, you can't infer all their stories from their historical stage. It's a nineteenth-century version of the twentieth-century anthropological argument of structuralism versus functionalism (either all cultures are comparable or each one is *sui generis*); and for Freud – who is very much on the universalising, proto-structuralist side – you can see how it translates into his account of the child's progression through several preordained stages of knowledge-seeking and theory-making. Freud calls these successive moments the oral phase, the anal phase, and the genital phase – and later (in the 1920s), he adds on a phallic phase (common to both sexes) to bolster his own final version of the conflicted, masculinity-centred path to adult sexual identities. He speaks of children as theorists and mythmakers, who in effect passes through all the phases of cultural development, from primitive to 'civilized' (and the scare-quotes are sometimes Freud's own), on their own individual journeys to adulthood.

This account of childhood development is one of the ways – I would argue – that Freud brings together science and myth, rather than setting them up as two distinct orders. All knowledge, all research, develops out of this juvenile curiosity that Freud explicitly says is the prototype of later scientific or philosophical work. Conversely, there is no science or philosophy that is not marked by all the particular drawbacks and advantages of the researcher's reasons, conscious and unconscious, for doing it.

I'd suggest as well that Freud partly goes against mythic 'grandeur' precisely because he brings myth down to the level of everyone's own story: each separate child will find out or create for themselves the standard theories of sexuality and identity that go with the particular stage of their development. The supreme example of Freud both levelling and at the same time recreating – or making use of – an established mythical grandeur, is what he does with the Oedipus myth. In his extraordinary new version, Oedipus is not the unique hero or anti-hero of an ancient story, but the name for a universal predicament, that of always harbouring or having had unspeakable childish urges. As Freud memorably puts it in *The Interpretation of Dreams* (chapter V, section D): 'It is the fate of all of us, perhaps, to direct our first sexual impulse towards our mother and our first hatred and our first murderous wish against our father.' We are now so used to the Oedipus complex – to hearing the phrase, at least – that the scandal of Freud's original claim, at the turn of the twentieth century, has faded. It's as if Freud, not Sophocles, were the primary author of Oedipus, and that's the measure of the way that the idea has made its way into cultural consciousness as a powerful myth of its own.

Freud took Oedipus the unique and uniquely afflicted hero, and reinvented him as a new kind of everyman (or everyboy): as a small child smitten with mother-love and father-hate, stuck in the triangle – yes, the 'Oedipal' triangle – that we have come to see as a part of family nature. But it could be said that the little boy whose primary world consists of his mother and father, on whom all his passions converge, is really only a twentieth-century (western) child – or to be even more specific, a mid-twentieth-century western child. At the time of Freud's writing *The Interpretation of Dreams*, in the late 1890s, families were still for the most part quite numerous, with many children being born (and not all surviving). Step-parenthood was extremely common, as a result of remarriages following a birth parent's death. But by the middle of the twentieth century, most middle-class families came quite close to the nuclear model that is implicit in Freud's hypothesis: there were few children (thanks to the general availability by then of reliable contraception for married couples); there were the two parents, living together to a fine old age (not much early mortality and not many divorces yet); and there was probably no one else living in the same household apart from the parents and children (no grandparents, no unmarried family members, no resident servants).

This pared-down minimal mid-century pattern – the one that is generally imagined as some sort of transhistorical if not transcultural norm – has now, in twenty-first-century reality, been superseded by any number of new modes, by choice and by happenstance: these range from gay parenthood, to single parenthood, both chosen and unchosen, to step-parenthood, now mainly because of the frequency of parental separation and remarriage. But it is still regularly held up as the standard of family life, as though since time immemorial. As well as the social changes, there are all the new ways of getting to be a parent biologically, through *in vitro* fertilization and other reproductive technologies: so even 'the facts of life', what Freud's cynical child researcher has decidedly not been told by its parents or teachers, have changed.

In particular: the reproductive differences between men and women have diminished. Freud emphasised the symbolic distinction enshrined in the Latin legal tag of *pater semper incertus est*: 'the father is always uncertain' whereas, implicitly, the mother is not. That is to say, you can never prove that a given man is or is not someone's father, but a woman is visibly the mother of a baby because she is seen to be pregnant and gives birth. Now, though, fatherhood is ascertainable, through DNA testing. And motherhood is no longer so sure, because IVF makes it possible for the two functions of egg provision and pregnancy to be divided between two different female bodies: making two biological mothers.

This mutation of parenthood, with mother and father no longer diametrically opposed, goes together with the social changes which have so dramatically reduced the practical differences between men and women over the course of the past century. Today, in most western cultures, it is taken for granted, for instance, that both parents will have paid jobs (rather than the father being the breadwinner and the mother staying at home, another model which in practice applied mainly just to the mid-twentieth century); and it is also, increasingly, assumed that men will to some degree share in the hands-on and time-taking activities of parenthood (Prince William changing baby George's nappies!).

As I've suggested, family set-ups prior to this mid-twentieth-century moment of the nuclear family were just as variable in their own ways as the ones we now think of as characteristic of a new complexity. What seems curious now, in light of the changes in family forms that we've seen across the past few decades, is Freud's focus on the trio of mother–father–infant. Even the model of the nuclear family tends to imagine a sibling or two! (And so does he, in the interstices of his general theory: sometimes, in fact, it's as if there is always going to be one more baby: no child is not faced by the threat of another one coming along.) But it was easier, then, to create an explanatory myth in that form when mother and father had clearly defined symbolic and social places that are now, whatever the real situation of a given household, or a given child, increasingly defunct. The distinctive Freudian mythology within which femininity is a state of hopeless longing (for masculinity), while masculinity is a fear of losing it (losing masculinity), must surely have shifted in its social and psychical mooring.

This is not to say that unconscious feelings to do with either a threatened or a rejected identity are not just as likely to be present as before, in both men and women. But they are more likely to be experienced across boundaries that would previously have separated (actual) men from women. The particular Freudian myth of girls' development to 'normal' womanhood involves the necessary repression of a masculinity initially shared by children of both sexes; girls who become women never get to move out of the emotional confines of the family, so as to enter the broader public world of cultural equality. Boys, on the other hand, are able to move on out of the restricting family triangle on condition of giving up their early fantasies of uniqueness and omnipotence. Today, those myths of gendered development no longer have the same cultural purchase – whereas previously they might have offered a very clear explantory story for differences in the psychical situations of the two sexes.

Something similar applies to the development of sexual orientations. Freud's developmental story was radical in its suggestion that initially, there was no differentiation of sex for the object of desire (because to begin with, there is no understanding of the difference of sex). To end up attracted to the other sex, as the culture prescribed and expected, was not a natural progression but the result of a series of turnings towards and away which were bound to involve the renunciation of other possibilities, notably same-sex attraction. Freud always stresses the lack of inevitability in any individual story of sexual development, and also – disarmingly – says that there is really no explanation for how it is that most people do end up with the heterosexual identity that is culturally expected of them.

This indeterminacy within the general shows up for instance within the particular myth of the castration complex, which involves, Freud says, every child's horrified realisation that one sex has it and the other doesn't (and hence, that they themselves may one day be lacking – or, if they are girls, that they already are). From the essay on 'Fetishism' (1927): 'Probably no male human being is spared the fright of castration at the sight of a female genital. Why some people become homosexual as a consequence of that impression, while others fend it off by creating a fetish, and the great majority surmount it, we are frankly not able to explain.' The combination here of (all but) universalisation at the same time as there are multiple routes is absolutely typical of Freud. It happens to all male human beings, this sighting and the fright it engenders. But there are three possible outcomes; and the most common one and the cultural norm is in fact the least not the most explicable. To begin with, a generalisation so sweeping that it cries out for contradiction, whether theoretically or empirically. But then, after that sure-fire certainty and the sense of constraint – it can't not have happened, no one escapes it – the reference to several possible subsequent developments, and an abandonment of certainty for the open acknowledgement of having no answer.

Freud does offer other developmental stories to account for (male) homosexuality than the one momentarily sketched here (the focus of the essay is on fetishism, the second of the three possible post-sighting eventualities). But in fact this particular myth makes homosexuality for men much more plausible in terms of the premises of the story – and strikingly, it offers no good reason at all for why men would ever become heterosexual: 'we are frankly not able to explain'!

Freud's account of the development of femininity was elaborated (in the mid-1920s to early 1930s) largely in response to criticisms of the boy-centredness of his general theory of the Oedipus and castration complexes. It would be interesting to speculate about what modifications to the story (or stories) he would have seen, or heard, or put forward in the different conditions of becoming a man or a woman a hundred years later.

DE CHAVEZ: I would like to ask about your thoughts on the future of psychoanalysis as a teachable subject in academia. Todd Dufresne has already pronounced psychoanalysis to be dead, claiming that as an intellectual activity it is now nothing more than 'another critical movement for bewildered undergraduate students in English to ponder.' Do you think that students now (most of whom are exposed to every (un)imaginable spectacle that dwells in the internet) are still moved or challenged or even shocked by the ideas of Freud? Or, like amazing sex that has inexplicably gone bland, has psychoanalysis lost its radical edge that once scandalised, threatened and perturbed? Has it become unsexy common sense; that is, has it turned into the very evil it once wanted to vanquish?

BOWLBY: It's curious, isn't it, how English is always the academic subject that seems to be where psychoanalysis might be taught or not taught. Not, for instance, psychology, or philosophy, or history – disciplines whose practitioners (apart from some notable exceptions) generally ignore psychoanalysis altogether. (But this wouldn't be true in the same way of French philosophy, or even French history, with a psychoanalytic thinking much more embedded in Francophone culture than it has ever been in English-speaking countries.)

And it is true that even within English – undergraduate English, let's say, to pick up on the quote – there has probably been a falling away from Freud in the past couple of decades. In this connection I now think of Sussex University in the 1980s and 1990s as a sort of golden age, when psychoanalysis was very much part of the intellectual culture, and students would be encountering different texts by Freud as a matter of course. And writing about them, and reading them critically and in detail – as you would with any other piece of writing. It's easy for me to idealise this period, because it was my own (teaching) youth, and in retrospect the students and the level of engagement have probably taken on fabulous colours they may not have really had at the time. Fabulously coloured those Penguin Freud texts surely were, though! In all the colours of the rainbow: bright orange for *The Interpretation of Dreams*, a rather off-putting dark brown for the volume on civilisation and culture; and a lurid bright green for the one called Sexuality. And some of these volumes got used so much – for so many seminars over the years – that they started to fall apart and I bought replacement copies. That would have been vol. 7, Sexuality, and vol. 8 (dark green), which included the 'Dora' case study. And as you might guess from that last example, the dominant use of Freud was in courses that had a feminist component.

During this time (the 1980s and 1990s) Freud was very much on the agenda (including the agenda that found its way into the content of university courses) as part of ongoing arguments about the origins and possible futures of human sexual differences. He had played a negative role in many of the second-wave feminist books of the 1960s and early 1970s as a sort of rhetorical straw man: Look what he said about women! That women all want to be men, that women are naturally secondary, always have been, and always will be. Then Juliet Mitchell made the counter-argument in her book *Psychoanalysis and Feminism*: not just that feminism can't dismiss psychoanalysis, but that it can't do without it. It can't do without it because Freud has the best account yet of the psychical determinations of the patriarchal culture we're in – which isn't immutable.

I think one reason that psychoanalysis may have dropped off the syllabus is that sexual difference (even the expression sounds a bit dated now) has ceased to be seen as the central question to be asked, whether politically or theoretically. Other kinds of difference and identity have weighed in alongside it – just as feminist questions, in their own time, were claiming a theoretical and political place in addition to the established category of class. This is where Marx comes in again, to go back to your first question; and this is another angle, perhaps, on the displacement of Marxism in theoretical enquiry. In the early 1980s Marx was still an automatic point of reference for thinking about history, but that was no longer so straightforwardly true by the end of the decade because feminism and other forms of identity politics had displaced it.

Psychoanalysis, unlike Marxism, did present a theory that made the difference of men and women the most fundamental of all human differences – even though it wasn't there from the beginning in the mindset. For Freud, as for Simone de Beauvoir, you become a woman (or man), you aren't born one; and therein lies the hope or possibility of change: that the woman (or man) you become is not innately given, is subject to cultural variations. But while it may not be a natural difference – becoming what culture considers a man or a woman does not follow from having a male or female body – it is still, Freud suggests, existentially the most fundamental aspect of human identity. In his lecture called 'Femininity' (1933), he says: 'When you meet a human being, the first distinction you make is "male or female?" and you are accustomed to make the distinction with unhesitating certainty.' The implication is that there is something primordial about this 'distinction': you can't not categorise every other person in this way, in terms of a particular binary opposition. And the further suggestion is that if and when you can't – when it's not clear whether a person is male or female – then there is a disturbance: only then, perhaps, do you become aware that there was a question at all (because normally the question is answered with 'unhesitating certainty'). Being certainly male or female, then, is on the one hand so basic that it does not have to be thought about; and on the other hand so basic that when it becomes an issue, it is unsettling – unlike, say, the feeling caused by being unable to work out a person's age or social position or anything else. One aspect of this is the binary insistence: unlike other distinctions, such as age or ethnicity, you have to be one or the other of two and only two mutually exclusive possibilities; to be one is (just as emphatically) not to be the other. Right down to the level of language, this primary determination of a gendered difference is maintained. 'He' and 'she' are separated and named; in English, you cannot be identified in a third-person pronoun without also being gendered (but you are not characterised in any other way). Other languages, of course, do much more automatic differentiating – in adjectives, in parts of the verb, in the plural, and so on.

In all his writing about sexual development – about how we more or less acquire an identity as being of one sex or the other – Freud is always looking at the misfit margins, at those who have come to differ and perhaps to suffer from their difference – whether in their own particular case, or (as in some of his sympathetic remarks on the situation of women, or homosexuals) because of the difficulties faced by the category to which they have come to belong. At the same time, he stresses that marginal or problem instances, whether individual or shared, do not imply that the norm is a settled place: no identity is fixed or assured, just as none is naturally there from the start. Normality, like its absence, is in need of explanation; as with the example of male heterosexuality, it doesn't just happen with the simplicity of a default position.

To return to the specifics of your question, I'd say that thinking with Freud, arguing with Freud, and reading his work in detail, was and is an excellent way into all kinds of topics and questions in feminist studies, in literary studies – and also in those other humanities disciplines where psychoanalysis is rarely given much attention. As far as the quote from Todd Dufresne is concerned, I would disagree from the outset with that assumption that a student in English will be bewildered by a proliferation of different theoretical movements. They will be, perhaps, if what they're presented with is like a checklist of options with not much relation to one another and no history to them, shared or otherwise: one week psychoanalysis, the next week postcolonial, another week queer theory, and so on. But there are other ways of teaching. In the case of Freud, there is a supplementary reason for spending more time. He was himself an outstandingly strong writer, whose work can be read with all the close attention that we might give to a conventionally literary text. Students are often delighted to discover this when they first take up a text by Freud, whether in the originsal or in James Strachey's translation: not intimidating after all! This too was one of the great bonuses, in the UK, of the publication of the Penguin Freud: Freud became for the first time a readable writer – in the sense of being available and also in the sense of being appealing.

I don't fully believe the line about a reduced shock value of Freud. It's true that the culture we live in now is over-sexualised, so that Freud saying that sexuality is everywhere, even where you least expected it, doesn't sound controversial in the way that it did a century ago. It's also true that Freud wasn't above playing the scandal card himself as a rhetorical device, in contexts where that can now only look dated – like when he says, near the start of the *Three Essays on the Theory of Sexuality*, that the existence of sexual attraction between men, and between women, is bound to come as a great surprise to his readers. And it's also the case that many Freudian ideas – as with the examples of the now Freudian Oedipus, or the Freudian slip – have worked their way into ordinary cultural consciousness: the shock is in some sense pre-registered, or pre-empted, or blurred. But I think that the challenge of Freud is still there in the force of his undermining of every naturalised assumption about human identity – which is why I dwelt on that seemingly casual remark about the primacy of sexual difference, its presence as as a submerged issue, in the most ordinary of social encounters.

BAYOT: Many readers have known you through your translations of Jacques Derrida: *Paper Machine* (2005), *Of Hospitality* (2000), and *Of Spirit* (1989; with Geoffrey Bennington). And in this connection, I'd like to ask you a few questions. Firstly, at what point in the trajectory of your scholarship did Derrida become a critical figure? And how did that come about – was it a conference with or on Derrida? Or was it a bookw? Could it be your PhD studies in Yale? Or was it via Freud? And, secondly, speaking of Freud, I'd very much like to know what accounts for your Derridean turn from Freud (without implying your abandonment of the latter in favor of the former)?

BOWLBY: No Derridean turn away from Freud that I'm aware of – but I'll try to answer this with some sort of narrative of where and when these interests (and related ones) began. With Derrida, it was while an undergraduate at Oxford. It wasn't that he was taught on the Classics or English syllabuses on my undergraduate courses – far from it! – but that I was involved with the small knot of people who were keen on theory – that talisman word that put together various mainly French thinkers: Foucault, Barthes, Kristeva and Lacan as well as Derrida. That group of people at Oxford, including Maud Ellmann, Ann Wordsworth and Robert Young, produced the *Oxford Literary Review*, which despite the name was a journal dedicated to theory. When I went to Yale as a graduate student in comparative literature, it was because – as I mentioned before – it was there that the wonderful thing called theory was happening. I hadn't yet read more than a smattering of either Derrida or Freud, but at Yale it became possible to think about both – in particular through Shoshana Felman's teaching of psychoanalytic texts, and through Derrida's own seminars in the department each year. And when I went for a year to Paris to do research for my dissertation, I was able to attend Derrida's seminars there as well. There were also other inspiring courses at Yale from the teachers I've mentioned before.

The contrast in all these opportunities couldn't have been wider between (what it was and is easy to caricature as) the intellectual dreariness of Oxford undergraduate studies in the late 1970s, and the openness and sense of something happening at Yale.

So to answer the specifics of your questions – I can't really remember a time (after I became a student) when Derrida *didn't* seem a critical figure. The same would be true of Freud, except that of course the difference – one difference! – was that one was long established and long dead, whereas Derrida was in the middle of his writing life.

BAYOT: Here is a continuation from the previous question. What does it take to be a translator of Jacques Derrida? And what does it mean to be a Derrida translator – to be an interpreter or disseminator of his ideas?

BOWLBY: I suppose I can only answer what it takes by trying to work out what in my case it took: everyone's arrival at a point of translation is going to be a bit different, involving a mixture of language skills, the chances of where you are based and what you are doing, a degree of devotion to the enterprise (translating French philosophy isn't a way to earn money), and more. For me, one thing that may well be slightly different from others who have translated Derrida is that I sort of grew up translating. I did Latin and Greek in secondary school, as well as for almost two years of my undergraduate degree. For much of that time I was doing almost nothing else (only one other subject, history, in the last two years of school, and nothing else at all, except a little philosophy, in the first five terms of university). So I spent a lot of my teenage years sat in front of very big dictionaries, 'doing translations'. When I did begin to translate French stuff, it felt like going back to something familiar.

Also, going back before the learning of other languages – I was born in a town (in the northeast of England – Billingham-on-Tees) where my parents were newcomers and spoke a very different English, southern and posh, from the language spoken by virtually everyone else in the place. From as early as I can remember I was conscious of speaking one way at school, and then switching to my parents' accent, more or less, when I got home – and also conscious that no one else I knew had this division, apart from my own siblings who did the same thing. One day when my brother had come home with a friend and my mother had overheard them, she said to me, 'Do you think Richard speaks like that *all the time* at school?' It never occurred to her that that was also how I spoke – and it hadn't, till then, occurred to me that it might be conceivable that he or I would speak at school how we spoke at home. At any rate, I always felt more at home in the non-home language, and wished it was really 'mine'. I'm sure this is some of the explanation for why I've always loved speaking French – or wanted to get away from my 'own' language. And in a simpler way, it is why it's always felt natural to me to be transferring between two languages.

I like the suggestion of your question that to be a translator is to be both an interpreter and a disseminator – but that also sounds too grand for what's essentially a job of work that you do as best you can. I think that I've always found translating a means of interpreting for myself as much as for the imagined reader. In other words, it's as if you get inside what's being said in a quite different way when you're trying to work out how to put it across in an English that doesn't sound forced or esoteric, while also staying close to the wording of the French. There was a time when translations of French theory into English all sounded as though they were written in their own special idiom – to the point that that curious pretentious style then got taken up in all sorts of writing in English by people who'd read the translation – that writing would include everything from books to journal articles to students' MA term papers (oh! those endless unreadable term papers on Lacan and Derrida from the second half of the 1980s!).

The tendency to over-literalism in theory translations isn't just about abstract expressions or philosophical language; it's also about very ordinary phrases and formulations. When I started translating from French myself, in the mid-1980s, I tried – when I could – to get away from this kind of practice, to let the French come over, as far as possible, in the more ordinary way that it read in its own language. Take *au fond*, for example, which is really common in both written and spoken French, and is often translated by 'at bottom'. At bottom! Who ever says that? And why go there anyway, when basically, the phrase just means . . . 'basically' – a perfectly good idiomatic equivalent, which even keeps the same metaphor – base, basic, foundational, fundamental – that's in *au fond* as well.

So 'basically' is what I've generally put for *au fond*, and it hasn't – as far as I know – met with objections. As far as I knows – but then I wouldn't necessarily know, and one of the impossibilities of translating as a task is that you can only really get it wrong, since everything you put is by definition a departure from the original, a poor distortion or at best a pale imitation. Or else, looking at this from the other direction, considering only the target language of translation, all the non-idiomatic phrases you use are open to criticism as stilted and distracting, rather than as an attempt, which in some cases they may honestly be, to do justice to what is distinctive about the French. In reviews of translated books, you rarely see praise for the translation, which is usually mentioned only if it's being marked out as bad – in style, or accuracy, or both. It is, in fact – basically and fundamentally – a thankless task.

Which leads me to one more thought, to do with what I call 'translator's narcissism'. Most translators of French theory start off with a built-in overvaluation of the French object. In other words, you love and admire it and regard it as intellectually important, and if you didn't you wouldn't be wanting to translate it in the first place. But there are times when even French philosophers doze, and you find that your admired author hasn't put something very well. Sometimes – in the case of one book that I translated (not by Derrida) – quite a lot of the time. So then you have a dilemma. If you fix up or clarify the sentence, and it's your work, your contribution, you'll get no credit for it. If you leave it in its malformed or unclear state, readers will think the fault is the translator's – you'll be blamed for it – because the clutsiness will be there in the translation. Either way, you can't win. But there is no point in dwelling on this too much. Narcissism isn't really a luxury that translators can indulge in; this work involves the most selfless kind of writing I know. And sometimes, if people do tell you they've found your translation useful or readable, it can give you the simple, rewarding sense of a job worth doing.

BAYOT: Situated at a historical point after deconstruction, when and where 'literature' has come under fire, is there still a place for aesthetic valuation and evaluation? Can we still speak of good or great literature? In short, do we still have the intellectual latitude to make distinctions and to do so unabashedly in recognition (of the necessity) of a hierarchy of values?

BOWLBY: Once again, several different responses to this. First, it all depends what you mean by the aesthetic. That's a word that seems to have come to the fore in critical debate in the past fifteen or twenty years, in part as a counter to (supposedly valueless) 'theory' but also, I think, because it has more of a serious philosophical history than words like criticism or appreciation. But my sense it that it's only recently – in this new context imbued with theory – that the word 'aesthetic' has been much used in relation to literature – as opposed to the arts more generally: painting and sculpture and music and architecture, with literature probably not the first example in anyone's mind.

I think you are right that there has been a return to questions of value, and often under the heading of the aesthetic. But my sense of the earlier history is not quite the same. I think deconstruction was always evaluative, in the sense that some texts were taken to be more worth deconstructing than others. Implicitly, there was a canon, just as there was in so-called traditional criticism. It was a somewhat different canon, and in the American context, where deconstruction was mostly happening in comparative literature contexts, it was generally a selective European canon of broadly modernist and Romantic-period philosophy and lyric poetry.

In the UK this story came out somewhat different. First, because such theory as *was* happening within institutions, at places like Sussex and Cardiff, was in departments of English rather than (as in the US) French and comparative literature (there was no comp. lit. to speak of in Britain at that time). And second, because the movement for embracing theory took the form of a repudiation of the Englishness of 'Eng. lit.' studies. English (meaning the study of English literature) was very often identified with the consciously moral, evalutative mode of F.R. Leavis; his work, and the work associated with him through the journal *Scrutiny*, had been hugely influential for the teaching of English at all levels (by which I mean, including seconday school teaching). For Leavis, a 'good' novel was morally good – it taught you about Life – as well as artistically good: the two reinforced each other. Then along came theory, which represented a sophisticated new language, wonderfully un-English in both its words and its subject matter. The canon of English literature – even for those teaching or taking a degree in it – seemed part of what needed to be rejected, sometimes wholesale (why bother with so-called literature at all?) and sometimes only in its established contours (it needed updating to include the works of more women, more working-class, more non-white writers – and so on).

In the decades since the first moment when theory broke in upon English, the more sweeping version of the anti-canonical argument has faded away. You don't now encounter many voices arguing that all texts, from Mills & Boon romances to Jane Austen novels, are equally complex and of equal literary value. There had been a famous example, at the height of the fashion for theory as anti-evaluative, of a well-known Shakespeare scholar, Terence Hawkes, who came out with a statement to the effect that an episode of *The Bill* – a hugely popular TV police drama at the time – was as good as *King Lear* any day. I don't think that now you'd find critics wanting to say something deliberately iconoclastic and levelling like that in relation to the canonical writers they've written on – with Shakespeare, of course,

being the top of the Englsih pantheon, which was why the provocation was so effective.

BAYOT: What do you personally and professionally think of cultural
studies and the way it is taught and practised in current times? Would
you consider the phenomenon of cultural studies in the history and
field of literary studies a blessing (albeit a mixed one)? As I ask you
this question, I have in mind someone like Christopher Norris who, on
the one hand, has been very much an advocate of deconstruction, but
yet on the other hand, has serious reservations about cultural studies
as regards its social constructionist tenor and its con-fusion of generic
bounds in the case of fiction and history, for instance.

BOWLBY: As a taught university subject, cultural studies has taken
many different forms in different places, so I wouldn't want to gener-
alise about the subject as any kind of whole. Although it is
notoriously a field which has no clear methodology or object of
study, it does have a generally recognised point of origin: the
Birmingham Centre for Contemporary Cultural Studies as it developed in the 1970s under the leadership of Stuart Hall. A lot of
groundbreaking published work came out of that moment, and this
was also part of the inspiration for some of the disaffection in Britain
with the then standard modes of studying English literature.

Where cultural studies has been less successful or less energising,
perhaps, is when it has lost that politically critical edge which was
very much part of its Birmingham identity. Christopher Norris is
right to complain about the contructionist model, which did become
repetitive: as Barthes would have put it, a matter of finding the same
story everywhere (the story of a low-key cultural conspiracy). On the
other hand, there was no more brilliant proponent of the contructionist theory (not called by that name) than Barthes himself, whose
working model through to the late 1960s was one of ideology as an
inverted relation between nature and culture. So in one way, it's only
because we're now so used to that idea, which has become a sort of
orthodoxy, that it seems to be something that needs to be cast out.
And in another way, it all depends on who's doing the constructionist
cultural studies: if those constructionist critiques are brilliant three-
page pieces *à la* Barthes's *Mythologies*, then readers are not going to
be bored – not even half a century later (it's amazing how many of
them still sparkle).

It's also important, I think, that (British) cultural studies came out
of sociology as much as English (after Birmingham, Hall took up a
chair in sociology at the Open University). Before theory – and before

cultural studies – sociology was seen as a cutting-edge subject in a way that it isn't now; to some extent English (after English went theoretical and cultural and professedly interdisciplinary) took over the mantle of radical social critique that had previously belonged to sociology. There was also a lot of fluidity between the two disciplines, both intellectually and in practical institutional reality. I think Hall had begun a PhD on Henry James at Oxford before being identified with sociology. Then at a later time there were sociology academics who were given jobs in English departments – when sociology was fading as a subject, and English (in some departments in the UK) was becoming consciously multidisciplinary.

Another strong spin-off from cultural studies has been the rise of media studies since the 1980s. What happened at Sussex University can tell the story best here. The first time media studies was proposed there as a potential degree subject, in the mid-1980s (no other university in England offered it at the time, though one Scottish university did), it was rejected on intellectual grounds. The next year, as a backdoor strategy, there was a new proposal, this time for 'English and Media Studies', and that was accepted. In fact, given the system that operated at Sussex at the time, that meant that only one quarter of a student's courses would be in Media Studies (since half the courses on any degree programme were interdisciplinary 'contextuals' – like Studies in Feminism, which I mentioned earlier. Even so, the first year that degree was offered, there were over a thousand applicants for twelve places! This was long before the days of universities marketing themselves to potential students, and also before the existence of a Media Studies A level course to act as a pathway to a degree (A level media studies has itself since become hugely successful). So there was evidently some sort of real demand out there for whatever might go by this name. And in the next few years the subject grew very quickly in every kind of academic form – from formalised university departments with BA and PhD programmes all the way through to GCSEs and A level qualifications offered by schools and sixth forms.

**BAYOT: Do you foresee any change in critical fashions – is it for better or for worse?**

**BOWLBY:** In this case I don't foresee anything, I know it! Changes in critical fashions, as you put it, have become part of a regular cycle, a sort of permanent roadmap or Satnav of literary studies whereby every decade or so, as though by common consent, it seems to be Time for a Turn. We've had several of these since the 1980s, and I'm not sure that I can accurately recall them in order: some resonated more in some national or local contexts than others, while some of them overlap either chronologically or in their object, or both. But there was the historical turn, the postcolonial turn, the ethical turn, the religious turn (or was it the theological turn?) – and all of them preceded by that mother of all turns, the linguistic turn – a.k.a. structuralism, or Theory. I would say that that first big turn was different from the later ones, initially setting up a would-be indefinite stand-off between a 'traditional' – or worse, 'traditionalist' – them and a theoretical us. That first Theory included any number of possible strands of French philosophy, psychoanalysis and cultural theory that were yet to be separated out into different components, or to branch out according to the different later twists and turns.

With the subsequent turns, theory was itself an established part of the terrain, so that the historical turn (which essentially referred to new historicism, a very particular kind of history) or the postcolonial turn, were not anti- or pre-theoretical, but rather were moving on from it and with it in specific directions. What has changed, I think, since the beginning of this, is that periodical turning is now seen as the natural way of critical life. There's no suggestion, as there might once have been, that we're looking to find 'the' way to study author X or text X, to find 'the' truth about X. (A qualification here, though. New authors are now always being brought in for study, and there is far more diversity of authors than there was in the past. But on the other hand, the challenge to long-established canonical names has if anything faded away. As I was suggesting before, no one really bothers arguing for or against the value of Shakespeare any more: it is simply taken as read.)

BAYOT: What do you think are the most important functions of scholarship in literary-cultural studies? And related (I presume) to that: what is the value of literary pedagogy in this age of technology and 'after' deconstruction?

BOWLBY: I find myself shying away from this one because of the echoes of Matthew Arnold and his grandly titled essay on 'The Function of Criticism at the Present Time', from the 1860s. At the same time I find myself drawn to it, because I've always been fascinated by Arnold's criticism (and poetry) in the way it articulates, in a sort of primary form, one of the long-standing justifications for the reading of literature: as a support or consolation in the face of a confusing, changing world. Literature is something to hang on to ('a surer and surer stay', Arnold says). It does not explain the (present) world, and nor is it itself in need of explanation or analysis.

I understand the pleasures of reading some particular loved book for the umpteenth time. In part, and I wouldn't kick against this now, it is the childish pleasure of going back to the same story, and probably the same physical book (no Kindles here!), one more time. But each time you read a book or poem again, you usually notice something different from other times – and that, as much as the repetition, is what makes it interesting. Also – and this is the more important point – I don't think that the comfort function could be any basis or justification for the academic study of literature, at any level. Current arguments in support of humanities subjects often adopt a version of the Arnoldian model by talking about the benefits of the arts for people's 'well-being' (a word that's shot up the scale of quasi-personal political discourse in the past few years). I'm sure it's not wrong – in other words, reading and other sorts of artistic consumption or participation do have therapeutic and sustaining uses for individuals and for groups. But the idea that reading helps us to feel better (about ourselves or the world), that it gives us a nice warm feeling about life, doesn't seem to me the right argument for teaching or studying literature. It puts reading in its separate, sphere marked 'leisure' or 'recreation'; rather than considering it as a form of critical thinking.

You bring up the changed – so changed! – context of reading in an online world, when getting out a book may itself come to have an air if not an aura of old-fashioned indulgence; and at the least now means something different – means more of a deliberate choice – when set against all the alternative reading devices that you turn off or turn away from in order to sit down with that one. The temptation for book reading to be experienced as a consoling retreat is probably stronger than ever (not that the internet doesn't, in its own way, offer the equivalent function in its own distinctive ways). But even though I'm old enough and old-fashioned enough to find it difficult to read seriously or with enjoyment from a screen, I know that's a personal preference and I don't think the medium fully determines the way that the message is read. What probably does make more difference is flipping about between websites when reading – or writing: and that's a result of the contingent fact that the site of reading or writing or typing is no longer a unifunctional surface that will only ever receive this one pageful of words, but one that can alternate back and forth all the time between an infinitely extendable number of different messages and images.

Your 'after' before deconstruction would require more unpacking than I could do in *these* pages (if pages is even the right word, other than by analogy, for whatever it is I'm looking at and now perhaps you're looking at on a screen). I'm not sure whether you mean that deconstruction, whatever it was, has disappeared from view, or that its work has been done, or that we're now on to the next (big or small) things in terms of critical practice? Or whether perhaps your scare quotes are there to suggest not so much a sequence as also a sense of fidelity: 'in the style of', 'in homage to'? Whichever – and probably you meant all of these possibilities to be there at once – I don't think that I've had the sense of a change of teaching practice that would be anchored to something that's happened with theory – or with deconstruction in particular. But on the other hand, there are probably fewer courses around than there were twenty years ago, say, that concentrate on deconstruction, or explicitly take their intellectual cues from some version of it.

Following the 'after' mode, it is true that in the years following Derrida's death in 2004, a lot of deconstructive work flowed into questions of mourning and commemoration – which had already been central to Derrida's own thinking. That's also one of the areas in which literary criticism more generally has taken up deconstructive ways of thinking. And technology is a deconsructive theme too! – not least in *Paper Machine*, which you mentioned. And in the first-person narrative of *The Post Card* (1980) the focus on the telephone – and on a particular phone box in New Haven, Connecticut – has now itself been changed by the anachronisation of that particular semi-public, semi-private space and all the changes in the conditions of personal communication which the mobile and the smartphone have brought about.

BAYOT: An interview that I personally find very interesting and insightful is the one with Roland Barthes conducted by Jean-Jacques Brochier (first published in *Le Magazine Littéraire* in 1975). There, Barthes was asked to discuss the key words that had been significant to him and his work. The words foregrounded for discussion in 'Twenty Key Words for Roland Barthes' were: pleasure, fragment, politics, Japan, and reading, among others. I'm wondering if we could have the pleasure of hearing you talk about the key words that define and invigorate the critical universe of Rachel Bowlby.

BOWLBY: This is the most enticing of all the questions so far, and that feels just right for the Barthes connection. Thinking about what my keywords would be, I've found that most of the ones I'm drawn to seem to come from the shorthand marks I put in the margins of books I'm reading – which haven't changed a lot in all the years since I first started reading for my dissertation. I also list page references under category headings in the back of the book, adding a page number whenever I come across something else. Many of these categories and all the margin notes are just initials; the most idiosyncratic ones perhaps are V. (for *vitrines*, or shop windows) and VQ (*vie quotidienne*, everyday life). There's also F for *flâneur* and P for *passante* (the female passer-by, or passing woman as seen by the *flâneur* – or occasionally, the (female) *flâneuse*. W is a bit uncertainly poised between Women and Walking; and there's also SD for Sexual Difference. Not always easy to know the difference between W and SD, but as long as I can find the passage again when I need it, the purpose is served. P = *passante* has suffered from too much P = 'parental' interference in recent years. C covers everything to do with consumers, commerce, consumption, shoppers and shopping (or at least everything apart from shop windows – ). The Greek letter ψ is for psychoanalysis, and NGψ for a passage when the narrator in a novel is making some general statement that comes from an identifiably psychological discourse. Then there is   for philosophy; that comes up mostly as a marginal marker in Freud texts, almost always with a minus sign in front of it, for when Freud is throwing out one of his anti-philosophy asides.

These then are some of my keywords:

**consumer**   I've been interested in the way that this word undergoes all sorts of meaning changes – not just historically, as what we now call consumer culture starts to get going (the boundaries are always being changed or disputed for that beginning), but also from one discipline or discourse to another. In our own time, there has been a shift from an image of consumption as overwhelmingly feminine – women were the consumers, and to be a consumer was to be duped or dizzy or thoughtlessly desirous – to the citizen-consumer, genderless if not male, who is the equivalent of the rational abstraction of *homo economicus* and makes the best possible decision based on the information available. That shift was happening in the 1980s – when I was first working on these matters – which were the Thatcher years in Britain. On the one hand there was the expansion, at that time, of marketised thinking into several domains, such as education and healthcare, which had before been treated as heterogeneous fields, each with their own ways of doing things. Now, instead of the student or parent or patient, all separate characters specific to their role and regime, you had the consumer, across the board; and that consumer was supposed, by that name, to be endowed with choices and reason (rather than seen as foolishly susceptible, as in the earlier model). Meanwhile, on the other hand, shopping itself, in most of its forms, both the regular activity ('doing the shopping') and the more exceptional kind ('going shopping') was starting to be seen as a fairly ordinary male as well as female activity: and that change was probably not unrelated to the general improvement in the status of the consumer at this time.

**domestication**   This was one of those words that I found myself noticing and back-of-book noting all the time in critical writing. If such and such an idea or practice had been 'domesticated', it had implicitly lost its primary radical nature. Very often those using the concept were either feminist or deconstructively inclined, or both – and it struck me that this was an interesting blind spot on both counts. In deconstructive terms, what you don't have is a pure origin or source which then, at a second moment, may be simplified or watered down or appropriated – all the things that domestication could imply. Yet that was exactly the structure that was suggested by a process of domestication. And in feminist terms, this made me realise, there's a long-standing myth, almost an underlying reverse grand narrative, that the women's movement is a movement away from home: feminism is a rejection of domesticity a leaving behind of the home which is defined as the literal and symbolic site of women's oppression and confinement. The feminist adoption of the negativity of 'domestication' went against the revaluation of a trivialised womanly sphere. But it also, thereby, exposed a contradiction in feminism's own model of freedom, which in this sense was consonant with the existing masculine order of things.

In the early 1990s I wrote an essay (included in the present book) about this curious concept of domestication), and since then I've found myself noticing other home-related topics and movements in representations of modern life. One of these is commuting, which I wrote about in *Everyday Stories*. Commuting started to become a commonplace way of life around the end of the nineteenth century as the new metropolitan transport networks made it possible for people to travel into the city centre to work from suburbs and semi-rural locations on the outskirts. With commuting, you have various models of double selfhood. Sometimes it's the idea that there is an authentic, natural self at home. The professional, working self is in effect a mask or performance; at the same time, though, the home life may also itself be something that has to be staged and built up. (The prototype of this scenario is the clerk Wemmick in Dickens's *Great Expectations*, who changes identity in the course of his long walk to and from his place of work, and whose home is quite literally a (pretend) castle, complete with a drawbridge and all kinds of other accoutrements.) Another model is that of a simple alternation between a city or working self and a domestic or rural self; this polarisation is almost built into the fabric of ordinary temporal as well as spatial conceptualisations of life's routines, with the working day, the working week and weekend – and so on. The gendered separation of the two modes or the two spheres used to be axiomatic, but now, with the norm being for women to work as well, that is not as clear as it was

**mythology**   This one is a real Barthes word – one that's even perhaps entered the English language in Barthes's own sense of something like an ideological narrative. Barthes's 'mythologies' of the 1957 collection are a wonderfully diverse collection of mini-essays about anything from new cars to striptease to washing detergents, and that appealed to me very much when I was first working on consumer culture and everyday life: there is nothing to match it. But the actual word 'mythologies' started to resonate much more with me when I was thinking about the book that was eventually called *Freudian Mythologies*, and I realised that theories of myth in the more traditional sense are all about the way that myths change as they move through different phases of a culture (whereas Barthes, as it happens, was more interested in analysing a certain kind of fixity in the contemporary ideologies he takes apart in *Mythologies*). Freud's model of individual development is based on a series of (overlapping) stages – the oral phase, the anal phase, and so on – that each has its accompanying myths or theories: these are the questions and stories through which small children conceptualise their world, and Freud uses both words interchangeably. As I described in response to an earlier question, he took this conceptual framework from his knowledge of comparative mythology, a new field in the nineteenth century, transposing to the individual and infantile level a model that had been formulated to describe the evolution of whole cultures. These Freudian childhood explanatory myths are always in process – but they follow a course that is absolutely set (there's no way that this or that myth is not going to kick in at more or less its appointment moment; but if you get stuck on one stage, as can happen, that's a 'fixation').

It was also interesting to think about the turns of myth in relation to Greek tragedy, which was the other focus – alongside Freud – of *Freudian Mythologies*. Freud had lifted the Oedipus myth from Sophocles' tragedy and converted it into something quite different (a theory of infantile desires). But in a sense, though not always nearly so radically, that revision or rewriting of myth was what every tragedy did: by presenting a new interpretation of a myth, or picking out one aspect of it for emphasis or storyline. So the notion of a core myth that can, in effect, be retroactively modified by the effect of a powerful new interpretation – a fundamental strucure of psychoanalytic thinking, as well as a description of what Freud did with *Oedipus* – that notion is itself one that has its origins, or at least antecedents, in what Greek dramatists did with their own stories.

**reading**    I like the versatility, if not instability, of the word reading. It seems such a fundamental idea in the study of literature, but it's probably one of the most slippery terms there are, as it moves about between the basic literacy skill to the suggestion of an arcane and intimate knowledge ('close reading'), to the social history of who read what when, or the media of reading; somewhere amongst all these is the practice, also known as reading, of making inferences from just about anything seen in the off-the-page world – by 'reading' a face or a street, for instance – and with different kinds of aptitude implied in each case. Reading can also mean doing that curious thing called 'a reading' (or a reading of a reading, even) that may appear to have no connection with either its own historical moment or that of the text it is talking about. Or reading can suggest a liberation or exploration: the scene of reading – in a picture or in a book – is always, potentially, an opening onto another world from the one the reader is presently in. At the same time, reading has often been represented as a form of addiction (generally female, and generally to novels) – all the way from the circulating libraries castigated by Coleridge (in the *Biographia Literaria*) to Q.D. Leavis's strictures about trashy Hollywood novels in *Fiction and the Reading Public* (1932). And on to contemporary denunciations of internet dumbing down, through the special distractions of on-screen reading. Then there's the way that novels themselves may censure the reading of novels in the course of their stories: that's a recurrent practice in the internal history of realism, whereby one kind of writing makes its claim to the fuller, more truthful representation of reality by mocking or criticising the reading of what it's not.

I feel some ambivalence about the sort of reading that's known as 'a' reading – in other words, a very particular genre of writing. I do readings of this type all the time; I'm not sure I really know any other way to write (though I'm trying to here!); or at least, I start to feel unmoored if I'm writing without the relative security or excuse of a text of some sort for interpretation. This probably stems from having come to criticism from unusual directions: starting from theory and philosophy more than from what are called primary texts in the traditional teaching of literature. Deconstruction, in a wonderful way, made all texts in principle equal: you did have to be 'reading', to be doing a reading, but what you read didn't need to be some already consecrated literary or philosophical text (although in practice, it most often was). That was my cue or permission for doing close readings of texts of a kind that possibly not many people had read before in an everyday sense, let alone in the lit-crit sense – I'm thinking about the marketing texts and trade journals and suchlike that I studied when I was working on the history of self-service shopping and supermarkets.

I'm very interested, though, in the history and sociology of reading – that started with my dissertation, which was on novels about art and the publishing industry, as well as on novels about department stores. A lot of the influential left-wing writing in (British) English studies in the middle of the twentieth century was about the the history and future of reading – as with Richard Hoggart's *The Uses of Literacy* and Raymond Williams's *The Long Revolution* – and those books were around when I was growing up; there was also the Leavisite critique of 'mass culture'. I'm sure all this must have filtered in as a background to my subsequent interest in advertising and the history of consumer culture, because the arguments about reading were always (especially with Hoggart and the Leavises and their offshoots) tied into some form of an argument about what consumer culture was taking away from a hypothetically more authentic culture.

**realism**   Realism is often – even routinely – dismissed as a boring topic, or used as a term of dismissal 'mere realism') in contrast to some implicitly more sophisticated or complex literary mode. I've never understood this, and not only because I've always been naturally inclined to nineteenth-century novels, which are where (in terms of the word itself and the movement in its name) it all started. Realism has always seemed to me the *most* interesting and complex of literary and literary-historical questions – not the least. What is the point or the pleasure of representing reality? – something that Aristotle (in the *Poetics*), sounding almost like a twentieth-century psychologist, says that all small children like to do. And realism is also one of the few semi-technical critical concepts which is also in everyday adjectival use: this or that story or episode isn't 'realistic'. The overlap with the use of the word to mean practical, and with the philosophical division between realist and idealist, is important too in the ways it has sometimes been important to the evolution of realism in literature and art, and of the word's use as a casual or careful critical term.

When I think of realism, though, my first image is kitchen-sink! – in the half joking name that was given to 1950s and early 1960s British films, and plays like John Osborne's *Look Back in Anger* (where there is ironing but, as I recall, no actual sink). I can study the sets of kitchen scenes in British TV soaps for probably almost as long as it took the producers to lovingly source and strategically untidy them.

**railways (or, more realism)** I love the historical alignment between railways and realism: both of them had their beginnings in the 1820s – when the word realism was first used (in French) and the first train journey was made, in northeast England, from Stockton to Darlington. Both of them, realism and the railways, show their passengers or readers to new places they might not have seen before. This isn't only or primarily about the passenger's destination; it's about the journey itself and what you see from the window. In Hawthorne's *Blithedale Romance* (1852) there's a passage about the backyard realities behind the houses that are now visible from a passing train: this new form of travel has exposed to view what had never been seen before and was habitually hidden behind by the contrastingly public presentation at the front, on the main road: 'Realities keep to the rear'! In that sense, railways are doing what realism itself does – and it's also a realist fiction (of sorts!) that points that out. Another point of connection is the speeding up of life that railways are seen to both symbolise and exacerbate. Realist novels often use the railway line to mark out distances of both space and time between a rural here and an urban there, or between an old time of relative changelessness and a modern time of ceaseless movement and urgency. Then there is the timetabling of trains, which demands a strict uniformity between places that could previously have gone by the variable times of their local clocks. Along with so many other modes of temporal standardisation, with the progressive reliance on clock-time (and watch-time), this development is part of the regular new life-world that nineteenth-century realism charts, and that the novels of the early twentieth century, with their multiple time-perspectives, consciously move away from.

In my book on Virginia Woolf, I used the train as an ongoing metaphor. The train goes against the usual association of modernist novels with a non-linear narrative mode, but I took my cue from Woolf's 'Mr Bennett and Mrs Brown', which is a fictionalised essay set on a suburban train going from Richmond (in south-west London) to Waterloo, and plays with the train journey as a metaphor for narrative and communications. Once this essay had got me started, I began to see trains and locomotive metaphors all over the place in Woolf's writing: that's the way it happens.

***vie quotidienne***   Pretentious though it may be, I have to keep this in French, because VQ has always been the abbreviation I've put in the margins of books I'm reading whenever I come across something about everyday life. Everyday life is almost in the position of being both the limit point of realism and its beginning. The limit point because when you stick into a novel a description of what happens day after day, unchangingly, always the same, then you have no story. As may very well be true, for most people, most of the time – but which doesn't make for the most page-turning of fictions. And the starting point, on the other hand, because one of the aims of realism was to bring into representation topics that had not been considered artistically valuable or interesting before. The daily domestic lives of women, as they began to be described in nineteenth-century novels, are a prime example of VQ in both these modes: the sheer repetition of day after day, and the showing of settings and experiences that had not had a place in literature before.

I suppose though that I'm attached to VQ because the letters themselves look somehow exotic, anything but the regular daily run of the mill ('daily life' is dull by comparison). And that's really what appeals to me about the idea of the everyday: that in the routine – precisely because it's so rarely looked at – there may also, potentially, be variation and difference. Especially once you start to put it into words or images.

**walking**   Like many others, in the 1980s I got interested in the nineteenth- and early twentieth-century walker in the city, the *flâneur*, and also in the dissymmetries attending his hypothetical female counterpart, the *flâneuse*, at a time when aimlessly walking around on her own was not a feasible occupation for a middle-class woman, even one with time on her hands (or her legs). The walking woman most often appears in literature not in her own right but as a *passante*, a (female) passer-by who comes and goes as a sighting for the (male) *flâneur*. In some ways, the department store provided a sort of indoor *flânerie* for women: they could wander around respectably in the city all day long.

The *flâneur* and associated females were almost always in French, in direct or indirect homage to Benjamin's use of Baudelaire in his writings about nineteenth-century Paris. *Flânerie* was one of those topics that was written about with such detail and intensity for a time that it afterwards seemed to fade away as if everyone had just got bored with it. These days, you'd be quite hard put to it to run into a *flâneur* of any description or sex on your critical travels. There is still plenty of literary walking to be had – but it's now much more likely to be located not in the city but in the poetically or philosophically fortifying countryside, the source of Wordsworth's or Rousseau's meditations. So there's been a move away from modernist (or proto-modernist) urban walking, back to Romantic rural walking. And also from looking at the walker as a sophisticated observer or consumer of metropolitan sights, to seeing walking as a way of thinking.

**shop windows**   This should really be another French word, *vitrines,* or shop windows – or V., in my marginal shorthand. Shop windows probably first struck me (in literature) when I began to read Zola's novel *Au Bonheur des Dames* (1883), about a Paris department store; Zola was fascinated by the transformation of shops that was so visibly shown by the comparison of the vast plate-glass display windows of the big new stores with the dingy and cramped little windows of the traditional ones. The glass of the big windows was like a new kind of flattering mirror, whose mannequins showed to the woman on the outside looking in a fashionable image of what she might become (by stepping into the store and purchasing the outfit).

At the same time, you could think of the shop window as a commoditised version of Lacan's 'mirror stage'. This was described (in an essay first published in the 1930s) as a sort of mythical proto-subjective moment when very small (pre-verbal) children supposedly get the first inkling of an integrated image of themselves through a mirror image which shows them (a picture of) themselves: it's me! A me for the first time seen as a whole, but seen over there, elsewhere, like someone else: it's an image. And as such the mirror self is aspi-rational: it's not me (here), yet it is me, it's a better me: I could be that, it's what I will be. You can see how this set-up might translate into the modern world of advertising images: posters, shop windows and (later) the screens of cinema, TV and subsequent devices.

Shop windows, once you start noticing them (or can't stop noticing them), turn up all the time in nineteenth- and twentieth-century literature, often in connection with scenes of recognition and desire like the paradigm scenario I've just sketched. But they're not always connected with women's (as opposed to men's) consumerly desires, and the best ones – the most artistic ones – aren't always to be found in literary books. Over the years I built up quite a collec-tion of glossily illustrated books from the first half of the twentieth century with titles like *Display for the Man's Shop,* and when I wrote a book about the invention of self-service and supermarkets there was a chapter on shop windows and passers-by. The passer-by, in the salesmanship literature, is the name of the character you're trying to get to stop and look at your window display (and then, hopefully, to be drawn into the actual shop). But with supermarkets, the shop window disappears. They are big stores but they have no display windows! – instead, they present themselves as functional, as anti-design. Yet while the window disappears, the psychological set-up connecting the consumer and the goods on display in the window is in fact like a preview of the windowless self-service scenario. This is because in both cases there is no store assistant showing you the things or persuading you to buy them; rather, it is the goods that appeal on their own – by their framing in the window, or by packaging or colour or brand recognition, and so on.

BAYOT: Having had the privilege of moving and being guided around your critical landscape, I would like to shift gears and drive to a more personal terrain: your family. What were your parents like? Are or were they readers of literature? Ar or were they supportive of your pursuit of literature, writing, and criticism?

BOWLBY: My parents *were* readers, yes – at least there were plenty of books in the house. Including a mixture of theology and sociology in my father's study – but he also read novels, and so did my mother. He was a Church of England clergyman, and the office was part of the house; it was drilled into us children (by my mother rather than him) that this wasn't 'our' house, but belonged to the Church. My interest in social history came from my father, who liked – and likes – ideas and argument about ideas, I was encouraged to go to the library, and I did, all the time. I also used to go round to friends' houses to watch TV – in particular, to watch ITV, the channel (there were only two!) which, among other things, had commercials. The set at home could only receive the BBC (no ads), and anyway watching was strictly rationed (a favourite word – and practice – for parents who had grown up on wartime and postwar rationing) – so commercials were transgressive and exotic. Not hard to see that that's one place where one of my interests comes from.

I don't think my parents really understood when I began studying English halfway through my BA degree. I don't think I did either, though probably not for the same reasons. For one thing, I hadn't done it at school. That was an advantage, in the end, as it meant that I didn't have to unlearn anything in the way that people who've gone through the GCSE and A level process do have to. Also, it meant – especially coming from classics, equally weird but in a quite different way – that the sorts of questions that the conventions of studying English literature always seemed strange to me. So I was a natural for theory.

BAYOT: Whither Rachel Bowlby and her shopping with Freud (or for more), if I may ask?

BOWLBY: Still close to those words, I realise. There's a book I never wrote about the wealth of consumer psychology literature that came out in the first half of the twentieth century. I call it a wealth not just because there's so much of it, but also because it is often interesting and socially engaged in a way that, by and large, later manifestations of the field are not. I've drawn on some of this material in the past, but there's much more to say (and much more to read). I think it would be worth doing, not least because it relates to a moment when economists' and advertisers' questions about subjectivity and choice were formulated in much more adventurous and searching ways than they are today. Maybe one day I'll write this book.

Recently, I've been writing about everyday stories. The starting point was that I wanted to counter the standard would-be-theoretical put-downs of literary realism. Either it's a mistaken enterprise, since language, by definition, can never achieve a likeness to non-linguistic reality. Or, if not wrong, it's banal and simplistic: it does not do any of the more complex moves which would make it literature by setting it apart from life. But the first complaint forgets that the reality up for representation is full of words to begin with: we're always in realism already as we pass round everyday stories and images. And the second objection ignores the way that literary realism has had the historical role of giving a value to people and places and parts of life that were not represented before.

I've already talked quite a bit about shifts in what counts as worth representing, as well as shifts in what is there to be publicly seen and described. The focus changes with new ways of seeing: with new intellectual or ideological 'views' gaining currency but also, more straightforwardly, with new means of looking and new sights exposed (Hawthorne's back yards as seen from the train). And to move away from the visual emphasis: typical stories, the likely sense of how people are and what they might do, are always in motion, at least potentially, however stable they may seem. The best example of a suddenly shifting but previously static story of this kind is that of parenthood. Until recently it seemed to be fixed in the mould of the nuclear family norm, as the natural and predictable sequel to marriage; today, there are any number of possible parental stories.

With DNA and the new reproductive technologies, even the so-called 'facts' of life, the biological bedrock beyond which no true-life story could go, have altered, now that fatherhood has become ascertainable and motherhood can be uncertain, because divided between two women (the one who provides the egg and the one who is pregnant).

These shifts in reproductive stories were the focus of my book *A Child of One's Own*. In *Everyday Stories* I talked about some of the different kinds of surrounding ordinary stories that have fascinated me over the years – from parenthood to shopping to commuting. Freud is part of this. He listened to patients talking on – every day. He also (most of the time) made the quotidian strange and weird. What more audacious and witty name for a book could you imagine than *The Psychopathology of Everyday Life*? It's Freud at the opposite extreme from the grand, universal theory derived from tragedy. Instead, the everyday is a mass of the most trivial and tiny details whose meaning, in any given case, is going to be far more idiosyncratic than general. And less predictable.

# Acknowledgements

Chapter 2, 'Half Art', was first published in *Paragraph* 34:1 (March 2011). Chapter 3, 'Readable City', and Chapter 20, 'Cultural Studies and the Literary', were published in *PMLA*, 122:1 (January 2007) and 112:2 (March 1997). Chapter 5, 'Shopping for Christmas', was published in the *Independent*, 12 December 1998. A different version of Chapter 6, 'Please Enter Your Pin', was published in the *London Review of Books*, 22 October 2009. Two chapters first appeared in *Textual Practice*: Chapter 7, 'Oedipus Today', as 'Generations', 21:1 (March 2007); Chapter 24, 'The Future of Literary Thinking', 30:7 (December 2016). Chapter 9 appeared as a review in *Journal of the History of Sexuality*, 2:3 (July 1992). Chapter 10 appeared as 'The Constancies of Kinship' in *Cambridge Quarterly*, 32:1 (2003). Chapters 11, 19, 21 and 23 were all published in *Times Higher Education* (15 August 2013, 16 October 2014, 12 November 2004, 4 February 2016). Chapter 12, 'Domestication', was a chapter in Diane Elan and Robyn Wiegman (eds), *Feminism Beside Itself* (Routledge, 1995). Chapter 13, 'The Joy of Footnotes', was published in *Women: A Cultural Review*, 7:3 (Winter 1996). Chapter 14, 'Clichés in the Psychology of Advertising', appeared in a French version in *GRAAT* (Publications des Groupes de Recherches Anglo-Américaines de l'Université François Rabelais de Tours), no. 16, *Fonctions du cliché: Du banal à la violence* (1997). Chapter 15, 'Who's Framing Virginia Woolf?' was published in *diacritics*, 21:2-3 (Summer–Fall 1991). Chapter 18, 'Ginny Whizz', appeared in the *New Statesman*, 19 September 2011. Chapter 22, 'Derrida One Day', was a chapter in Simon Glendinning and Robert Eaglestone (eds), *Derrida's Legacies: Literature and Philosophy* (Routledge, 2008). Chapter 26, the interview with David Jonathan Bayot and Jeremy De Chavez, appeared on its own as a short book edited by Bayot and published in Manila by De La Salle University Press in 2014.

I would particularly like to thank Thomas Baldwin, Gillian Beer, Jonathan Derbyshire, Simon Glendinning, Matthew Reisz and Karen Shook, for writing or speaking invitations which led to many of the pieces collected here.

# Index

adoption 67–71, 85
advertising 3–4, 30–1, 110, 122–31,
    145–6, 173, 235, 236, 237
Amossy, Ruth, and Elisheva Rosen, *Les
    Discours du cliché* 130
Angé, Louis, *Pour bien faire sa publicité*
    125
Aristotle, *Poetics* 232
Arnold, Matthew 225–6
Arren, J., *Sa Majesté la publicité* 128
Athill, Diana 16
Auerbach, Erich, *Mimesis* 137, 150
Austen, Jane 222

Bachelard, Gaston, *The Poetics of Space*
    98–9, 100
barcodes 51
Barthes, Roland 128, 144, 182, 184,
    197–8, 218, 223, 227–8
Baudelaire, Charles, 9, 234
    'Le Flacon' 27n5
    *The Painter of Modern Life* 8, 12,
    16–17n2, 18–32
Bayot, David Jonathan viii
Bazin, Nancy Topping, *Virginia Woolf
    and the Androgynous Vision* 139
Beaumont, Matthew, *Nightwalking*
    16–17n2
Beauvoir, Simone de, *The Second Sex*
    100–1, 107–9, 216
Beer, Gillian 94
Benjamin, Walter 9, 14–15, 158,
    234
Bergson, Henri 98–9
*The Bill* 222–3
Billingham-on-Tees 219
biography 141, 152–4, 196–200
Birmingham Centre for Contemporary
    Cultural Studies 223
Bloom, Harold 168, 169, 182,
    194
Bloomsbury 137–8, 152, 197
Bowie, Malcolm 25
Breuer, Josef 202

Brewster, Arthur Judson, and Herbert
    Hall Palmer, *Introduction to
    Advertising* 126
Brooks, Peter 182
Brown, Louise 76
BT (British Telecom) 3
Butler, Judith, *Antigone's Claim* 82–5
    *Gender Trouble* 95–6

Cambridge, University of 94–5
Cardiff University 222
car 7, 15, 33–41, 48, 208
Carrefour 49
Certeau, Michel de 158
checkouts 50–1, 119–21
childlessness 68, 76–7n16
Cholodenko, Lisa 88
Cixous, Hélène 183
Clarke, Stuart N. 39
Chodorow, Nancy, *The Reproduction
    of Mothering* 73n5
cliché 122–31
Coleridge, Samuel Taylor, *Biographia
    Literaria* 231
commuting 229–30
comparative literature 182–3,
    222
comparative mythology 210
computers 41, 109, 204–5
Conan Doyle, Sir Arthur 193, 195
consumer, changing figure of, 206–8,
    228–9
consumer culture 42–6, 48–55, 72,
    109–10, 173, 183–4, 204–8,
    228–9
contraception 60–2
Coogan, Steve 87
Crimean War 24–5, 27n8
cultural studies 157–9, 223–4

Darlington 233
Darwin, Charles, The *Origin of Species*
    20, 27n4
deconstruction 93–114, 135, 160–3,

164–7, 168–9, 218–22, 225–7, 231–2
department stores 14–15, 49, 51, 109, 183–4, 235
Derrida, Jacques 94–5, 115, 135, 160–3, 164–7, 168–9, 182, 218, 227
DeSalvo, Louise, *Virginia Woolf* 79–81
designer babies 76
diaries 199–200
Dickens, Charles, *Great Expectations* 229–30
Dinnerstein, Dorothy, *The Mermaid and the Minotaur* 73n5
domestication 93–114, 229–30
dual form 84–5
Dufresne, Todd 217

egg donation 63, 70–2, 75n18, 77
Elkin, Lauren, *Flâneuse* 17n10
Ellmann, Maud 218
Engels, Friedrich, *The Origin of the Family* 82, 102–03, 107
Esso 125

family, changing forms of 61–2, 65, 82, 85, 86, 102, 189–90, 211–12, 237–8
fatherhood 62, 67–8, 71, 77, 85, 120, 212
faxes 109
Felman, Shoshana 168, 218
feminism 59–60, 64, 95–6, 100–5, 108–12, 139–40, 149–50, 183–4, 206
Fenton, Roger 27n8
Fielding, Henry, *Tom Jones* 26n3
*flâneur* 8–10, 14–15, 17n10, 21, 24, 234
Fontane, Theodor, *Effi Briest* 192
footnotes 115–21, 150
Forster, E.M., 137, 141
   *Howards End* 45–7
Foucault, Michel 141, 182, 194–5, 218
Franklin, Sarah 71
Freud, Sigmund, 59, 65–8, 73n6, 80–1, 82, 86, 99, 116–17, 181–2, 184–99, 201–3, 208–19, 228
   *An Autobiographical Study* 186
   *Civilisation and its Discontents* 202
   'Creative Writers and Daydreaming' 185

'Delusions and Dreams in Jensen's *Gradiva*' 186
'Dora' case 215
'Family Romances' 62, 67
'Female Homosexuality' 66, 74n14
'Femininity' 216
'Fetishism' 213
*The Future of an Illusion* 202
*The Interpretation of Dreams* 68, 99, 187, 209, 211
*Leonardo da Vinci* 197
*The Psychopathology of Everyday Life* 209
*Studies on Hysteria* 185
*Three Essays on the Theory of Sexuality* 217–18
*Totem and Taboo* 202
Friedan, Betty, *The Feminine Mystique* 100, 109–10
Fry, Roger 141

gender, as term of argument 59–60, 73n2, 206
generations 60–1
Gissing, George 184
Glendinning, Simon 167
Glendinning, Victoria 152
Goody, Jack 97, 98, 103
Gowers, Sir Ernest, *Plain Words* 156
Grafton, Anthony, *The Footnote* 121n2
Gros Frédéric, *Marcher, une philosophie* 6, 13
Grossberg, Lawrence, *Cultural Studies* 157
Grossmith, George and Weedon, *Diary of a Nobody* 199
Guiguet, Jean 138
Guillory, John, *Cultural Capital* 169
Guys, Constantin 18–27

Hall, Stuart 223
Harris, Alexandra, *Virginia Woolf* 152–4
Hartman, Geoffrey 168, 169, 182
Hawkes, Terence 170–1, 222
Hawthorne, Nathaniel, *The Blithedale Romance* 233, 237
Hayden, Gary, *Walking with Plato* 5
Hegel, G.W.F. 82
Herbin, Pierre 122–5
history 200–3, 206
Hoffmann, E.T.A., *The Sandman* 192
Hogarth, William 26n3

Hoggart, Richard, *The Uses of Literacy* 98, 232
home 38, 41, 86, 93, 97–110, 229–30
Homer 123
housework 101–3
Hoyland, Graham, *Walking through Spring* 5
Huxley, Aldous, *Brave New World* vii

*Illustrated London News* 18, 26n1
Inglis, Anthony 138
interdisciplinarity 60, 184, 224
internet 3, 41, 71, 204–5
interviews 52, 172
Irigaray, Luce 108, 183
IVF 62–3, 70, 71, 74n7, 75n18, 76–7, 212
Ixion 13

James, Henry
  'In the Cage' 51–2
  *What Maisie Knew* 86–9
Jameson, Fredric 182–3
Jensen, Wilhelm, *Gradiva* 186
John O'Groats 4
Johnson, Barbara 168
Joyce, James, *Ulysses* 191–2

Kaplan, Cora 182
*The Kids Are All Right* 88
Kierkegaard, Søren, *Diary of a Seducer* 199
kinship 61–3, 67, 70, 74n15, 82–5
Kristeva, Julia 108, 183, 218

Lacan, Jacques 82–4, 115, 119–21, 130, 181, 183, 186, 218, 235
Land's End 4
language and social change 156
Lawrence, D.H. 137
Lazarus 22, 27n5
Leader, Darian, *Why Do Women Write More Letters Than They Post?* 115–21
Leavis, F.R. 137–8, 222, 232
Leavis, Q.D., *Fiction and the Reading Public* 231, 232
Leclerc, Annie 183
Lee, Hermione, *Virginia Woolf* 153–4
Lévi-Strauss, Claude 82–3, 97, 206–7
literature 143–8, 149–51, 170–1, 172–80
  and advertising 123–6

study of, 150, 157–9, 214–15, 225–6

McDonald, Ronan, *The Death of the Critic* 176
Macfarlane, Robert, *The Old Ways* 6
McGehee, Scott 87
Man, Paul de 168–9
Marder, Herbert, *Feminism and Art* 137–8
Marxist theory 60, 101–2, 158, 170, 182, 184, 194, 198, 205–7, 216
media studies 224
Mill, John Stuart 104
Miller, Alice 80–1
Miller, Arthur, *Death of a Salesman* 49
Miller, C. Ruth, *Virginia Woolf* 132–42
Miller, J. Hillis 168, 182
Miller, Michael B., *The Bon Marché* 183–4
Mitchell, Juliet 65, 73n1, 73n2
  *Psychoanalysis and Feminism* 60, 73n3, 181–2, 215
modernism 192–3, 233
Montesquieu, *Lettres persanes* 12
Montrelay, Michèle 183
Moore, Julianne 87, 88
motherhood 60–4, 67–8, 77, 85, 119–20, 212
Murray, Jenni 164, 167n1
mythology 201, 208–14, 230–1
  *see also* Barthes, Roland; comparative mythology

naturalism 192
Nelson, Cary, *Cultural Studies* 157
Newbolt Report on teaching of English 174–5
Nicholson, Geoff, *The Lost Art of Walking* 6, 7
Norris, Christopher 223
*Norton Anthology of Theory and Criticism* 25
Nowell Smith 174

Oedipus 66–73, 74n15, 187, 211
Open University 223
Ordnance Survey 6
Osborne, John, *Look Back in Anger* 233
Ovid, *Metamorphoses* 20
Oxford, University of 218–19
*Oxford Literary Review* 73n2, 218

Packard, Vance, *The Hidden Persuaders* 128

parenthood 61–2, 74n11, 76–8, 85

Parsons, Deborah, *Streetwalking the Metropolis* 18n10

Patmore, Coventry 100

Penguin 73n3, 181–2, 215, 217

philosophy 160–3, 186, 194–5, 206, 228

photography 24–5, 129

Pinker, Steven 155–6

Poe, Edgar Allan, 'The Man of the Crowd' 21, 29–30

Poffenberger, A.T. 127

posters 24, 31, 164–5, 235

propaganda 128

Proust, Marcel, *A la recherche du temps perdu* 191–2

psychoanalysis 59–60, 80–1, 99, 181–99, 201–18

psychology 122–31, 184, 187–8, 206–7

Quiller-Couch, Sir Arthur 174

radio 109

RAE (Research Assessment Exercise) 176

railway 7, 8, 16, 233–4

reading 28–32, 157–9, 194–5, 226, 231–2

realism 192–3, 202, 231, 232–3, 237

Redfield, Marc, *Theory at Yale* 168–9

REF (Research Excellence Framework) 178n11

reproductive technologies 62, 70–1, 76–8, 85, 212

Rose, Jacqueline 182

Rosen, Elisheva, *see* Amossy, Ruth

Rousseau, Jean-Jacques 7, 8, 2235

Ruskin, John, 'Of Queens' Gardens' 103–5, 106–8

Rybczynski, Witold, *Home* 105–7

Sam, Anna, *Checkout* 48–55

Scritti Politti, 'Jacques Derrida' 167n2

*Scrutiny* 137–8, 222

self-service 48–55

sexual difference 73n2, 201, 212–14, 215–16, 218

sexuality, as term of argument 59–60

Shakespeare 222–3, 225
  *Hamlet* 188

shop assistants 48–55

shopping 14–15, 42–7, 48–55, 107–8, 109, 119, 128–9, 183–4, 200–1, 204–8

shop windows 143–8, 235–6

siblings 65, 66, 83–5

Siegel, David 87

silent salesman 50

Sinclair, Iain, *London Orbital* 17n2

Sinclair, Upton, *The Jungle* 113n9

Sisyphus 13

slogans 122–7

*Social Text* 183

sociology 158, 223–4

'soft option' 173–4

Solnit, Rebecca, *Wanderlust* 6

Sophocles 195
  *Antigone* 82–5
  *Oedipus at Colonus* 84
  *Oedipus the King* 67, 185, 188, 195

sperm donation 63, 64, 70–2, 75n18, 88

stagecoach 7

Steiner, George 94

Stendhal, *Racine et Shakespeare* 26–7n3

Stockton-on-Tees 233

Strachey, James 217

Strachey, Lytton 141

Struther, Jan, *Mrs Miniver* 44–6

supermarkets 15, 42–4, 46, 48–54, 109, 119–21, 128, 204–5, 207, 236

surrogacy 62–3, 71–2, 77

Sussex, East 153

Sussex, University of 182, 200, 215, 222, 224

Sutherland, John, *The Boy Who Loved Books* 173

Tansley, Mark 169

telephones 3–5, 109, 227

Tesco 49

*Textual Practice* 170–1

Thacker, Andrew, *Moving through Modernity* 33

Thatcher, Margaret, and figure of consumer 207–8, 228

Thoreau, Henry David 6

theory 60, 168–9, 175–6, 218, 221–3, 224–5

*Times Literary Supplement* 140–1

Toohill, J.C., *The Art of Advertisement Copy Writing* 126–7

translation 18, 23, 25, 111, 160–3, 219–21

Treichler, Paula, *Cultural Studies* 157
Troy, Ohio 51

walking 3–17, 229, 234–5
wet-nursing 75n19, 78
*What Maisie Knew* (film) 86–9
  see also James, Henry, *What Maisie Knew*
Wilde, Oscar, and literary canon 151
Williams, Raymond, *The Long Revolution* 232
Wollstonecraft, Mary, *A Vindication of the Rights of Woman* 78, 100
*Woman's Hour* 164–5, 167n1
Woolf, Virginia 33–41, 79–81, 100, 132–42, 143–8, 149–51, 152–4, 195–8, 233–4
  'Evening over Sussex' 33–41
  'How Should One Read a Book?' 147
  *Moments of Being* 79, 140
  *Mrs Dalloway* 10
  'Mr Bennett and Mrs Brown' ('Character in Fiction') 35, 38, 233–4

*Orlando* 39, 141
  'Reviewing' 143–8
  *Roger Fry* 141
  *A Room of One's Own* 38–9, 147, 150, 153, 196
  'Street Haunting' 10–11, 38–9
  *Three Guineas* 144s, 196
  *To the Lighthouse* 152, 191–2
  *The Voyage Out* 139
  *The Waves* 100
Wordsworth, Ann 218
Wordsworth, William 235
  *The Prelude* 28–30
work 22, 62, 102, 109, 229–30

Yale University 162, 168–9, 182–3, 218–19
Yellow Pages 3–4, 16n1
Young, Robert 218

Zimmerman, M.M. 48
Zola, Emile, *Au Bonheur des Dames* 48, 51, 54, 183, 235

www.ingramcontent.com/pod-product-compliance
Lightning Source LLC
Chambersburg PA
CBHW071557110726
47908CB00007B/2137